Organizational Change Management

is the key to

BRIDGING THE GAP

between strategy development and strategy execution

Ali ElKattan

An organizational change management guide based on
ElKattan's Model for Change Management

ElKattan Consulting
32 Anson Road, Walsall
West Midlands WS2 0DH
England, UK
info@elkattanconsulting.uk

www.elkattanconsulting.com

Book Training on Udemy: https://bit.ly/3Eogevj

© ElKattan Consulting 2021 – V1.6b

ISBN: 9781658670951 (black & white)

ISBN: 9798602068252 (color)

Imprint: Independently published

Contents

List of Tables

List of Figures

List of Examples

List of Skill Practices

Welcome to Bridging the Gap!

After encountering upper management resistance to corporate change initiatives as a company CEO, while simultaneously preparing for my doctorate, it became clear to me that the ideal topic for my research would be to question what makes people resist change.

This book is a product of that research intertwined with my own experiences in numerous projects; the intention being to present a complete reference on the topic of change management that adds value to the aspects of theoretical knowledge and practical techniques.

This book is about leading organizational change. When we decide to lead a change, we accept the responsibility of effectively transitioning people into the new desired state. We accept this obligation, irrespective of the ambiguity and risks that come naturally with change. Achieving successful change requires managing the people side to develop and engage the stakeholders, and to convert resistors to be supporters.

Bridging the Gap attempts to examine various situations I encountered, wherein management moved from strategy development to strategy execution without properly embedding the change management component into the equation. The objective of this book is to assist managers in recognizing this gap by building a bridge toward the successful implementation of strategic initiatives.

It is my hope through Bridging the Gap, to support change leaders by providing them with the knowledge and tools that will serve as a guide in managing change.

Ali ElKattan

Cairo, April 2020

Acknowledgments

This project was initiated by my dear friends and brothers, Tarek Ezzat and Nagy Hamamo. Were it not for their support, as well as their continuous encouragement, this book would never have seen the light of day. My gratitude remains boundless.

I would like to thank my lovely family (Maha Abdelfattah, Omar, Alia, and Ahmad) for giving me all the support and freedom to work on this book for so many long hours.

I also want to record my thanks to the following people who reviewed and commented on the book in different stages of its development.

REVIEWERS

Ahmed Rafaat

Ahmed Samir

Aishah Schwartz

Donia Abdelaziz

Ehab Saad

Emily Richardson

Huda Hassan

Omar Badr

Mohamed ElHamamsy

Nagy Hamamo

Randa Samir

Tarek Ezzat

Yassir AbdelBaseer

DESIGNERS

Alia Maged

Donia Abdelaziz

Goran Tovilovic

CHAPTER 1
INTRODUCTION

Chapter 1 - Introduction

1.1   OVERVIEW

Let's start our journey in the world of change management! Are you ready to explore this mysterious landscape and connect between its different continents? Hopefully, by the end of this book, you will be able to influence and lead successful changes within your organization.

The principal aim of this book is to help others be successful in managing new organizational change. Helping others has always been one of my personal core values. Even though I work as a change management consultant, to the degree that I am able, I will share the knowledge and tools that have helped me navigate change management programs. I do not promise that everything will be valuable to everyone; it will be up to you to choose what might be most beneficial in your particular circumstances.

I sincerely hope this book, presented as a guide and reference for senior managers, change leaders, project managers, and management consultants, will benefit those involved in managing and delivering new strategic programs within their organizations.

Widely regarded as the foremost speaker on the topic of change, John Kotter contends that new organizational changes are always required for organizations to win in both the present and the future. However, managing a new transformational change is not that easy. For an organizational change to be successful, numerous aspects must be taken into consideration, such as managing engagement of the target group, adjusting the organizational side, navigating organizational politics, considering the hidden agendas of the different stakeholders, addressing cultural barriers, selecting the right motivational factors, understanding perception, managing resistance to change, and assuring the right leadership.

A research-based change management model is the core of this book, bringing the cultural component under full investigation, in terms of both national and organizational cultures, which is missing in many change management models. ElKattan's 5-Theme Model, which tackles a number of the pitfalls in existing models, demonstrates how the culture can be managed to enhance the various stakeholders' willingness toward change.

This book will also help organizations successfully implement their strategies. Most organizations move from strategy development to strategy execution without properly managing the strategic initiatives from the change management perspective. It is the intention of this book to help managers recognize this gap; supporting them in building a bridge to ensure the successful implementation of their strategic initiatives.

1.2   PURPOSE

The main purpose of this book is to provide:

- An overview of change management and why it is needed.

- A discussion of the general concepts of change theories, types, and concepts.

- Clarification on the relationship between change management and project management, program management, benefits management, and strategic management.

- Descriptions of the most famous change management models.

- Reflections from real case studies.

- Descriptions of the national and organizational culture models and how they influence implementation of change initiatives.

- Details of the 5-Theme Model and why it is essential for change management.

- Details of the themes, components, practices, and activities of the 5-Theme Model and how they can be applied in practice.

1.3   DOES THE WORLD REALLY NEED THIS BOOK?!

With all of the other books, articles, and references addressing the varying aspects of change management, what makes this book relevant?

Carefully check the following points below that summarize the value of adding this book to your collection:

- To my knowledge, there is no other publication that links between change management and other areas like stakeholder management, culture management, project management, program management, benefits management, communication management, and strategic management in one reference.

- It fills the gap in literature between strategy development and strategy execution, as the model presented in this book can be perfectly applied to the strategic initiatives that are formulated during the strategic planning process.

- It not only provides a research-based change management model, but its related techniques and templates also help translate academic and theoretical knowledge into real-life applications.

- It highlights the influence of both national and organizational culture on change, which is scarcely available in existing literature.

- It summarizes different change management models in a way that allows readers to choose the one that best fits their specific context.

Throughout this book, we will review a variety of knowledge areas, explore different models of change and culture, and hopefully, along with the 5-Theme Model, advance the knowledge areas of change management from a fresh perspective.

1.4   STRUCTURE OF THE BOOK

This book is a reflection of the author's own experiences, as an employee witnessing the downfall of companies unable to implement change; from managers making fatal mistakes; a researcher reading tens of articles and references, analysing case studies and interviewing change leaders, experts, and employees; and a practitioner giving advice and developing change management tools and templates. Table 1-1 lists the chapters of this book along with a summary of each chapter.

Table 1-1. *Book Summary*

Chapter	Title	Summary
1	Introduction	Summarizes the purpose and structure of this book; indicates the target audience; gives a brief introduction to all the chapters. Presents the first real-life case study that the author experienced as a change leader.
2	Change Management Basics	Presents fundamental concepts about change management.
3	Bridging the Gap	Identifies the most fatal change management mistakes. Presents the second real-life case study that the author experienced as a change leader.
4	It is Crucial to Understand Culture	Discusses basic knowledge and fundamentals of culture and its relationship with change; describes the differences between national and organizational cultures.
5	Influence of National Culture on Change	Describes the influence of national culture on change. Presents Hofstede 6-Dimension Model for national culture.
6	Influence of Organizational Culture on Change	Describes the influence of organizational culture on change. Presents Hofstede Multi-Focus Model for organizational culture.
7	ElKattan's 5-Theme Model	Gives a description of the 5-Theme Model along with its five themes, components, and three-phase change life cycle.
8	Vision and Sponsorship Theme	Explains the purpose of the Vision and Sponsorship theme along with its components, deliverables, techniques, and templates.
9	Assessment Theme	Explains the purpose of the change Assessment theme along with its components, deliverables, techniques, and templates.
10	Strategizing Theme	Explains the purpose of the Strategizing theme along with its components, deliverables, techniques, and templates.
11	Tactics Theme	Explains the purpose of the Tactics theme along with its components, deliverables, techniques, and templates.
12	Planning and Appraising	Explains the purpose of the Planning and Appraising theme along

Chapter	Title	Summary
	Theme	with its components, deliverables, techniques, and templates.

Appendices		
A	A Quick Orientation About Change Management Models	Presents seven change management models along with some reflections, insights, and links with ElKattan's 5-Theme Model.
B	Project, Program, Benefits, and Strategic Management	Clarifies the relationship between change management and project management, program management, benefits management, and strategic management.
C	Expected Behaviors in Organizations Based on Cultural Measurements	Expected behaviors in organizations based on the measurements of the six cultural dimensions of the Multi-Focus Model.
D	Research Methodology of the ElKattan's 5-Theme Model	Brief description about the research methodology that was used to develop the model as well some information about the research case studies.
E	ACE Survey	The ACE (Awareness, Competence, and Emotion) survey that is used by ElKattan's ACE Model to assess the individual's engagement and readiness to change.
F	The 5-Theme Model's Components, Deliverables, and Workflow	List of the 5-Theme Model components and deliverables.

The book is divided into three parts:

Part 1 (Chapter 1 to Chapter 3)

The first three chapters cover basic knowledge about change management, and introduces the two main case studies of the book.

Part 2 (Chapter 4 – Chapter 6)

These chapters cover basic knowledge about culture; explaining select culture models and issues that the reader needs to be aware of before we discuss the culture aspect discussed in the model.

Part 3 (Chapter 7 to Chapter 12)

This part presents the change management model, along with its templates and tools. It also includes select, real life examples, in addition to introducing two other case studies.

1.5   MY PERSONAL CALL

"Where do you see yourself 10-years from now?" It was at my farewell party that I received this question from one of my colleagues. This was very unexpected for me. As I used to ask the same question while interviewing new candidates joining the company.

At that moment, I flashed-back 20-years when I had an inner passion for the academic field, where I believed I could have a positive impact on others, which was one of my core values.

As the son of a well-known professor at the School of Engineering, I was inspired to follow in his footsteps. I recall him saying many times that he saw me continuing my post-graduate education in the United States.

After graduation, my low GPA wasn't promising regarding pursuing my post-graduate education; and it was a difficult moment facing my father with that news. And because persistence had been a core value for me, I decided to move forward by submitting many applications to different universities, but I was rejected.

Next, I spent two years working in the USA. During this period, I was attending masters' courses in two universities hoping they would help me get accepted, but eventually, I was rejected, returning back to Egypt with another failure.

Back to my colleague's question, I wanted to say, "In 10-years, I see myself teaching at one of the well-known universities.", but I held back, thinking the idea was unrealistic. I had been away from academics for more than 20-years; while taking a different career path, ending with being a CEO.

Although I do not recall my response to the question, it gave me a pause to rethink my future.

Six months later, I joined a master's degree program, completing it in two years. I then realized that having the master's degree alone would not help me achieve my goal, so I decided to enter a doctoral program.

Time-wise and financially, it was a challenge. I was so busy in my work, while managing a family with three children.

Returning back to school 20-years post-graduation was not really based on what my father wanted me to do; it was based on the values that had been instilled in me as a child – driving me toward my interests and goals.

I went through another four years of hard work while I was a CEO of a large company.

While I was searching for my doctoral topic, an event happened that changed a significant aspect of my life. The chairman and I proposed a new change initiative that was met with very strong resistance; and in spite of all my previous track record of success in managing similar initiatives, I ultimately failed to manage this resistance to change.

This event drove me to select change management as my research topic and to focus on developing a guide to support managers surviving even the strongest resistance to change.

I ended up having my model, which has been published in an article and in this change management guide: BRIDGING THE GAP.

After my doctorate, I served as an Assistant Professor and the Director of Graduate Studies at Nile

University, where I teach my change management model along with its applications and tools.

I currently serve as the Managing Partner of ElKattan Consulting, which is a UK-based company specializing in change management consultation and capacity building.

It was my personal values that drove my choices and decisions at certain key moments to achieve these results, which I am really proud of.

In the end, it is all about your values and how much you believe in them.

1.6 THE BOOK CASE STUDIES

As a change leader himself, the author includes four case studies in this book. Three of them are personal case studies written by the author: Global Trans, News Media, and Polytechnique University. The fourth one (Rally) was initially written by one of my graduate students. The purpose of including these four case studies are to show the main essence of change management and reflect on using the knowledge provided.

While analyzing the case studies, the book will also highlight personal, common change management mistakes made by the author himself. By sharing his case studies, the author hopes to encourage reader engagement throughout the journey with personal reflections.

1.7 GLOBAL TRANS CASE STUDY

1.7.1 Background About Global Trans

In early 2012, I joined an international translation and localization company, which I will refer to hereafter as Global Trans. I was appointed by the board as a new CEO to replace the chairman, who had also been serving as a CEO for over 10 years.

This company developed an extensive industry-specific translation and localization expertise in many different fields in more than 120 different languages, rendering services for the world's largest language service providers serving companies like Microsoft, Oracle, Google, Samsung, Ford, Olympus, Canon, and many other international organizations.

Internally, this company had more than seven localization and translation brands, with five offices in key locations around the world. Every one or two brands belonged to an independent business unit inside the company. Each business unit had its own managing director responsible for defining strategy, managing the budget, and deciding how to launch a new service or penetrate a new market. In total, it had more than 250 employees, with a 2014 turnover of around US $6M. The structure of this company was more of a divisional structure, where every business unit had its own managing director.

1.7.2 Transformational Leadership

The chairman was a transformational leader who excelled in making dramatic changes and expanded the business accordingly. In less than seven years, the company was able to establish a network of professional translators in more than 50 languages in different industries. The chairman also successfully entered the Asian, European, and North American markets in a relatively short time. When I joined Global Trans, he was looking to expand the company's presence in Africa.

Our vision was to be one of the 50 top global players in the localization industry within five years. However, I did not personally believe that organic growth would get us to this position, which is why I advocated for an acquisition strategy for the development of new markets. This required focused market research and analysis, especially in a potentially promising market like China.

1.7.3   The Change Initiative

Global Trans had three independent business units. Each business unit was managed by managing director, and had its own identity, project management, marketing, translations, vendor management, and branding in the market, focusing on specific languages in four regions: The Middle East, Africa, Asia, and Europe.

Complaining that adding a new service or developing a new industry consumes a huge amount of effort, money, and time from all business units, the chairman held a meeting with the executive board to explain how the current status was hindering corporate growth strategy, presenting his analysis of the problems:

1. Developing a new industry requires almost the same effort from all business units, which consumes excess time and financial resources.

2. Inconsistencies among the business units as far as the process, regulations, and quality.

3. Isolation within business units hindering sharing of knowledge and experience.

4. Lack of coordination among different teams in different business units providing similar services.

5. No existing backup for key persons in each business unit due to difficulty in finding qualified professionals familiar with the industry.

Figures 1-1 shows the structure of the company.

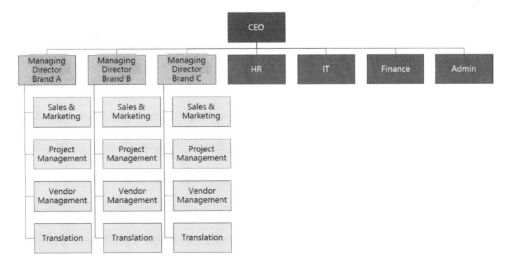

Figure 1-1. Organizational Structure (Before the Change)

During the meeting, I proposed to change the current divisional organizational structure with a matrix structure in which similar functions in the three business units were to be merged into one centralized function.

The current structure of the independent business units, along with the managing director position, would be replaced by a new Brand Management function that was to be added to the structure. Figure 1-2 gives the structure of the new proposed matrix structure. As illustrated in Figure 1-2, employees in the new matric structure will report to two managers.

Figure 1-2. Matrix Organizational Structure (After the Change)

I commented on my suggestion by saying:

> *"... the matrix structure is a dual management concept in which some employees report to two managers, a vertical manager and a horizontal manager. In our new structure, the vertical manager would be the new appointed functional manager while the horizontal manager would be the brand manager; replacing the position of business unit managing director."*

1.7.4   Change Management Mistakes

The newly proposed matrix structure was criticized and resisted by some colleagues because they believed that it would destroy accountability, as employees would not be able to work for two bosses! As an inside observer, it appeared that the new change initiative was met with resistance largely due to organizational politics.

Later, one manager commented:

> *"... there were some layers of the middle managers who were not convinced, nor completely aware of the need for this change. Hence, the managers of these layers did not feel enthusiastic about the change and therefore they did not exert efforts to convince their subordinates of such a change."*

The employees were not engaged with the change as they worried that the proposed restructuring would result in layoffs. In addition, they did not really know the driver for the change and had different versions of the vision of the change.

I, as a CEO and change manager, met with all different departments to communicate the new change through face-to-face and online meetings. Clearly, I had not effectively communicated the vision and the need for change. It was sort of one-way communication with no understanding of the message's perception and its implication on employees. Also, another critical mistake that I did was that I ignored the lack of continuous sponsorship by top management to daily conflicts, which was a major factor that impacted the momentum for the change.

Organizations are political even if they do not seem so. Politics in organizations is how employees exercise their power to achieve what they want. The impact of the change on the power and political situation inside the company was a very important to be considered, which I did not.

It was clear that I was facing emotional resistance from the key managers, which led to disconcerting confrontations. One of my mistakes that I kept managing the resistance mainly from a rational perspective, which did not work.

1.8   BARRIERS TO CHANGE

Let us hypothetically imagine the meeting in which I was announcing the new change initiatives in our Global Trans case study.

I called for a meeting with managers who were very secured, empowered, and had key positions in the company. I gave the following message:

> "... we will change our business unit structure as this structure does not support our growth strategy. The new structure will be a matrix one, in which we will group all similar resources from all business units to have one centralized function. We will not have independent business units anymore."

After my previous introduction, I presented a very well-prepared presentation about the many issues that were associated with the current structure, and how they were causing the current problems.

Now, I want you to think for a moment – what were these managers thinking of when I was giving my presentation?

I had no idea at that time of what can be called the *perceived loss;* and that was one of my greatest mistakes in managing the introduction of the change initiative.

Perceived loss can be loss of benefits, loss of control, loss of territories, increased workload, etc.

Everyone in such a moment would be mostly concerned with their own perception. Everyone would first think of *how will this impact me?*

I am sure you can easily guess that they were thinking of one or more of the following questions:

- I used to be a managing director, what will my next position be?

- Will I stay in my department?

- Will they increase or decrease my salary?

- Will I be promoted?

- Will I be laid-off?

- Should I postpone my resignation to see what will happen?

I am sure part of my message was received by my audience, but it was definitely distorted as the minds of those around me were busy putting all the bits and pieces together, away from the business message, to assemble their own perceptions and conclusions in case the proposed change was implemented.

Later, I realized that any change, in life or in business, is bundled with *uncertainties*. My message was full of *uncertainties* and ambiguity about what would happen during the change.

Managing new change requires enough support, discussion, and reassurance to deal with the uncertainty and ambiguity. When people face uncertainty, they often feel conflicting emotions (this will also depend on culture, which we will review when discussing the influence of culture on change).

From one perspective, some people may be worried that things will go wrong; some may fear from the unknown, others may just have a low degree of accepting *uncertainties* in their life; thus, the natural reaction of needing to feel protected from the unknown. On the other hand, some people may also be curious and/or excited about new challenges that may impact them in a positive way.

Furthermore, most people did not have freedom of choice.

Did such imposition cause more resistance in addition to the perceived loss and uncertainties?

Yes, this is usually true. Imposition provokes resistance as people do not get the sense of commitment or the sense of *"we are all in it together."*

However, it is worth mentioning that *imposition* will not have that much effect in a large power distanced culture, in which people accept and expect to have a big distance between them and the "big boss." In such a culture, people accept and expect not to have much freedom of choice. The question is: will people really be committed or not? (We will discuss this in more detail in Chapter 5.)

Change has, in reality, so many barriers that create obstacles and resistance. However, in this section I wanted to highlight three barriers that I consider very critical for any change. Always remember these three key words whenever you approach any change: perceived loss, uncertainties, and imposition.

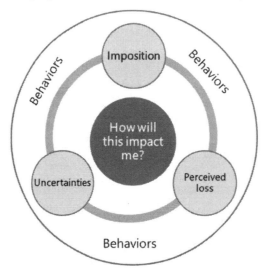

Figure 1-3. The Three Main Barriers to Change

People will not always resist change; most people will not resist if the change is not imposed and they have a sense of ownership, no sense of perceived loss, and the long-term benefits are clear, achievable, and rewarding compared to the effort that will be made.

1.9   CHAPTER IN A BOX

- This chapter offers the purpose and structure of the book, with an emphasis on its relevance for inclusion in contemporary change management literature.

- The book is written to clarify what change management is, how to apply it, and how it differs from project management.

- The book also covers national and organizational culture in demonstrating their interrelation to change.

- Three main change barriers were highlighted: perceived loss, uncertainties, and imposition.

CHAPTER 2
CHANGE MANAGEMENT BASICS

Chapter 2 - Change Management Basics

2.1 OVERVIEW

In addition to imposition, uncertainty, and perceived loss, as discussed in Chapter 1, change leaders face failure for many other reasons. The change may fail even if the outputs of the related projects are delivered successfully and on time. Change is considered successful only if the new capabilities are subtle, outcomes are enabled, change benefits are realized, and the new behaviors are fully integrated into the culture.

In the Global Trans case study, the organization was restructured, new positions were introduced, and new processes were developed. However, the change itself was a total failure. The organization went back to its previous structure three years after the attempted implementation.

No one can deny that in some situations, changes can be applied by imposition using the power of management, especially the power of owners. However, a transformational change requiring new behaviors and ways of doing the work cannot be achieved solely by power of management. Rather, it requires that its stakeholders have alignment, commitment, and motivation. None of these conditions can be expected to materialize exclusively through imposition.

Important Note

Change is a lifelong practice for any successful organization, but it usually has many barriers that prevent its successful implementation. (Merrell, 2012).

2.2 FAILURE IS PART OF THE LEARNING PROCESS

Southern California's Orange County is an adventurous place to live. One of its amazing features is that you can switch between going to the beach and skiing on the snow in the same day. It's true!

When I lived there back in the 1980s, while at the beach one day, my friends and I decided to organize a plan to go skiing at a resort about 50 miles away. I had never skied before. I remember listening to some skiing tips, and being told that if I want to stop, I should move my feet inward toward each other.

On my first attempt to ski, I went up the mountain and started heading downhill. When I reached the bottom, I started moving my feet inward to stop; unfortunately, it did not work out as planned – I had one of the worst falls I experienced in my life. Discouraged, I declared it to be my last ever attempt to ski.

Learning to manage an organizational change, as well as any other life endeavor, is like learning how to ride a bicycle or to ski. Simply, you will not learn without falling (or failing), which is an essential part of the learning process. You might read about learning how to ski, educating yourself, and afterward take a few lessons before setting out on your own skiing adventure. While it is important to know the how, it is essential to practice, and while practicing, falling (or failing) is to be expected – it is part of the learning process.

With skiing, as well as any other life endeavor, no matter how well you are prepared, sooner or later you will fall (or fail). The real moment of truth comes when you are faced with picking yourself back up and deciding whether or not to try again.

Figure 2-1. Falling is Part of the Learning Process

When you fail, don't let yourself become irreparably discouraged and frustrated, as I did with skiing. We all need to fail a time or two in order to learn. Failing is part of the learning process. Similarly, this is how we learn any new practice, including change management.

Can you reflect on how your failures contributed to your learning journey?

2.3   WHY DO WE NEED CHANGE AND CHANGE MANAGEMENT?

Why do we need to change? This is a big question for anyone who tends to play it safe in their personal or professional lives because understanding the reason behind the change is motivational in reaching your goals.

In the present era in which we live, no one really needs to highlight the importance of the word "change." History itself proves the fact that nothing ever stays the same.

Therefore, change management is becoming more significant than ever. It is easy to see its importance in light of the fast pace of current environmental and technological changes.

For every change management success story, there is an example demonstrating the failure of adapting to change. Before 2010, nearly everyone owned a Nokia mobile phone. The original Nokia models are now obsolete; replaced by smartphones from companies like Samsung and Apple – neither of whom had a large share of the market in the beginning. But why did this change happen?

Organizations must keep adapting to external and market changes; otherwise, diminishing their ability to survive

When I go to any change management workshop, my audience is usually more aware of the importance of managing new changes than I am. With the rapid pace of change, it is difficult to argue whether or not managers need to master the competency of change management.

Important Note

Change in any organization is typically linked with change in the external environment. However, organizations should also implement new internal developmental or continuous improvement programs, even if the change in the external environment is currently not impacting the organization satisfactorily.

While the implementation of organizational change is crucial for survival, change is also accompanied by risks and uncertainties particularly, when it affects marketability, customer base, or industry.

Every change is accompanied by a transition period. The transition period is needed to build new capabilities and establish new behaviors. Change management is needed to help leaders manage this transition period, while an organization moves strategically from one state to another.

Generally, change management is needed to:

- Establish readiness for the change initiative.

- Assure having the right awareness, competence, and engagement.

- Manage both the people and organization sides.

- Provide the right change narrative.

- Assure achievement of the change outcomes and benefits.

- Establish and reinforce the new behaviors and mindsets into the organizational culture.

- Embed new capabilities within the operations.

All of these terms will become increasingly familiar, and you will begin to use and identify them with ease as we continue through the book.

Simply put, change management is required whenever there is an uncertainty, complexity, anticipated resistance, moving out of comfort zones, changing existing behaviors and norms, and building new capabilities.

In the Global Trans case study, I had mistakenly thought that I could use my experience to manage the change, without following traditional change management processes or practices.

In retrospect, I have to confess that my extended experience in management was not enough, by itself, to lead the change correctly.

It was not a matter of change management maturity; most of the Global Trans management team had not ever heard about change management. During the implementation of the change initiative, we were reactively responding to new issues; more focused on fire-fighting, rather than proactively planning the change – thus, the benefits anticipated by the chairman were not realized.

Moral of the story: in order to avoid the obstacles and hindrances in achieving effective implementation of big projects and initiatives, consideration must be given to change management models.

2.4   DOES CHANGE MANAGEMENT REPLACE PROJECT MANAGEMENT?

Change management is not another dimension or replacement of project management. It is, however, an area that needs to be considered in addition to project management for successful implementation of strategic initiatives.

The change management body of knowledge is a combination of many knowledge areas designed to manage a change initiative to realize its benefits.

As we keep progressing, we will cover different knowledge areas. These knowledge areas are: Stakeholder Management, Culture Management, Organizational Alignment, Communication Management, Benefits Management, Resistance Management, Coaching, Performance Management, Leadership, Risk Management, Value Management, Strategic Management, Program Management, and Project Management.

Some of these knowledge areas are the core of the ElKattan's 5-Theme Model as we will see starting from Chapter 7. Figure 2-2 shows the knowledge areas that are applied in change management.

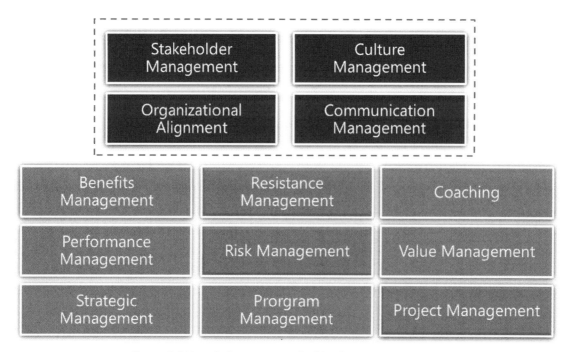

Figure 2-2. Knowledge Areas Applied in Change Management

2.5   WHAT ARE CHANGE AND CHANGE MANAGEMENT?

Change management is a way to manage the change in projects, specific to current circumstances, based on predefined processes, practices, and techniques.

In the absence of a change management, an organization typically uses an ad hoc process depending entirely on the leadership of specific individuals; an approach that can lead to setbacks in achieving long-term success. Having a standard change management model helps the organization learn from previous change initiatives.

Any organizational change has a transition period. Why?

Because a transition period is needed to establish and support the new capabilities and behaviors.. A change initiative, on its face, indicates moving the organization in a transition period between two different states.

By definition, a change is moving the organization in a transition period from a current state, to a future state engineered to achieve specific benefits.

Change management is the practices and tools designed to manage a change. As defined by the Association of Change Management Professionals (ACMP, 2019), change management is the practice of applying a structured approach to the transition of an organization from a current state to a future state to achieve expected benefits. Figure 2-3 shows the classical pattern of any change.

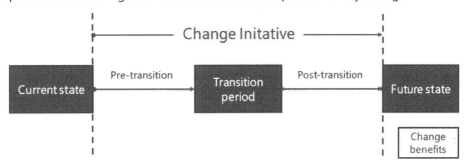

Figure 2-3. Change Classical Pattern

There are many types of change initiatives, the main types are:

* **Strategic initiative** – This may involve change in the mission, vision, business model, or key strategies of the organization. Typically, such a change is a transformational one and will affect most elements of the organization.

* **Restructuring initiative** – Normally, change in the structure follows the change in the strategy. However, top management, as in the Global Trans case study, may attempt to restructure the organization to tackle a set of issues to achieve greater overall performance.

* **Systems/Process improvement initiative** – These are change initiatives affecting internal processes, procedures, and IT systems.

* **Culture initiative** – Generally the most problematic, as this change deals mainly with the people side.

2.6   CHANGE CLASSIFICATIONS

Present-day change management literature classifies change in various ways.

Some researchers assert that change can be classified into three categories:

- **Incremental change** – fine-tuning existing processes to increase efficiency.

- **Continuous change** – the evolution and improvement of processes and operations.

- **Radical change** – primarily driven by external environmental factors.

Other researchers support categories that include two factors:

- The first factor is planning, whether it is a planned or unplanned change.

- The second factor is impact, whether high or low.

As presented in Figure 2-4, these two factors comprise the following four change types:

1. The first type of change is transformational, a planned change with projected high impact.

2. The second change type is transactional or planned with the expectation of having a low impact.

3. The third type of change is revolutionary, unplanned, but with a high impact.

4. Lastly, we have an evolutionary change, the type of change that is unplanned but with low impact.

Most change management model focus primarily on planned changes, which are the transformational and transactional types.

Transactional change can be classified into two sub-categories depending on the magnitude of the change and length of the transition period:

- **Incremental** – occurring at short intervals, addressing smaller changes, improvements, or just fine-tuning processes.
- **Transitional** – requiring a longer transition period to move from the current state to the future state.

Typically, incremental change has low organizational impact, but should be maintained continuously to keep improving processes and operations. This is similar to the "Kaizen" concept which was introduced by Toyota in the lean manufacturing methodology.

On the other hand, the transformational change, may require capabilities that may not be available and may have major impact on an organization's mission, vision, business model, strategy, leadership practices, and culture.

Numerous researchers have notably argued that incremental or transitional changes could accumulate and create a substantial transformational change.

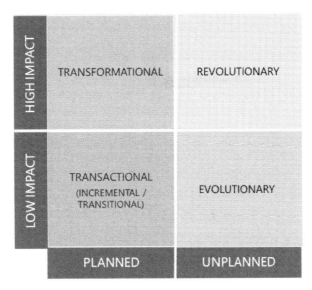

Figure 2-4. Plan vs. Impact Change Classification. Note. Adopted from Burke (2010)

2.7   CHANGE CLASSICAL PATTERN

The change classical pattern is one of the important concepts of change management.

Many change management scholars agreed that any change must follow a certain pattern of three phases – pre-transition, transition, and post-transition. So, achieving a successful change requires managing these three phases of the change pattern.

The first phase is the pre-transition phase, which I will call it as the Readiness Phase. The aim of this phase is to assure the individual and organizational readiness to the change and to identify the values and behaviors that need to be managed. At the beginning of this phase, we determines the degree to which people are prepared and willing to accept the change.

A high level of readiness means the stakeholders are ready to proceed with the change.

The second phase is the transition phase. Before this phase begins, the leadership team should assure that the driving forces are greater than the anticipated resistance.

The third phase is the post-transition phase, which I will call it as the Sustaining and Realizing Benefits Phase. The aim of this phase is to assure the change is sustainable and the intended benefits are realized.

Figure 2-5 shows the change classical pattern that is used in ElKattan's Model.

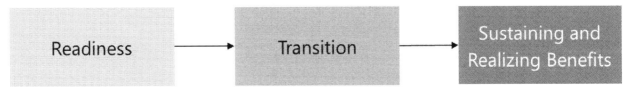

Figure 2-5. The Change Classical Pattern (Readiness – Transition - Sustaining and Realizing Benefits)

2.7.1 Readiness Phase (Pre-Transition)

As the name implies, the main purpose of this phase is to assure readiness on both the organizational and individual levels; put simply, this phase determines the degree to which the organization, culture and people are prepared and willing to accept the change.

The objectives of this phase are as follows:

- Forming the change leadership team.

- Identification of the change vision and objectives.

- Assessing individual, culture, and organizational readiness.

- Formulation of change management strategies and tactics.

- Conducting training and orientation.

- Initiation of the communication plan.

- Increasing the level of dissatisfaction with the current status.

The readiness phase is similar to Lewin's unfreezing phase. A high level of readiness means the stakeholders and organization are ready to proceed with the change. The readiness is normally correlated with both support from management and a willingness by the individuals to begin moving toward the new desired state.

2.7.2 Transition Phase

The second phase is the transition phase. During this phase, senior managers are required to continuously support the change and remove obstacles as they arise. The change management plan must be integrated with the project management plan. Continuous monitoring of the change management plan is crucial to accommodate adjustments and refinement as needed.

At the beginning of this phase, a full awareness of the anticipated changes during the transition period must be clearly conveyed. Even though the project ends in this phase, achieving the outcomes and realizing the benefits may occur later in the third phase.

The objectives of this phase are as follows:

- Execution of the technical solution as well as the change management tactics.

- Building new capabilities and demonstrating new behaviors.

- Initiating improvement processes required by suggested solutions.

- Developing a competent team.

- Enabling the change outcomes.

- Managing the stakeholder engagement and resistance.

- Managing the organizational alignment.

2.7.3 Sustaining and Realizing Benefits Phase (Post-transition)

Whenever the difference between project management and change management is discussed, the sustaining and realizing benefits phase almost immediately becomes a focal point of the discussion. Here, the role of change management is crucial where it pertains to the form of reinforcement of the new behaviors and realizing the planned change benefits.

Project management considers its processes completed once the new service or product has been delivered according to the schedule, budget, and scope. This phase assures that the new behaviors are secured and embedded in both operations and culture.

For example, when implementing a new Enterprise Resource Planning (ERP) system, the project ends once the new ERP is deployed. However, it must be accompanied by a change management plan to ensure that the staff are already familiar with the features of the new system. This phase also guarantees that the benefits are realized in both the short term and the long term.

This phase is important to make sure people do not revert to their previous habits and behaviors. In this phase, we also track the intended benefits to make sure that the change provides the expected value. The objectives of this phase are as follows:

- Analyzing feedback and taking corrective action.

- Revisiting the change strategy for the next phase of implementation.

- Achieving the change outcomes.

- Ensuring the realization of the intended change benefits.

- Institutionalizing the new change (new systems, new incentive scheme, etc.).

- Making sure the new change is embedded into the organization's culture.

Some change management models suggest that new change initiatives be introduced in this phase to prevent people from attempting to return to the pre-change state.

2.8 MISCONCEPTIONS ABOUT CHANGE MANAGEMENT

Below are some misconceptions about change management:

- **Change management could replace project management** – Change management complements project management. The change management plan must be integrated into the project management plan.

- **Organizations need to select one change management model for its programs** – There is no singular way to manage all change initiatives. Change management activities must be tailored to fit local circumstances.

- **Change management function must be established inside organizations** – The role of change management could be integrated with other organizational functions, such as the offices of project management and strategic management.

- **Change is intangible and cannot be quantitatively measured** – Change benefits must be quantified and measured in order to assess the success of change implementation.

2.9   RESISTANCE TO CHANGE

When it comes to change, resistance emerges as one of the most common factors. Resistance, as discussed in Chapter 1, is primarily derived from perceived loss and uncertainty, thus, change must be managed at the individual level, as well as the organizational level. If resistance is not managed properly at the individual level, those resisting will exercise considerable effort and energy in convincing others to support their position.

The question is: do all people invariably resist the change and its uncertainty? The answer is no; people may react with fear or respond with hope based on how they construct the meaning of the change. Also, culture comes into the equation. As we will see in Chapter 5, some organizations have more of an uncertainty-accepting culture than others. In these scenarios, people like new, innovative ideas and embrace challenges.

Also, resistance may not be a resistance. Some people may believe it is part of their responsibilities and they have the right to accept or not; or they just see the risks are too high for such a change.

2.9.1   My Electrical Metaphor

As an electronics engineer, I will attempt to explain the resistance concept using a metaphor involving a simple electrical circuit. Rest assured, you will understand this metaphor without a degree in engineering. As shown in Figure 2-6, any simple electrical circuit has a battery, wire, and a lamp.

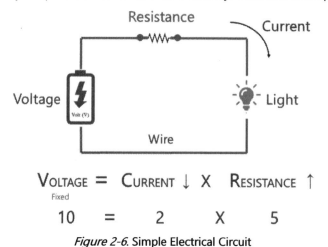

$$\text{VOLTAGE} = \text{CURRENT} \downarrow \text{ X } \text{RESISTANCE} \uparrow$$
$$\underset{\text{Fixed}}{}$$
$$10 = 2 \quad X \quad 5$$

Figure 2-6. Simple Electrical Circuit

The equation which governs this circuit is:

> Voltage = Current x Resistance

Assume that the Voltage value of the battery is constantly fixed. What happens to the amount of Current when Resistance increases or decreases?

The more Resistance you have, the less Current present; accordingly, *less light* from the bulb. On the other hand, the less Resistance you have, the more Current present; accordingly, *more light* from the bulb.

Now, the critical question is what will happen when Resistance decreases to zero?

If Resistance decreases to zero, this means the wire has no resistance at all. The Current will be extremely high and the bulb *will burn out!*

And what will happen if Resistance = infinity, which means that the wire does not allow the current to pass through. This means the current will be zero and the bulb will have *no light.*

Therefore, you cannot have a circuit with zero resistance; similarly, you cannot also have a circuit with a very high resistance. As shown in Figurer 2-7, change management has its own equation.

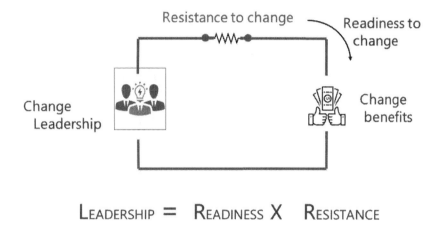

Figure 2-7. Change Management Circuit

The equation which governs this change management circuit is:

Change Leadership = Readiness to Change x Resistance

Similarly to what we discussed, you can think of what will happen when the amount of resistance to a change decreases and increases. The intention of this metaphor is to demonstrate that, the right amount of resistance is required to achieve successful change.

Important Note

Resistance in general, despite what is found in much of change management literature, is *not* a bad thing! Rather, the right amount of resistance can enhance, challenge, and mature the original idea of the change initiative.

Having the right amount of resistance to change is healthy; however, if the resistance increases to a certain threshold, it can become a real obstacle to change. Thus, resistance should be neither avoided or removed, rather, it must be managed and utilized properly.

The moral of this metaphor is that resistance to change is similar to the resistance obstacles facing electricity – you do not want to have zero or high resistance – but in balance, change can be effectively implemented.

The question of how to anticipate employee resistance will be outlined as we delve into the different components of the ElKattan's Model.

2.10   SOURCES OF RESISTANCE

Change comes with positive and negative consequences. Typically, change initiatives and resistance go hand-in-hand.

Previously, we discussed three factors that cause resistance to change: imposition, uncertainty, and perceived loss. However, one of the critical sources of resistance to change occurs when the change conflicts with values, basic assumptions, norms, and ways of doing things; otherwise known as culture.

Resistance to change can be anticipated under the following conditions:

- If the change requires a behavior that is not favored by the norms of the company.
- If the change conflicts with the way people relate to each other.
- If there is no transparency inside the organization.
- If there is a management practice that fails to clarify potential negative issues within a proper timeframe.
- If people are unwilling to accept risks.
- If negative discussions arise concerning an organization's management or any previous change initiatives that have failed.

Generally, these resistance indicators reflect on the culture of the organization itself.

Three chapters of this book are dedicated to culture and its influence on change within business environments, in addition to a chapter explaining how to manage culture.

Now we have established culture as a main source of resistance, in addition to perceived loss, uncertainty, and imposition.

There are additional sources of resistance like: power struggle, fear of complexity, lack of competence, etc.

Coping successfully with resistance is on the hardest parts of change management. Managers usually think if they present the change idea logically, employees will accept the change. However, they shortly discover that resistance remains no matter how clearly they present the change vision and objectives.

The key is to understand that the nature of resistance, as will be explained later in more detail, is a reaction of emotional and rational process within the stakeholders.

2.11   TYPES OF RESISTANCE TO CHANGE

Kruger maintained that up to 80 percent of change resistance consists of intangible soft factors related to culture and emotions, with the remaining 20 percent visibly seen – or hard factors – primarily related to differences in rationale, logic, and ideologies. Of course, these percentages are just indicators, and subject to variance depending on the context of the change initiative.

Figure 2-8 shows Kruger's change iceberg.

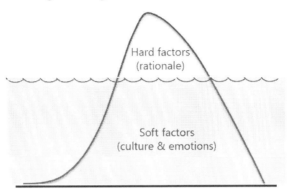

Figure 2-8. Kruger's change iceberg

Based on Kruger's change iceberg, resistance can be categorized into three main types:

- **Emotional resistance** – emerging from fear of the unknown, fear of losing any benefits, political issues, a sense of insecurity, any threat to one's comfort zone or territory, mistrust, etc. This form of resistance can be managed through reassurance, reinforcement of trust, negotiation or trade-off. Researchers agree that emotions play a powerful role in the most successful cases of change.

- **Rational resistance** – stemming from a lack of awareness, intellectual or logical differences, opposing ideologies, etc. This type of resistance can be managed through persuasion based on clear data and facts.

- **Incompetence resistance** – manifested through fear of complexity or lack of technical knowledge and/or skills; managed by providing training, mentoring, and coaching.

Table 2-1 summarizes the three types of resistance.

Table 2-1. *Resistance Types*

Type of resistance	Sample of resistors	How to address
Incompetence	Those who are afraid of the change complexity or believe that they do not have the right competence.	Development through training, mentoring, and coaching.
Emotional	Those who might lose benefits, power or the comfort zone.	Reassurance, building trust, Negotiation and/or trade-off strategy.
Rational	Those who have different beliefs, ideas, and philosophies or not convinced with the details.	Factually based persuasion strategy.

2.12 REFLECTION ON GLOBAL TRANS CASE STUDY

Referring to the Global Trans case study discusses in Chapter 1, it quickly became clear that I was facing emotional resistance within key management, which led to disconcerting confrontations. My mistake was that I kept managing the resistance mainly from a rational perspective, which did not work.

Why was I worried about this resistance?

Because most organizations are built on control and authority even when involvement is a common practice. That is why I was worried as I perceived it as a direct threat to my control as a CEO.

Organizations are political even if they do not seem so. Politics in organizations is how employees exercise their power to achieve what they want. The impact of the change on the power and political situation inside the company was a very important to be considered, which I did not.

2.13 THE DRIVING FORCES OF A CHANGE

Most researchers agreed that having a clear and well-communicated vision is one the most important practices in change management. Also, the first step in the implementation is usually the most challenging. Most people are resistant to, or will be unsupportive of change, unless they are already dissatisfied with the current status. This occurs largely on an individual level.

Most researchers conclude that the three driving forces required in any concept for change to be successfully implemented are:

1. A clear and well-communicated vision.

2. The right capabilities for the first step.

3. A high level of dissatisfaction with the current state.

Now, I will put these three drivers in what is called in change management: "the Change Formula" as shown in Figure 2-9.

Change happens when:

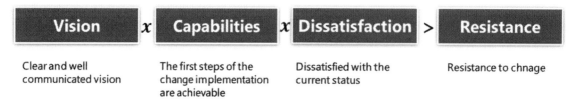

Figure 2-9. Change Formula

This formula compares one specific variable – change resistance– to three other variables: (1) Clear and well communicated **vision**, (2) The right **capabilities** of the first steps of the change implementation, and (3) **Dissatisfied** with the current status. In this sense, the formula maintains that a product of the three variables "on the left side of the formula in order for a company to arrive at an optimal start for any change initiative.

This formula demonstrates that if dissatisfaction is missing or close to zero, the product would certainly be smaller than the right side of the equation (i.e., Resistance), and the change would therefore encounter multiple difficulties in the implementation process. Thus, a change leader must increase the level of dissatisfaction with the current state in order to move people out of their comfort zone.

Meanwhile, the vision for the intended change must be created and communicated to all concerned stakeholders, along with the capabilities cornerstone, which is to begin implementation with practical and simplified actions.

Therefore, the formula is simply stating that the driving forces must be greater than the anticipated resistance. The change leader should analyze the context and culture before initiating the change initiative, to determine what other driving forces are critical to focus on.

Based on this formula, a change leader must ensure that the change vision is very clear; that there are enough influential people who are dissatisfied with the status quo; and, finally, to ensure that the first steps in any change implementation are achievable and well-understood.

2.14 CHANGE CURVE

Organizational change simply means moving from one state to another. This could be change in behaviors, attitude, the way people work, systems used, authorities, or the distribution of power. People should be ready to move ahead and disengage from what needs to be changed about their working conditions or management; stepping out from the past into a brighter future. That said, the past is not always all bad, and it is to be expected that when a person has previously excelled at what they do for an extended period of time, it will be difficult to get detached to what he/she was doing.

Some people will struggle with leaving their "territories" – those places or positions where they felt validated for their contributions to the organization and/or were held in high esteem by their colleagues – requiring a period of understanding and transitional support by management as change begins to take shape.

Management could also, for example, organize an event celebrating organizational achievements and offering individual recognition of those achieved specific goals or excelled in their commitment to the company's success.

The Kubler-Ross model shown in Figure 2-10 assumes a series of emotions and correlating phases, that people may experience one or more of, in the course of change implementation: Shock, Anger, Denial, Frustration, Bargaining, Depression, Letting go, and Acceptance.

Based on the Kubler-Ross model, once a change has been decided on and announced, some will see it as bad news and feel immense "shock" – followed by a period of "anger" or "denial" depending on the context. If people go to the "denial" phase first, they tend to strongly believe that, ultimately, the change will not occur. When the change moves forward, people may enter the "anger" phase, followed by the "frustration" phase, especially if they perceive that the change was forced on them.

Enter the "bargaining" phase; a period through which some people may begin to negatively project their own perceptions regarding the problems with change, and actively seeking ways to stop or avoid it. Ultimately, with the change process being unstoppable and unavoidable, they arrive at the "depression" phase, requiring time, patience and support from management as they work their way through to the "letting go" and "acceptance" phases.

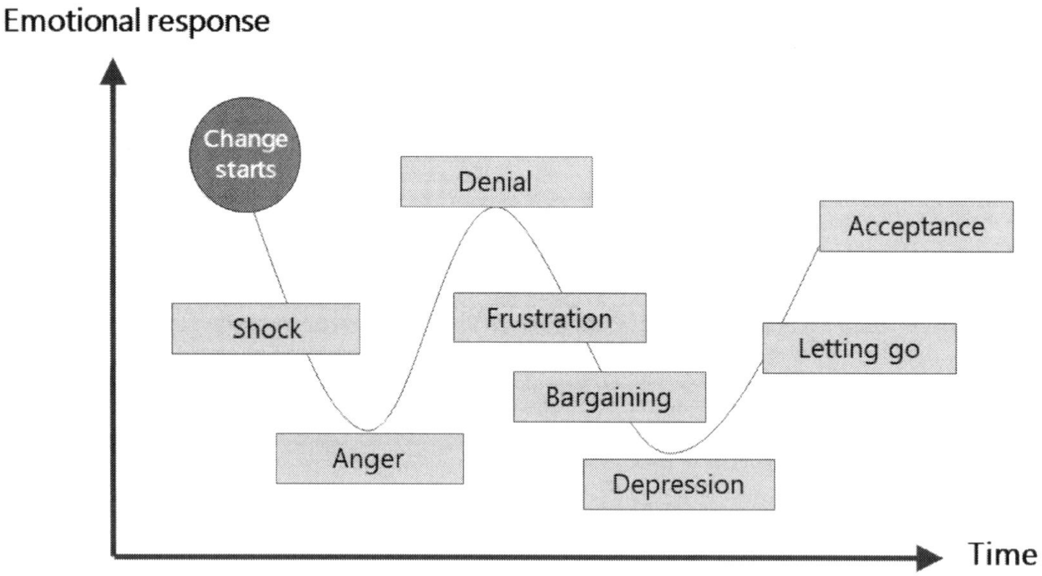

Emotional response

Figure 2-10. Kubler-Ross Change Curve

The start of 2020 became an in-our-face example of real-time management of these emotions as many people were forced into self-isolation, social distancing scenarios, and working from home due to the Coronavirus (Covid-19) pandemic; creating a crisis situation that no one asked for or imagined.

Self-reflection

Have you ever experienced any of those emotions in Figure 2-10 as a response to social or an organizational change due to the Coronavirus pandemic? If yes, how was it handled?

People who are shocked by the change will be concerned about the perceived loss. What impact will it have? How will it affect them? During this phase, the change leader should observe, listen, and show facts.

Ultimately, people reach different levels in the acceptance phase. While some suffer through negative emotions, others will carry onward and forward with either neutral or positive emotions; finding their way through determining what works, and what does not.

In any organization, change leadership should be trained to individually identify the emotional phases employees may be passing through.

As mentioned before, not all people will move through all emotional phases before accepting change; they may also pass through them in random order and obviously, with varying degrees of intensity as Kubler-Ross points out.

Depending on the position of the stakeholders, change leaders should be able to anticipate the behaviors and perceptions – appropriately selecting strategies to assist them in disengaging from the past – while leading them through the emotional phases until they reach acceptance, with positive emotions and renewed determination in striving toward personal goals, and, ultimately, newly empowered corporate success.

2.15   CHAPTER IN A BOX

In this chapter, we discussed some concepts and definitions of change management. One primary takeaway was that we need the change to adapt to the external environment in addition to continue improving our internal processes. This chapter also outlined the importance of change management. It also set out the following change management basic concepts:

- Engage in due diligence in preparing for the change project.

- Provide proper awareness, competence, and engagement for all stakeholders.

- Demonstrate proper and balanced mental and emotional engagement.

- Assure the enablement of change initiative outcomes, realization of the benefits, and achievement of the strategic objectives.

- Establish and secure the new or appropriate behaviors with minimal culture conflict.

- Embed new change management capabilities within operations.

- Reinforce new behaviors; firmly establishing them within the culture.

It was discussed that a change requires a transition phase and is defined as moving the organization in a transition period from its current state to a future state engineered to achieve specific benefits.

And we knew that change management is about applying structured approach to manage the three phases of the change classical pattern: pre-transition, transition, and post-transition phases. These three phases are called the change life cycle, and we will be referring to them as the Readiness, Transition, and Sustaining and Realizing Benefits.

We also discussed the four classifications of change: (1) Transformational, (2) Transactional, (3) Revolutionary, and (4) Evolutionary mentioning that change management models like ElKattan's model focus only on the planned changes.

Resistance is generally classified into the following types: rational, incompetence, and emotional.

Sources of resistance are: imposition, uncertainty, perceived loss, culture, power struggle, deep structure, fear of complexity, and lack of competence.

Despite what is described in most change management literature, change is not always a bad thing. The change requires a balanced degree of resistance to enhance and mature the concept of the change initiative.

CHAPTER 3
BRIDGING THE GAP

Chapter 3 - Bridging the Gap

3.1   OVERVIEW

This chapter offers a brief background outlining common mistakes in leading strategic change initiatives as well as the differences between change management and project management. Also, differences between project outputs, change outcomes, and change benefits will be discussed. In addition to introducing a secondary case study.

Chapter 1 introduced the Global Trans case study. The News Media case study will be introduced in this chapter. We will reflect on both case studies in other chapter. Of course, change lessons learned from the case will be highlighted.

3.2   NEWS MEDIA CASE STUDY

In early March 2010, Aly Fady, a board member of News Media, requested a private meeting with me in Doha. Fady – who was the manager and sponsor of a new transformation program – asked me to support him to save the program and promised to promote me to whatever position I liked in the future.

In recalling the News Media transformation program, marketing director Hassan Abdel Hamid stated:

> "... at the beginning, the employees welcomed the change and were fully engaged; they were looking forward to turning into a huge profitable organization similar or identical to the BBC. However, with what happened later, these employees lost their passion for the change and became totally disengaged."

A senior member of the transformation program team also commented on it in an interview, saying:

> "... the organization went into a huge fight; it was unfortunate that we took part in this transformation program. We had carefully planned for this change, but when it came to the implementation, everything collapsed."

Background

Employing roughly 450 personnel and operating on an annual budget of approximately $6.5 million dollars, News Media, founded in 1997, was a non-profit organization dedicated to developing websites and content.

By 2010, the organization owned one of the world's most successful and stable news and Islamic-themed websites, garnering more than 120,000 visits per day.

The organization was owned by a Qatari association based in Doha, Qatar. However, it was located in Cairo, Egypt. In 2010, the organization, along with its catalogue of websites, suffered one of the most significant setbacks in the history of Arabic websites as a result of fatal mistakes in change management.

In 2007, I joined the organization as managing director, reporting to the CEO. I split my time between Cairo, where I managed an Egyptian team, and Doha, where I managed an Indian team.

Implementing a New Transformation Program

A newly elected board of directors contracted two international consulting companies and announced the launch of a new transformation program. The initiation of the change was not presented in advance for debate or discussion. No one from the Cairo office, where 90% of the production was managed, was consulted before the change was initiated.

There was a wide gap between the announced vision – which was to make the organization more institutionalized, more developed, and more dependent on its own funds than on donations – and the one that was being implemented.

A governance for the program was established, consisting of an executive committee composed of five board members headed by Aly Fady, and a leadership team composed of two board members, the two external consultants, and two executives from News Media: the president and the general manager. Figure 3-1 shows the governance of the program.

Figure 3-1. Governance of the Transformation Program

One of the consultants who joined the program commented on the governance by saying:

> *"... the top management of News Media did not want the employees to be involved in the communications. Because of this, the negative perception of this change was escalated."*

The Vision

There were many versions of the reason for the new program. One explanation offered was that it was to change the company's business model to emulate that of the BBC. However, many employees had alternative views as to why this program was initiated. Nagy Younis, the head of the project management unit, commented on this by saying:

> *"... the idea to be like the BBC did not sufficiently clarify what the results that should be achieved in the short and long term. It was an ambiguous idea. In addition, the absence of a shared vision between the leadership team was one of the main factors that impacted the success of the change."*

Even though one version of the vision was an inspiring one (converting to the BBC model), it wasn't clear to anyone what changes would be made, how they would be implemented, or who would be impacted. In addition, rumors spread through the organization that the Cairo team would be replaced by another team in Doha. The employees felt that the change had been imposed on them, and that it swirled with ambiguity and uncertainty.

Meanwhile, the staff was busy fulfilling the high demand for the organization's successful websites, with many seeing no need for change; in retrospect, maintaining the momentum of success would have been the wiser decision. The head of editors commented: *"... employees knew nothing of what the vision was about."*

The Leadership Team

Hisham Gaber, the general manager, said:

"... there was supposedly an executive committee formed by the board of directors to lead the new program. However, only one person from this committee was actively involved in the program."

This one person referred to by Gaber was Aly Fady, who was a new member of the board. The staff in Cairo did not really know who the sponsor and the change manager were.

Neither the change manager nor the leadership team mobilized any sense of urgency about the change, and employees in Egypt were not sure why the change was happening at all.

Commenting on the change manager, the head of the project management unit said in an interview:

"... this leader lacked experience in both how to manage change and how to lead such an organization."

Another key manager commented:

"... credibility is built upon accumulated experience in relevant areas. However, in the case that we are discussing, the change leader had no such accumulated experience. As such, it was not possible for him to build credibility."

Scope of the Transformation Program

In order to get the buy-in from the managers, the external consulting company hired by the board to implement the program conducted intensive workshops with the managers to come up with the scope of the change initiative, which were to be submitted to the board for approval.

Regarding the efforts of the change team to engage the staff, Nagy Younis commented:

"... the change team wanted to get the employees engaged, but this was not achievable, especially with the large number of employees who felt disengaged and consequently became inactive over the course of this change."

The transformation initiative consisted of two programs that were projected to take approximately 18 months to implement; each program was to be implemented through a number of projects (see Table 3-1 for the purposes, projects, and estimated durations).

Table 3-1. *Program Description*

	Program 1	Program 2
Purpose	The key purpose of this program was to build a solid business foundation. It also aimed at establishing a strategic level of alignment between the different functions.	The key purpose of this program was to build long-term sustainability enablers to ensure that the organization had what it takes to transform to the next phase of its development.

	Program 1	Program 2
Projects	Project 1: Strategic and operation assessment Project 2: Corporate strategy Project 3: Corporate governance Project 4: Business development strategy Project 5: Financial strategy	Project 1: Organizational development and cultural program. Project 2: Organizational restructuring Project 3: Legal structure model implementation Project 4: Operational business planning
Duration	6 months	12 months

The main goal, as indicated by one of the consultants, was to determine whether or not the organization was expanding in accordance with the mission under which it was originally established and to set it back on the track of this mission, if necessary.

You Cannot Stop Rumors

Rumors are always associated with a lack of information.

A comprehensive assessment was conducted at all levels of the organization in order to create a clear picture of which areas needed improvement. The assessment started with no prior notification or explanation of the reasons for it. Omar Abdel Halim, the head of IT, made this comment about why the resistance emerged:

> "... An assessment started with no prior explanation of the reasons for it. The resistance emerged after the assessment results came out. At this point, the directions to be followed were not clear."

Upon finalizing the assessment, the executive committee asked the News Media management to lay off some employees. This request was not acceptable to the management in Egypt, as the employees in question had been with the company for a such a long time and they were of the opinion that the organization could not get rid of them in this way. On the other hand, the members of the executive committee, whose members were all Qatari, assumed this to be an act of defiance.

Away from the assessment, the board shut down the TV channel owned by News Media and laid off all the channel's employees without warning. As there was little information provided about what was going on, negative rumors quickly spread.

One of these rumors was that the new program had a hidden agenda, which gained traction after some messages were sent by unknown employees to everyone that all production would be moved to Doha.

The Confrontation

Recalling the confrontation, an executive from the external consulting company said:

> "... at first, we maintained an open-book policy. Further, we attempted to come up with a shared vision. However, with the mistrust between all parties, we could not go on. In other words, we were able to handle such resistance for a few months, but we later came to stop implementing the new program."

The transformation program was perceived very negatively by the employees. The objectives were vague and unclear, even though the leadership team considered the objectives to be very clear! Therefore, the change came with a very damaging skepticism; it felt like a threat to the existing status of the organization. Thus, the employees felt frustrated, and uncertain about their future in the organization.

Staff started sending messages of complaint to the board, to no avail. The board's silence with regard to staff concerns intensified staff resistance. The head of editors, Magdy Saad, said:

> *"... at the outset, the organization's readiness for the change was not strong enough; there was no one to reply or to communicate to the employees what was going on."*

To make matters worse, the executive committee headed by Fady did not understand the culture of the organization, resulting in resistance to the newly implemented program. Younis commented about the cultural conflict by saying:

> *"... if the change-leading people had understood the culture embedded in the organization, they would have been able to ground their decisions; without an understanding of the culture, their decisions were obscured and arbitrary. Thus, these decisions increased tensions and inflamed the situation."*

The board decided to move the organization's CEO and general manager – who were also in the leadership team – from their executive positions and to remain as consultants in the organization and to join a supervisory committee. They hired the director of planning, Ayman ElMasry, as the new general manager reporting directly to Aly Fady. A few weeks later, the previous CEO, who was very popular as he was considered to be its real founder resigned as a result of a conflict with Aly Fady

As the resistance grew, Doha was finally compelled to send a representative to hear staff concerns. That was taken as a good sign; however, as soon as the representative had departed Cairo, it was announced that hundreds of layoffs would take effect and that all operations would be transferred to Doha.

Employees naturally felt betrayed and deceived; they refused to leave the Cairo office building, with the intention of continuing their mission. A sit-in commenced.

News Media was a non-profit organization with a good mission. Everyone in the organization believed in the mission and considered it to be part of their personal mission; the staff were unwilling to give up everything they had achieved for the community without a fight. Because of this belief in the organization's mission, they were determined to continue to seek funding for the many programs that were already in place to benefit the community.

3.2.1   Reflection

As I will be reflecting on this case study as we move through the book, it would be useful for the reader to consider the following:

- How clear was the future state of the program? How did this impact the alignment between all the stakeholders?

- What are the common issues between this case study and the Global Trans case study that we looked at in Chapter 1?

- What are the mistakes that caused the program to fail?

- What would you do if you were in my position? Would you accept the offer from Fady to support saving the program? And what would you advise him to do?

- A change initiative may have a single project, and it may also have – as in the News Media case study – a group of related programs and projects managed in a way to achieve the strategic organizational objectives. A program is a group of related projects and activities that together achieve a specific goal for an organization.

Below are photos from the News Media strike and sit-in.

3.3   WHY DO CHANGE INITIATIVES FAIL?

The change vision, which is completely different from the organizational vision or long-term goal, should resemble a compelling shared story that describes how the change will achieve its goal. The change strategies and tactics are the choices and directions that will be adopted to achieve that goal.

Reflecting on the News Media case study, we first notice that the three elements discussed in Chapter 1 are all very clear: (1) uncertainty, (2) imposition, and (3) perceived loss. It was indeed these three elements that caused the resistance to happen.

Before writing the case study, I did my own research to better understand what happened in News Media; while conducting my research, I did the following:

1. Conducted face-to-face open-ended interviews with four consultants.

2. Conducted face-to-face interviews with five stakeholders who lived through the experience of the change.

3. Completed a survey with 75 employees.

Upon completion of the interviews and surveys, I collected all the problems that caused the change to fail and categorized the data. Based on this categorization, I was able to determine the five main mistakes that caused the change to fail: (1) Lack of a clear and well-defined vision, (2) No understanding of the culture, (3) Poor leadership/sponsorship, (4) Poor resistance and power management, and (5) Wrong Implementation Strategy and Tactics. Below I will discuss in more detail each of the five change management mistakes.

3.3.1   Mistake #1: Lack of a Clear and Well-Defined Vision

Many participants believed that this mistake was the number one problem; it was essentially a lack of clarity and vision. Below is one of the quotes I received during the interviews:

> "... the idea to be like the BBC did not sufficiently clarify what the desired change was meant to do. It was an ambiguous idea. In addition, the absence of a shared vision was one of the main factors that impacted the success of the change."

Kotter, who developed the famous 8-Step change management model, claimed that one of the steps of his model corresponds to a common change management mistake, which is *underestimating the power of vision*.

According to Kotter, if there is clarity of the vision of the change, the inability to make decisions can disappear. Therefore, a vision must be developed to direct the change's effort and decisions. Once the vision of the change is clear, implementation strategies can be formulated.

3.3.2   Mistake #2: Poor Resistance Management

Many stakeholders agreed that the resistance was very poorly handled, which helped inflame the situation until everything collapsed. As one of the leadership team said:

> "... we were able to handle such resistance for a few months, but we later came to stop implementing the new program."

The leadership team should have asked: Are the employees dissatisfied with the current situation? Do they really need such a change? What problems and challenges are they facing? Why are they resisting? Is the resistance related to lack of awareness of the vision and strategy? Is it related to skills and knowledge? Is it related to personal issues and lack of motivation?

The leadership team also underestimated the resources of the staff in Egypt, which translated into power. These included knowledge, skills, network, and expertise. Power is not only related to the decision-making authority.

3.3.3   Mistake #3: No Understanding of the Culture and Change Readiness

Various problems related to readiness and culture were mentioned during the interviews. As the head of editors said:

> "... at the outset, the organization's readiness for the change was not strong enough."

Regarding the culture, one manager explained:

> "... without an understanding of the culture, their decisions were obscured and arbitrary. Thus, these decisions increased tensions and inflamed the situation."

The culture is the underlying set of key values, beliefs, practices, and norms shared by employees. It strongly influences their behavior and commitment. Having worked together for more than 12 years, the employees at News Media had a strong and homogeneous culture with a very high level of identification with the organization and its mission that resonated with their personal values. In retrospect, it was clear that the new board of directors was not really aware of this culture.

The case also shows a clear cross-cultural conflict, which we will analyze further in Chapter 5 when we discuss the influence of the national culture on change.

3.3.4   Mistake #4: Incorrect Change Strategy and Tactics

It was obvious that the tactics used to implement the change were not successful. One of the reasons was that they did not understand the culture of the organization. By implementation tactics, I am referring to the strategies used to implement the change to achieve the desired vision.

At one point, the leadership team had a strategy that involved the employees to facilitate commitment and buy-in. However, as their actions were contradictory, this strategy was perceived as manipulative.

3.3.5   Mistake #5: Poor Leadership/Sponsorship

During my analysis, I categorized many issues under poor leadership/sponsorship. These included mistakes related to mistrust, communication, motivation, alignment, and governance, in addition to credibility and experience as mentioned below in the case study:

> "... this leader lacked experience in both how to manage change and how to lead such an organization."

The bigger the impact of the change, the more important the leadership. As Kotter indicated, successful transformation programs rely 70% to 90% on good leadership. Therefore, when it comes to a change such as the one in the News Media case study, nothing can replace the absence of good leadership.

3.4   CHANGE IS A BAD THING

At the conclusion of a training program I held at a multinational organization in Egypt, we discussed the lessons learned through the News Media case study. One attendee interestingly concluded that it had become clear to him that change is a bad thing that should be avoided to prevent potential organizational downfall.

Commenting on Kotter's findings that only 30% of change initiatives are successfully implemented, another workshop attendee asked:

> *"... if you were told by a surgeon that the possibility of success for an operation that you will have is only 30%, would you go ahead with this surgery?"*

Comments such as these crystallize that there remains room for improvement in helping managers form a better understanding of change management concepts.

3.5   CHANGE MANAGEMENT AND PROJECT MANAGEMENT

If you feel confused, or would like clarification about the difference between change management and project management, you are not alone. Whenever I conduct any training, I often find there is confusion between change management and project management. Even though the differences are clear (at least for me), as I attempt to clarify, the more it becomes apparent that my audience remains confused.

Building a new university is just a project; however, building a new university could be part of a change initiative if it strives to achieve the objective of applying a new philosophy to the education system, or providing long-term benefits related to improving the education system. Realizing the short and long-term benefits is more relevant to change management than to project management.

Project management ends when a project delivers the required outputs (solution or deliverables); while change management ends when the new behaviors are secured and the benefits are fully realized.

For example, when implementing a new system, the project does not end until the system is deployed, however, the change does not end until the intended benefits are realized.

A change initiative contains one project or more; each project has its own scope and objectives; each project is to be managed according to the project management process of the organization.

3.5.1   Outputs, Outcomes, and Benefits

As a change management leader, remember to begin with the end result in your line of vision. In other words, determine what specific outputs, outcomes, and benefits are needed to achieve optimal goals after the change initiative ends. It is crucial to be aware of the differences in these three elements. We will discuss in this section how to differentiate between change outputs, outcomes, and benefits. In Chapter 8, we delve into knowing how to identify and monitor each.

A project is managed by the project management methodology, which is defined by the APM Body of Knowledge (APM, 2013) as the application of processes, methods, knowledge, skills, and experience to project objectives. Achieving the project objectives means delivering the project outputs) the agree on scope, budget, and time. Project management has its own knowledge areas iefly described in Appendix B.

Project outputs are combined to build new capabilities and behaviors, which enable the outcomes and eventually realize the benefits. Accordingly, we should note the following:

- Project outputs lead to the project outcomes.

- Theoretically, a certain period is required between getting the outputs and enabling the outcomes and also between demonstrating the outcomes and realizing the change benefits.

- The project outputs will finally help realize the benefits. Therefore, projects should not be planned in isolation of the change benefits.

- You can think of the benefits as how the world will look different after solving the problem and implementing the change.

- The change benefits should lead to the achievement of the organizational strategic objectives.

Figure 3-2 presents the change life cycle while positioning the outputs, outcomes, and benefits.

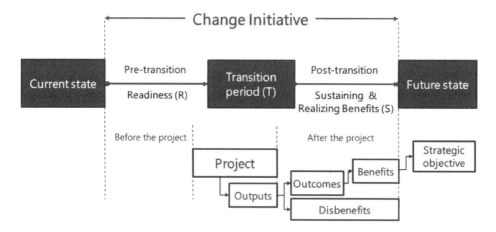

Figure 3-2. Change Life Cycle Including the Outputs, Outcomes, and Benefits

What is an outcome?

An outcome is the result in operations archived by a change after a transition period based on the quality of the projects' outputs.

What is a benefit?

A benefit is a gain from a change through outputs and resulted outcomes that contributes toward achieving the strategic objective.

The benefits are more than outputs or outcomes, there are the improvements and the added value brought to the business. The benefits are supposed to be the motivating factors for the organization to make a certain change.

To understand the relationship between outputs, outcomes, and benefits, assume that an automobile manufacturer installs a clean air filtering mechanism in a model developed for a high pollution level country.

Can you figure out what are the output, outcome, and benefit of such a project would be?

* The output would be air filters installed according to the agreed-on scope and schedule.

* Based on the quality of this output, we get the required outcome: reduced harmful material entering the vehicle.

* Based on the achievement of the outcomes, the change benefits realized are improved manufacturer image, and increased sales among health-conscious buyers.

Figure 3-3 shows the relationship between the outputs, outcomes, and benefits.

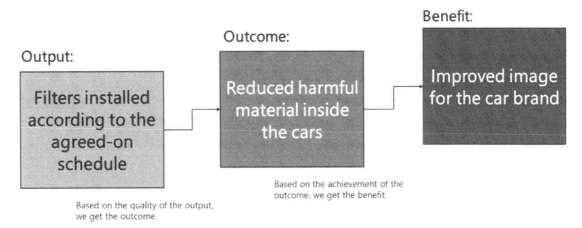

Figure 3-3. Relationship Between Outputs, Outcomes, and Benefits

Always keep in mind that the outcomes are not the outputs of the projects. The outcomes depend on the quality and sustainably of the project outputs as well as the new capabilities. The benefits are the ultimate gains and improvements.

Table 3-2 has the description and examples of the outputs, outcomes, and benefits.

Table 3-2. *Outputs, Outcomes, and Benefits*

	Output	Outcome	Benefit
Description	A deliverable from a project. Note: A project is temporary work undertaken to create outputs.	A result in operations achieved by a change after a transition period based on the quality of the projects' outputs.	A gain from a change through outputs and resulted outcomes that contributes toward achieving the strategic objective.
Rationale	Answers the question: *What do we need to have to achieve the change?*	Answers the question: *What is the new state?*	Answers the questions: *Why is the change justified?*

	Output	Outcome	Benefit
Example 1: Deploying new system	Output: - A new system tested and ready to go into operation - New business processes - Staff training	Outcomes: Faster processing and fulfilling of orders	Benefits: Customers are more satisfied Note: This benefit may help achieve "Increase Revenue" strategic objective
Example 2: Installing a clean air filtering mechanism	Output: - Filters installed in windows	Outcomes: - Reduced harmful material inside factory	Benefits: - Improved image for the factory - Healthier employees

Note. Modified from MSP, 2011.

Therefore, realizing the benefits is not in the scope of project management. Any project that aims at moving an organization from its current state to a future state should be considered as a change.

Project management should focus on resources to deliver the outputs; while change manages should focus on resources to increase individual and organizational readiness, assure the right behaviors and mindset, manage resistance, enable outcomes, realize benefits, and sustain the change.

3.5.2   Main Differences Between Change Management and Project Management

Table 3-3 shows the requirements that exist in change management, but do not necessarily appear in project management.

Table 3-3. *Main Differences Between Project Management and Change Management*

	Item	Project management	Change management
1	Achieving outcomes	X	√
2	Realizing benefits	X	√
3	Linking change benefits with strategic objectives	X	√
4	Establishing individual readiness	X	√
5	Establishing organizational readiness	X	√
6	Reinforcing new behaviors into the organizational culture	X	√
7	Developing communication campaign and	X	√

	Item	Project management	Change management
	change narrative		
8	Managing resistance	X	√
9	Assuring sustainability	X	√

Important Note

Project management largely avoids the "people side" during implementation, i.e., organizational politics, hidden agendas, cultural barriers, motivation issues, lack of communication, conflict resolution, resistance to change, ambiguous roles and responsibilities, poor leadership, and insufficient sponsorship.

3.6 BRIDGING THE GAP

Revisiting Kotter's research, it is evident that the strategic transformation initiatives have a success rate of only 30%. This occurs primarily because oftentimes management tends to jump straight to the execution phase without properly managing the people and culture aspects, creating a gap that needs to be bridged.

This gap can be bridged by adding change management practices. Change management is the bridge between the strategic initiative and its execution through managing culture, engaging people, and enabling the organization to successfully achieve change.

In writing this section, I decided to take its name (Bridging the Gap) as the book's title, as change management models can serve as an achievable bridge between strategy development and strategy execution. Figure 3-4 below shows how the change management represented in steps 5, 8, and 9 bridges the gap between strategy development and strategy execution.

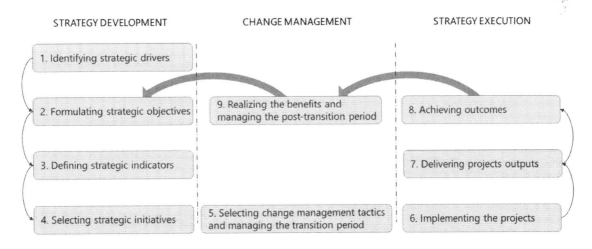

Figure 3-4. Bridging the Gap

Important Note

Change should not be implemented in isolation from the strategy. Therefore, the link between the change and its benefits with the strategy must be clearly identified.

A change should not be implemented in isolation from the strategy. Therefore, the link between the change and its benefits must be clearly identified.

Example 3.1 - Relationship Between Change Benefits and Strategic Objectives

In this example, I will explain the relationship between the change, change benefits, and the strategic organizational objectives.

Recalling the Global Trans case study introduced in Chapter 1, in order to address the problem of isolated business units causing delay and extra cost when introducing a new service, or to have consistent quality among all brands, a new matrix structure was suggested.

The purpose of the restructuring initiative was to help achieve two strategic objectives: (1) to introduce new services effectively, and (2) to achieve a high ranking in key services.

The benefits that we identified from the change initiative were to:

- Reduce the cost of the operations

- Improve the quality of services

- Deliver consistent processing to customers

- Improve the capacity of middle managers

- Increase knowledge sharing between units

The relationship between the change, benefits, and strategic objectives is presented in Figure 3-5 below:

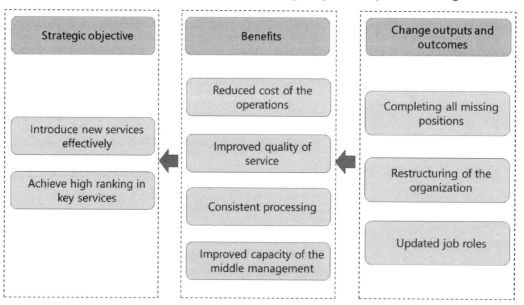

Figure 3-5. Relation Between Change, Benefits, and Strategic Objectives

In evaluating my own mistakes as a change leader, I observed that:

1. I did not put sufficient effort in quantifying and monitoring change benefits. This was one of the reasons that the chairman and other key stakeholders did not really envision a tangible return from the change.
2. I did not make sufficient effort to identify the cause-and-effect relationship between the intended change benefits.
3. I attempted to implement the new structure without initiating projects with assigned project managers. The implementation did not have a clear-cut plan with schedule, phases, milestones, tasks, and deliverables.
4. I mistakenly assumed that my plan was complete at the beginning of the change.
5. I did not have an agile plan, which caused numerous problems when the organization faced new issues as a result of pre-existing uncertainties. It is better to have an Agile plan for the change; change plans never begin as a complete plan.

3.7   CHAPTER IN A BOX

This chapter outlined the differences between outputs, outcomes, and benefits. It was explained that a project ends when the outputs are delivered, while a change ends when the outcomes are achieved, and the benefits are realized.

Outcome is defined as a result in operations achieved by a change after a transition period based on the quality of the projects' outputs.

Benefit is defined as a gain from a change through outputs and resulted outcomes that contributes toward achieving the strategic objective. Benefits management is a very valuable tool that should be used to assure successful implementation of the change initiative.

In this chapter, we presented the difference between change management and project managment. Project management is considered a key tool that are used to manage a change initiative. A change initiative should follow the project management process by having a well-defined plan with a schedule, phases, milestones, activities, and deliverables.

The five critical change management mistakes are:

1. Lack of clear and well-defined vision.

2. Poor resistance and power management.

3. No understanding of the culture nor the organizational readiness.

4. Incorrect change strategy and tactics.

5. Poor leadership/sponsorship.

Change management should be the bridge between the strategy and its execution by managing culture, engaging people, and enabling the organization to achieve successful change.

Change should not be implemented in isolation from the strategy. Therefore, the link between the change and its benefits with the strategy must be clearly identified.

CHAPTER 4
UNDERSTANDING CULTURE IS CRUCIAL

Chapter 4 - Understanding Culture is Crucial

4.1   OVERVIEW

Back in 2004, I was appointed as the managing director of an Egyptian company called Future Soft. The company specializes in developing animation and software applications. A few weeks after joining them, the company delivered a large project. As a manager, I decided to have a celebration and give awards to the two graphics designers who I noticed had done a great job. They were peers and do not report to each other.

Shortly after the celebration, I received a phone call from the owner reproaching me for the mistake I had made. The mistake was that I had called both employees together while giving them the awards while one of them was more senior than the other. Seniority and status must be respected in the company. This is part of its culture. I recall that the senior employee completely avoided me. I assume he never forgave me for the great mistake of having him stand next to his junior colleague.

Culture is such a complex phenomenon. It is a living thing that controls and directs, behind the scenes, many of the practices and behaviors inside an organization.

Understanding culture is crucial to the successful implementation of a change initiative. Leading a change without understanding the culture is like playing darts while blindfolded.

Most managers do not realize the importance of culture in respect to change implementation; they may even turn a blind eye to it. It is crucial to understand and manage culture while leading a transformational change. If you do not manage the culture, it will manage itself and you will end up as a blindfolded leader.

Any transformation will face certain challenges based on the culture of the organization.

In literature, there are many definitions for culture, and I will discuss few of them in this book.

When we discuss our ElKattan Change Management Model starting from Chapter 8, I will bring the cultural component under full investigation. However, in this chapter and the following two chapters, I will give an introduction about three cultures that have impact on implementation of the change initiatives: national culture, organizational culture, and organizational culture.

4.2   WHAT IS CULTURE?

4.2.1   Overview

Each person has his unique personality, while every group of people will have their own unique relationship or culture; this group could be a group of kids in a kindergarten, a group of teenagers in a high school, a family, an organization a tribe, a city, a region, or a country.

4.2.2   Definition

According to Waisfisz, culture can be simply defined as how people relate to each other, and how they related to the external; world. It can also be seen as a set of dominant norms which drive most of the behaviors inside an organization.

Culture was defined by Wilkins and Dyer (1988) as follows:

Culture is the values, beliefs, mindsets, attitudes, practices, customs, norms, and behaviors which are commonly shared by any group of people.

The four elements: values, beliefs, mindsets, attitudes are unseen; while the remaining elements: practices, customs, norms, and behaviors can be seen and observed. I prefer to merge the three unseen elements: beliefs, mindsets, and attitudes into the mindset element. Also, I prefer to merge the three seen elements: practices, customs, and norms into the practices element. Therefore, we end up having the following definition:

Culture is the values, mindsets, practices, and behaviors which are commonly shared by any group of people.

By mindset, we refer to the assumptions, beliefs, or the ways of thinking of the people inside the organization. It is the mind's predisposition to certain ideas. The beliefs are how the employees add meaning to data and then make their assumptions and come to their conclusions. An example of a mindset is the growth mindset. This means that people inside the organization accept failure as an opportunity to learn.

By behaviors, we mean the daily and regular actions as well as the way of doing work.

4.2.3   Culture and Programming

Back in the 1990s, I worked for quite a long time as a software programmer. C++ was my favorite programming language. I liked programming and how coding can make great applications and provide interesting features. The first application I managed was awarded best application in the world, simply because it was almost the only one available at that time. It was an application for displaying and searching Quranic text. Coding is totally invisible to the application users; as they use it, they are unaware of it and how the application was programmed to perform.

Culture is the same as the coding that I used to write. Culture programs our minds and controls our practices and behavior accordingly. Any human being who is in the right place at the right time will be subject to cultural mental programming from their moral circle.

This meaning is emphasized in Hofstede's definition of national culture, which is as follows:

National culture is the collective programming of the mind distinguishing the members of one human group from another.

For further understanding of the above definition, I will refer to the paper *Personality and Culture Revisited: Linking Traits and Dimensions of Culture* authored by Hofstede and McCrae in 2004. In this paper, the authors wrote about the famous Arabic scholar Ibn Khaldun, who was known as the father of sociology. In his well-known book *The Muqaddimah* (an Arabic word for *the introduction*), Ibn Khaldun referred to a saying (or Hadith) by Prophet Mohammed, peace be upon him. The first part of the saying says:

"... the human being is born in a natural state."

Natural state is a translation of the Arabic word *fitra*. This term *natural state* indicates why Hofstede used the keyword *programming* in his definition. When people are born, the mind is in a natural state that is ready to be programmed by the person's surrounding culture.

As shown in Figure 4-1, mental programming happens is a way so that the culture is transferred to the new members of a society so they will all generally look alike from a behavioral perspective to an external observer.

Figure 4-1. Transferring of Culture

It is important to mention that culture is not the only element involved in mental programming. There are other elements that also contribute to this mental programming and impact our behavior. The other two elements are human nature and personality.

Human nature is comprised of the common characteristics that are inherited and common to all of humankind, including the way we eat, love, express fear, and so on. These common human characteristics are not the culture. Figure 4-2 shows the three different aspects of mental programming.

Personality also affects our behavior. It is essential to distinguish between culture and personality, as both impact the way we behave.

If we assume that these three elements form 100% of my behaviors, what do you think the percentage of the contribution of each element when I was a newborn and when I was 40 years old?

When I was born, I had literally zero culture. Therefore the culture score is 0%. However, I came into this life with some personality traits inherited from many parents and I was also born with some characteristics that are common to all of humankind. For sake of simplicity, let's assume that both od these two elements equally influence my behaviors with 50%.

As I grew, I started acquiring the culture of my social surroundings. I acquired this culture in the same way I acquired language: it gradually penetrated my brain, which became programmed.

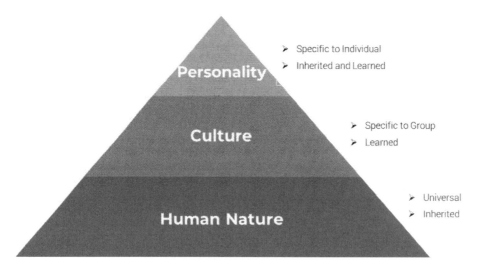

Figure 4-2. Aspects of Mental Programming. Adapted from *Cultures and Organizations, Software of the Mind* by G. Hofstede, G. Hofstede, and M. Minkov, 2010.

As I continued to grow, my personality changed and has not been totally based on my inherited traits; it developed according to the parental directions, education, religion, and experiences that I was exposed to. Hypothetically speaking, I would say when I am 40 years old, the percentages of the three elements as the following: Human nature (10%), Culture (50%), and personality (40%). This 40% cultural element is what we will discuss in this chapter. It is what I acquired from the society in which I was raised. We will discuss the society culture in a broad way using the Hofstede Model for national culture in next chapter.

Important Note

Culture is only learned; however, personality is both inherited and learned. Personality is inherited through our unique set of genes and is formed through external influences such as experiences and education.

4.2.4   Culture Can Only Be Seen Collectively

Two other important keywords in Hofstede's above definition are *collective* and *group*, these keywords indicate that the culture can only be seen collectively, not individually. To understand it, behavior comparisons must be made between different groups. Culture can only be understood through group comparison.

Important Note

Culture will be magically transferred to the newcomers of any group, slipping into their minds and hearts and directing most of their practices and behavior.

There is a famous metaphor about the jungle and its trees that explains the relationship between culture and personality. Every jungle, as seen in Figure 4-3, has its own characteristics but every tree within the jungle has a unique shape.

Figure 4-3. Culture and Personality vs. the Jungle and Trees Metaphor

People usually have one perception (stereotyping) about other nations. This is because people look at other nations as they look as the jungle; they only see and observe the general characteristics or culture. However, every person in every nation has their own unique and different personality.

4.3 ORGANIZATIONAL CORE VALUES VS. CULTURAL VALUES

One day, I was conducting a culture management workshop at Vodafone. I did my homework and studied the company's five core values, aiming to conduct an exercise with the participants to see if the values were really reflected in the culture.

When I started talking about their values, many of them commented anxiously:

"... these are not our values; these are old values; we have just been given new values. They are customer

obsession, innovation, ambition, speed, simplicity."

Perhaps they had a new CEO who had replaced the values selected by the old CEO, or perhaps they just had a new strategy that required new values. It is likely that when a board hires a new CEO, they will implement a new set of values.

Similarly, after Dell bought EMC in a historic US$70b deal, a new set of core values replaced the old set of core values that EMC had before being acquired by Dell.

I also did the same. Shortly after I was appointed CEO of Global Trans, I started the strategic development and planning processes (refer to Appendix B for more information about strategic management). The company had four values and I added a fifth value (strategic management does not usually require more than five values). I called a meeting to review and confirm the values we would use in our strategy moving forward. Most of the key managers who attended the meeting did not even realize that I had added a fifth value.

Even though these core values can be translated into the culture, some of them may only be cosmetic, as I indicated in the Global Trans case study. Cultural values are deep tendencies within societies, groups, and organizations that are extremely difficult to change. They cannot be changed overnight, as our Global Trans CEO discovered.

Does this mean an employee who moves between different organizations will personally acquire all these core values? Of course not. They become part of their practices within the organization.

Important Note

The organizational core values could be translated in the form of cultural practices, not cultural values. Employees do not necessarily embrace these announced core values in their personalities.

In other words, the cultural values are different from the core values associated with the establishment of each organization (i.e., integrity, customer centric, employee satisfaction, innovation, etc.), as these core values are mainly suggested by managers to be used for marketing purposes or to enforce certain practices and/or behaviors inside the company; also, they often change when top management changes.

4.4   CULTURE IS A MIX OF VALUES AND PRACTICES

There is another definition of culture that simplifies this complex phenomenon. Culture is simply different sets of values and practices, referring to what Hofstede and his fellow researchers indicated. It is these different combinations of values and practices that make the differences between societies and groups.

So, what are the differences between practices and values?

They both drive our behavior. However, practices are more superficial; they are seen and noticed, and relatively easy to change.

On the other hand, values are deep inside us; they are unseen. They can only be seen and noticed through behavioral alternatives. They are very hard to change. Values are the core of any culture and are defined by Hofstede in this way:

Values are the sense of broad feelings and emotional tendency toward pairing of the same dimension.

The most important keyword in the above definition is the word *dimension*. When we study culture, its values or practices could be expressed in the form of different set of dimensions. I wrote the following random samples of what cultural dimensions can be:

* Assertive vs. caring

* Open-minded vs. closed-minded

* Rational thinking vs. irrational thinking

* Low-context communication vs. high-context communication

* Long-term oriented vs. short-term oriented

* Conservative vs. liberal

* Work-oriented vs. people-oriented

* Internally driven vs. externally driven

Figure 4-4 shows how the values and practices form the culture from a very abstract perspective.

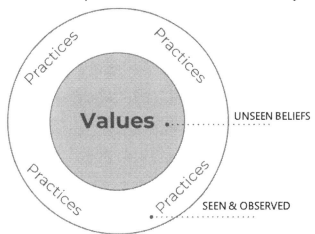

Figure 4-4. Values and Practices

Hofstede identified national values using six dimensions and classified national practices into three categories. I will not discuss the six value dimensions here, as the whole next chapter is dedicated to them. The three classifications of the practices are:

1. Symbols

2. Heroes and stories

3. Rituals

4.4.1   Symbols

Symbols are a superficial layer in the culture, such as the spoken language(s), dress, etc.

When it comes to organizations, symbols could be banners or slogans with simple and inspiring statements that refer to what the management wishes to change or emphasize. Figure 4-5 shows how banners, as a cultural practice of an organization, can be used to emphasize or identify a culture. The picture is not the best quality as I took it myself while conducting a change management workshop at one of the multinational companies.

Figure 4-5. Banners as a Cultural Practice

When it comes to change, symbols help make the change goals clear to all stakeholders. For example, as we see in Figure 4-5, the organization wanted to change their culture to be more innovative. Like this organization, most multinational companies have banners all over the walls with statements about the values they wish to transfer into the culture.

When I was a CEO to one company, I dreamed of having a more inspiring culture. Therefore, I used to use the statement, "*Have you inspired someone today?*" during my written communication. Such a statement is considered a practice that may or may not encourage the adoption of certain behavior.

4.4.2   Heroes and Stories

Heroes are people who are highly prized and act as examples for others due to their behavior and actions. In organizations, heroes represent those employees who are favored by management and thus get promoted. People usually tell stories about individuals that reflect the essence of the culture.

I often tell the story of a security man working for an American company called Hughes Aircraft for which I was also working in the late 1980s and early 1990s. This man was always making jokes with the senior executives. Such a simple story reflects certain important cultural tendencies in this organization. I will elaborate more on this story in the next chapter when we talk about the six value dimensions.

4.4.3   Rituals

Rituals are an excellent way of identifying different cultures. Rituals include ways of greeting, social events such as wedding parties, and religious ceremonies. When foreigners come to Egypt, they may have the opportunity to see an Egyptian wedding. This is a new experience for them that reflects a different culture.

In organizations, rituals include the way management and employees meet and gather. When it comes to change, rituals are used to emphasize the change. This can be done by communicating the need for the change or the required new behavior in every meeting and gathering in a variety of ways. Figure 4-6 shows the three categories of cultural practices.

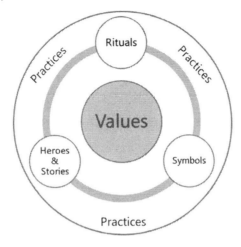

Figure 4-6. Hofstede's Categories of Cultural Practices

Figure 4-7 summarizes all the national culture elements we have discussed.

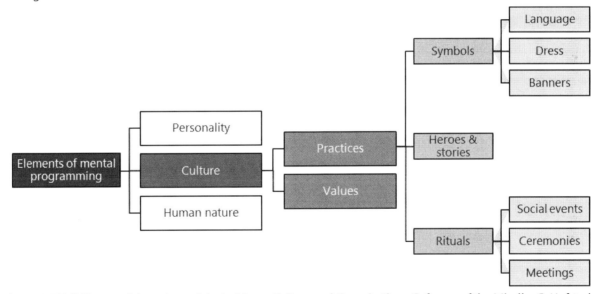

Figure 4-7. Full Picture of the culture. Adapted from *Culture and Organizations, Software of the Mind* by G. Hofstede, G. Hofstede, and M. Minkov, 2010.

4.4.4   Globalization of Culture

People who refer to the tendency of culture globalization among nations are, intentionally or unintentionally, referring to the globalization of practices involving areas such as fashion, products, commonly used words (especially in English), movies, and sports. However, values are, and will remain, different. A person from Africa may see the European countries as one nation, as they look and dress the same; however, they are definitely different from each other because of the differences in their values.

Values will remain different between nations.

4.5   WHAT IS ORGANIZATIONAL CULTURE?

4.5.1   Overview

When I started my academic research about the influence of culture on change, I intended to study only the influence of national culture, which mainly distinguishes between societies. However, as Geert Hofstede indicated, organizations are affected by the national culture as they are part of society. Michael Schachner from Hofstede Insights convinced me to add the organizational culture element to my research.

According to Waisfisz (2015), organizational culture can be strong (homogenous) or weak (heterogeneous). Strong organizational culture influences both the satisfaction and commitment of employees which are necessary for any organizational change (Alas and Vadi, 2014).

4.5.2   Definition

Organizational culture is defined in a similar way to national culture. As such, almost the same definitions apply, with minor changes. For example:

Organizational culture is the values, mindsets, practices, and behaviors which are commonly shared by any group of people who together form the organization, or

Organizational culture is the collective programming of minds that distinguishes the members of one organization from another.

Organizational culture reflects the history of the organization and it is not easy to change.

4.5.3   What Elements Shape the Organizational Culture?

An organization is part of the society, and therefore it is normal that its culture will be influenced by the surrounding national culture.

However, national culture is only one element that influences the organizational culture. The organizational culture is influenced by many external and internal factors.

Key external factors are the industry and national culture, while the main internal factors are organizational design (systems, procedures, etc.), staff skills and qualifications, unit tasks, leadership and key managers personalities, the strategy, and past management practice. The past experience is a key factor, which remain deep-rooted in the culture.

On the other hand, the organizational culture influences many aspects of the organization, such as the level of formalization, centralization of management, strategy, hierarchy, and processes.

Figure 4-8 illustrates some of the elements that influence and influenced by the organizational culture.

Figure 4-8. Elements that Shape the Organizational Culture. Adapted from Industry Determinants of Organizational Culture by G. Gordon, 1991.

4.5.4 Culture Transfer

Similar to the transference of culture to the newcomers of any society, the process of cultural transference occurs to newcomers on a smaller scale in organizations. If newcomers cannot adapt to the organizational culture, it is unlikely that they will continue in the organization. It also happens with small groups of friends; if a newcomer does not fit in with their culture, they will be kicked out. That is why we hear the statement: "Nothing is stronger than peer pressure!"

4.5.5 Values and Practices

According to Hofstede, behaviors stemming from national culture is driven primarily by its values, while behaviors in an organization are driven primarily by the practices. That is why culture in organizations can be changed much more easily than culture in societies.

4.5.6 Organizational Sub-cultures

Each unit within an organization will have its own sub-culture. The marketing unit wants to create awareness and invest in branding. This will create a different sub-culture than the one that exists in the finance unit, for example.

Therefore, organizations have sub-cultures that influence the implementation of any change in different ways. Therefore, three types of culture need to be understood before leading a change:

1. National culture
2. Organizational culture
3. Organizational sub-cultures

4.6   CHAPTER IN A BOX

- Culture is only learned; however, personality is both inherited and learned. Personality is inherited through a person's unique set of genes and is learned through external influences such as their culture, experiences, and education.

- The organizational core values could be translated in the form of cultural practices, not cultural values. Employees do not necessarily embrace these announced core values in their personalities

- There are three elements that contribute to the mental programming which drives our behavior:

  4. Human nature
  5. Culture
  6. Personality

- Human nature is inherited; culture is learned; and personality is both inherited and learned.

- Culture is different sets of values and practices.

- Practices can be broadly classified into the following three categories:

  1. Symbols
  2. Heroes and stories
  3. Rituals

- Understanding the three types of culture is crucial to achieving success in the implementation of change. These types are:

  1. National culture
  2. Organizational culture
  3. Organizational sub-cultures

- National culture is one of many elements that influence the organizational culture. Other important elements include the personality of the founders and key managers, the maturity of the organization, and industry.

CHAPTER 5

INFLUENCE OF NATIONAL CULTURE ON CHANGE

Chapter 5 - Influence of National Culture on Change

5.1   OVERVIEW

No one on earth can deny that different nations have different cultures. This difference in cultures, along with the diversity of our languages and the color of our skin, is one of God's signs to human beings. Researchers have been studying the subject for a long time. Until recently, it was called the "national character," and there are important culture references that still use this term.

National culture refers to the personality of each nation or country, much like the personality of each individual. Understanding a country's culture helps to reduce negative perceptions of culturally specific behavior.

The term national culture was introduced in the middle of last century when the US government called on researchers to study the subject in order to understand the behavior of its enemies, especially the Germans, during World War II. If you need to understand the culture to win a war, then it would follow that you also need to understand culture to lead a change.

Many aspects influence the national culture of a country, such as historical, political, social, religious, educational, and economical aspects. It is clear that some countries with the same religion share common values; similarly, from a political perspective, we can easily observe some common values in poor and developing countries.

From the beginning of the 20th century, researchers started defining culture by using dimensions to better understand cultural values. I explained these dimensions in the previous chapter and provided some examples.

One more example of cultural dimension is "conservatism." Of course, different nations may interpret "conservatism" in different ways, but you can easily see that some nations are more conservative and stick to traditions more than others.

In the 1980s, the World Value Survey (WVS) was conducted to better understand cultural values. It was a huge survey covering around 43 societies in many different areas. As we will see later, it is available for researchers to study to reach their own conclusions about cultural dimensions.

To understand national culture, several models have been developed. Each model describes culture using certain dimensions. Each dimension has a score from 0 to 100 and can be measured relative to other cultures. The two most famous national culture models are:

1.   Hofstede Model

2.   GLOBE Model

In this chapter, I will explain the Hofstede Model in detail. The description of the GLOBE Model is outside the scope of this book.

The Hofstede Model is good to study as many researchers have confirmed that it is very helpful in identifying the influence of the national culture on the business environment as well as the implementation of the change initiatives. I will mention some of my personal stories to highlight the concepts of the model we discuss.

Incidentally, in 2016 – in collaboration with the Hofstede Insight and MediaCom – I participated in an assessment of the national cultural dimensions throughout the world. The purpose of the project was to update the Hofstede Model to find the most relevant cultural map explaining the world today.

5.2   HOFSTEDE MODEL

Hofstede first came up with his model with four dimensions in the 1970s after the analysis of the IBM survey databank relating to international employee attitudes was made available for academic research. IBM had been conducting worldwide comparative attitude surveys on its employees since 1967.

Based on the analysis of more than 116,000 questionnaires in 20 languages from 72 countries, Hofstede concluded that there are four dimensions that determine the values of different nations. These four dimensions were:

- Power Distance
- Individualism
- Assertiveness
- Uncertainty Avoidance

A fifth dimension was added in 1991 based on research that Michael Bond conducted on the Chinese Value Survey. This fifth dimension was called:

- Long-Term Orientation vs. Short-Term Orientation

Michael Minkov studied the extensive data of the World Value Survey and extracted three dimensions. It was found that two of these dimensions correlated with two of the dimensions in the Hofstede model. However, one dimension was different to the other five dimensions already included in the Hofstede Model. This dimension was called:

- Indulgence vs. Restraint

Accordingly, in 2010 Hofstede added this new dimension to his model to expand his 5 dimensions to 6 dimensions.

I will only go through the first five dimensions, as my research did not find much influence of the indulgence dimension on change.

While discussing each dimension, I will reflect on the culture in which I was raised: Egypt. The objective of this reflection is to clarify the concepts and encourage readers to reflect on their own culture.

Table 5-1 describes Hofstede Model.

Table 5-1. *Hofstede Model*

Dimension	Description
Power distance	This dimension reflects the degree to which the less powerful members of an organization or society accept and expect that power is distributed unequally.
Individualism	This dimension reflects the degree to which societies value personal independence over group membership..
Assertiveness	This dimension reflects the degree to which assertive behavior is encouraged vs. encouraging considerate and nurturing behavior.
Uncertainty avoidance	This dimension reflects the degree to which people feel threatened by uncertainty and ambiguity and try to avoid these situations.
Long-term orientation	This dimension reflects the degree to which a society exhibits a pragmatic or long-term-oriented perspective rather than a conventional or short-term point of view...
Indulgence	This dimension reflects the degree to which free gratification of people's own drives and emotions is encouraged.

Note. Source: Hofstede, et al. (2010)

5.3   D1: POWER DISTANCE

5.3.1   Overview

At one stage in my career, I worked for an Egyptian company owned by one the most famous businessmen in Egypt, who sold his mobile operator company to Vodafone in the 1990s. Whenever we received a message from his office, we would get a statement headed with: "A Memo from the Chairman's Office." That was quite normal and acceptable to all of us, as the message was coming from the big boss.

It is normal that power is not distributed equally everywhere, including in families, groups, organizations, and nations. However, some societies are more unequal than others. Remember: culture can only be seen by group comparison.

In a large power distance culture, the big boss is supposed to know everything. Their followers rely on their guidance and directions. They can also be seen as the parent of a big family. Therefore, in the workplace, subordinates expect protection from their managers when problems arise.

Power distance culture involves change from the top. You can expect that in a large power distance culture, the big boss will make most of the decisions alone, without involving too many people.

Important Note

Therefore, when a change initiative is launched in such a large power distance culture, it is normal that people do not really feel committed to it and it is difficult for them to find a sense of ownership for it.

5.3.2   Definition

Power distance is defined by Hofstede as follows:

Power distance is the degree to which the less powerful members of an organization or society accept and expect that power is distributed unequally.

This dimension has an index in which each country is characterized by a score from 0 to 100. A score of 100 indicates a very high power distance culture.

It is important to emphasize that power distance is mainly defined from below, not from above.

5.3.3   Examples of Countries

Examples of large power distance cultures are China, Malaysia, Mexico, Kuwait, and Egypt. Everybody in these countries knows their rightful place, which corresponds with the importance of their position. Examples of small power distance cultures are Britain, Germany, the Netherlands, the USA, and Scandinavia.

5.3.4   Influence at Business Environment

As we discussed in Chapter 4, there is no good and bad when we talk about cultures, as many factors need to be considered when analyzing a culture. In large power distance cultures, one's social status is very important and people like to be addressed by their titles. Therefore, "prestige" is a keyword for senior staff.

In a high power distance culture, seeking help and getting feedback from employees in some context could be seen as a sign of weakness and less competency.

Important Note

Large power distance could be perceived as a bad thing as it may impact the employees' sense of ownership. However, this should not be generalized as it could be perceived in some countries as inspiring and motivating.

Table 5-2 has a summary of behaviors of the power distance dimension in business environments.

Table 5-2. *Power Distance Behaviors in the Workplace*

Small Power Distance	Large Power Distance
Hierarchy means inequality of roles.	Hierarchy reflects inequality between higher and lower levels.
Decentralization is popular.	Centralization is popular.
Fewer supervisory positions.	More supervisory positions.
There is a narrow salary range between the top and bottom of the organization.	There is a wide salary range between the top and bottom of the organization.

Small Power Distance	Large Power Distance
Subordinates expect to be consulted or involved.	Subordinates expect to be told what to do.
Consultative, participative, and democratic leadership styles are common.	Autocratic, authoritarian, and paternalistic leadership styles are common. The ideal boss is paternalistic.
Subordinate-superior relations are pragmatic.	Subordinate-superior relations are emotional.
Privilege and special status for seniors are criticized.	Privilege and special status for seniors are normal and popular.
Manual work has the same status as office work.	White-collar jobs are valued more than blue-collar jobs.

Note. Source: Hofstede, et al. (2010).

Example 5.1 - Influence on the Egyptian Culture

In Egypt, where I was raised, the power distance is relatively high, scoring 70 in this dimension. This implies that Egyptians prefer a society in which the hierarchy is clearly set and observed. There are significant differences in power and wealth, and people in the lower strata of society accept this.

Successful leaders are often paternalistic leaders (godfather figures) who take care of their subordinates inside and outside the work environment and just justify their decisions to them even though they do not really have to. However, a common leadership style for large power distance cultures is autocratic, with the ideal boss being a paternalistic figure, as in the case of Egypt.

In Egypt, there is also a difference in power between men and women. Old movies show how in the old days there was a very large power distance between husbands and wives. Women used to accept men's decisions and could not even argue with them. However, the younger female generations are behaving differently. Nowadays, Egyptian men would think twice before making any decision without first consulting their wives.

In Egypt, titles are important and should always be maintained. For example, when greeting Egyptians in a professional setting, formal titles should be used. As the power distance is high, you always need to use the title, such as Mr., Mrs., Doctor, Muhandis (male engineer), and Muhandisa (female engineer).

Example 5.2 - Call me Ali!

I worked in California at Hughes Aircraft. I worked there with a group of other Egyptians representing a big customer in Egypt.

One day, the company decided to take a photo of the whole team. Under the photo, each person's name was written with no title, except for the Egyptian team members, whose names were preceded by titles as they knew that having a title is very important to the Egyptian people. Before my name, the title "Eng." was written (Eng. stands for engineer).

Similarly, in Egypt, when I ask my colleagues to call me Ali rather than Dr. Ali, they refuse and say they cannot call me just Ali.

5.3.5 General Influence on Change Initiatives

Below are the main influences of the large power distance culture on change:

- It is easy to authorize and initiate a change initiative.

- It is normally not easy to complete the change smoothly.

- Less formal planning will be required for the change.

- There is low engagement due to lack of commitment and ownership.

- Subordinates are not actively involved in the change.

Example 5.3 - Big Guys are not Signing in!

As an undergraduate student, I travelled to Finland to work for Nokia. I used to punch in my time card when I arrived at work. Everyone working at the company, including the executive directors, was expected to punch in with a time card.

Around 13 years later, I was appointed general manager of a Kuwaiti company based in Cairo. The employees were from Egypt and Jordan, with the majority being Egyptian. Before I was appointed, only the middle managers and frontline employees signed in when they arrived at work. The senior managers and top management were not required to sign in, which was totally expected and accepted by all employees. Why? Because they were the big guys, and this is how you deal with them in a large power distance culture.

On the first day of my new position, I made it known that all employees, including myself, would henceforth sign in at the security desk when they arrived at work.

Can you imagine the reaction of the senior managers to that decision? Most of them were totally against it. The decision wounded their pride!

At the same time, the employees did not really appreciate the decision or my efforts to introduce equality to the company.

I remember one manager telling me he felt as if someone was stabbing him in the back when he was signing in next to his subordinates.

This personal story illustrates the core of the power distance culture.

5.3.6 Influence of Power Distance on Organizational Structure

In cultures with small power distance, like that of the United States, subordinates generally prefer a horizontal organizational structure rather than structures with numerous reporting levels.

For example, in a company like Dell EMC, which has around 60,000 employees, there is maximum of six levels between Michael Dell himself and anyone else in the company. In small power distance, subordinates are comfortable providing feedback to their bosses as they are not that distant from each other.

In large power distance cultures, such as in Egypt, centralization is the norm.

5.4   D2: INDIVIDUALISM

5.4.1   Overview

During elections that take place in Egypt, which has a low individualistic culture, candidates may present their programs and explain their views. However, most people do not care much about these programs and often don't even bother to read them. People's decisions are mainly based on trust in the people who belong to their "in-groups."

In highly individualistic cultures, people tend to differentiate themselves from others; they develop unique personalities. In contrast, the need for harmony with their "in-groups" in low individualistic cultures (collectivistic) makes people tend to conform to others.

Highly individualistic cultures value personal initiative, privacy, and autonomy.

Important Note

That is why in a collectivist country, people mainly belong to "in-groups" that take care of them in exchange for loyalty. Therefore, loyalty overrides rationality.

The lower the individualistic culture, the more serious the external emotions are. Why? Because there is some level of social control in these collectivistic cultures. On the other hand, social pressure has a relatively weak influence on individualistic people.

5.4.2   Definition

Individualism is defined by Hofstede as follows:

Individualism reflects the degree to which societies value personal independence over group membership. Its opposite pole is collectivism, in which societies value group goals over individual preferences.

This dimension has an index in which each country is characterized by a score from 0 to 100. A score of 100 indicates a very high individualistic culture.

5.4.3   Examples of Countries

Americans and Northern Europeans tend to be individualists, while Southern Europeans are moderately collectivistic. Meanwhile, people in Asia, Latin America, and Africa are generally more collectivistic than Europeans. Most of the world's population tends towards collectivism.

5.4.4   Influence on the Egyptian Culture

Egypt is a relatively collectivist country, which, as previously mentioned, means that people belong to "in-groups" that take care of them in exchange for loyalty. People are loyal to their tribes and groups. Family and old friends are the glue of society.

Most people who currently live in Cairo come from other cities and small villages. Those people identify with the villages they come from, even if it was three generations ago. Where you come from – the place to which you belong – determines your identity and the way people will treat you.

When you deal with people in a collectivistic culture just as Egypt, you need, most of the time, to read between the lines to better understand what people mean. There is a lot of indirect communication. This high-context communication culture is typical in collectivistic cultures. On the other hand, individualistic cultures have a low-context communication culture with explicit verbal communication.

5.4.5   Influence in the Business Environment

Table 5-3 compares the influence of both low and highly individualistic cultures in business environments.

Table 5-3. *Individualism Behaviors in the Workplace*

Collectivist (Low Individualist)	Highly Individualist
Hiring and promotion decisions take the employee's in-group into account.	Hiring and promotion decisions are supposed to be based solely on skills and pre-defined requirements.
Employer-employee relationship is based on emotions and ethics, much like a family.	The employer-employee relationship is a contract between parties in a labor market.
Managers should build a relationship and trust with employees before proposing new ideas.	Managers should persuade their staff and get to the point quickly.
Management is management of the group.	Management is management of individuals.
Relationships prevail over tasks.	Tasks prevail over relationships.
Employees are members of in-groups who will pursue the interests of the in-group.	Employees are "economic persons" who will pursue the employer's interests if they coincide with their self-interest.
In-group customers receive better treatment (particularism).	Every customer should receive the same treatment (universalism).
E-mail is less frequently used to connect individuals.	E-mail is frequently used to connect individuals.

Note. Source: Hofstede, et al. (2010); De Mooij & Hofstede (2010)

5.4.6   General Influence on Change Initiatives

Below are the general influences of individualism on change:

- In a highly individualistic culture, it is not easy to develop an effective team and sustain a change.

- A highly individualistic culture motivates and accepts new and innovative ideas for change.

- In a low individualistic culture (collectivistic), new changes are generally accepted based on trust and feeling rather than on facts and rationality.

- In collectivistic incentives, it is preferable for the change to be part of a common mission for which at least part of the incentive is given collectively for achieving shared goals.

- In collectivistic cultures, change should not conflict with employees' group loyalties.

- Change communication strategy should be more rational in an individualistic culture and more emotional in a collectivistic culture.

- In collectivistic cultures, it is necessary for a change leader to build a relationship and trust before communicating the change. In this culture, people generally acquire most of their information via interpersonal communication and tend to make their decisions based on feelings and trust.

Example 5.4 - Advertising of Cars in Japan vs. in the USA

As an example, the advertising of cars in Japan focuses on inducing positive feelings rather than providing information. On the other hand, the advertising of cars in the USA focuses on specifications, as most people want to actively gather information about the product.

Example 5.5 - Family Together

In one of my training sessions at Vodafone Egypt, one participant told me that the most successful advertisement Vodafone ever had in Egypt was not about the powerful network or the number of retail outlets; it was about human relationships and getting the whole scattered Egyptian family together.

This is because in collectivistic cultures, effective advertising should focus on in-group benefits, harmony, and family; whereas in individualistic cultures, effective advertising should focus on individual preferences and independence.

Example 5.6 - You are Our Next CEO

Recalling the News Media case study introduced in Chapter 3, during the conflict that occurred between the employees and management in Egypt and the new board in Qatar, I received an invitation to go to Qatar to discuss some technical issues. After the meeting, a board member told me that if I took their side, I would be made the next CEO. I did not reply to him. The next day, I submitted my resignation.

Egypt is a relatively collectivistic culture. In such a culture, companies often function more like families, which was the case in this situation. In addition, team members are usually loyal to their boss and may speak with one voice: the voice of their most senior manager.

People's identity is based on the social system to which they belong.

Example 5.7 - Why Do Young People Leave Their Parents' Home?

My European culture coach told me that he kicked his son out of their house when he reached 21 years of age. He believed that his son should be more independent and should not stay living with his parents at that age.

In individualistic cultures, young people are much more independent from their families than in collectivistic cultures. In Egypt, for example, it is very normal for young people to stay living with their families until they get married. Every time someone argues with me that Egypt's culture has changed to become more individualistic, I ask them whether or not it is normal for young people to stay living at home till they get married.

Example 5.8 - Do You Follow the Crowd?

As I live in a collectivist country, it is normal to see on my Facebook page a post from one of my friends asking what type of mobile phone they should buy, and then start receiving replies to their question. Getting advice is common in all cultures, but some cultures depend heavily on what their inner group recommends, and they do not put any effort into a detailed comparison between the specifications of the different models.

I am one of those people by the way!

5.5   D3: ASSERTIVENESS

5.5.1   Overview

Hofstede originally called this dimension "masculine vs. feminine," as it was based on the values of both genders. "Assertiveness" is another name for the dimension, which reflects the meaning of the dimension and avoids the reader assuming that this dimension is about feminism-related issues.

This dimension reflects masculine values such as assertiveness and competitiveness vs. feminine values such as modesty, caring, and nurturing.

The more assertive a culture is, the more it is focused on the desire for achievement and success, and the less it is focused on caring for others and being people-oriented.

5.5.2   Definition

This dimension is defined by Hofstede (1980) as follows:

Assertiveness reflects the degree to which tough and assertive behaviors are encouraged vs. encouraging considerate and nurturing behaviors.

This dimension has an index in which each country is characterized by a score from 0 to 100. A score of 100 indicates a very highly assertive culture.

5.5.3   Examples of countries

Examples of masculine cultures are Britain, Germany, the Gulf states, Italy, Japan, and the United States. Examples of feminine cultures are the Netherlands, Portugal, Egypt, Sweden, Finland, and Spain (De Mooij & Hofstede, 2010).

5.5.4   Influence on Egyptian culture

Egypt is considered a relatively low assertive culture; you can easily observe that most Egyptians are not really assertive people. They prefer harmonious collaboration over conflict and in general try to find middle ground in arguments so that conflicts can be resolved through compromise and negotiation.

They would rather socialize with friends and family and they work to live, rather than the other way around. Jealousy can play a hidden and obscure role in Egyptian society, especially between women, and is a force to be reckoned with when dealing with groups of Egyptians.

On the other hand, Egyptians work very hard to get ahead in life and, in that sense, strive to achieve.

5.5.5   Influence in the Workplace

Table 5-4 shows a summary of behaviors of high and low assertiveness in the workplace.

Table 5-4. *Assertiveness Behaviors in the Workplace*

Low Assertiveness	High Assertiveness
Management is more by intuition and consensus.	Management is more decisive and aggressive.
Resolution of work conflict through compromise and negotiation.	Resolution of work conflict by letting the strongest win.
Rewards are based on equality.	Rewards are based on equity.
Preference for smaller organizations.	Preference for larger organizations.
People work in order to live.	People live in order to work.
More leisure time is preferred over more money.	More money is preferred over leisure time.
Careers are optional for both genders.	Careers are compulsory for men.
Higher share of working women in professional jobs.	Lower share of working women in professional jobs.
It is less important to demonstrate achievement and status.	It is desirable to demonstrate achievement and status.
Dominant values are compassion and good relationships.	Dominant values are achievement and success.

Note. Source: Hofstede, et al. (2010); De Mooij & Hofstede (2010

5.5.6 General Influence on Change Initiatives

Below are the general influences on change:

- A culture of high assertiveness is best motivated by change-based incentives.

- A culture of high assertiveness may help increase the pace of implementing new changes.

- A culture of high assertiveness usually neglects the people side and soft factors while implementing and focusing on achieving the benefits of the change. This may negatively impact people's engagement with the change.

- A culture of low assertiveness may focus too much on the people side and soft factors, which may compromise the achievement of the change's benefits.

Example 5.9 - Middle Ground

In one of my business interviews, the interviewer asked me to give an example of a weak point in my character. I immediately replied that I am not an assertive person and need to have more balance. Feminine culture, which I strongly belong to, prefers harmonious collaboration over conflict. In general, it tries to find middle ground in arguments so that conflicts are resolved through compromise and negotiation. However, too much focus towards a feminine culture is not healthy as it sometimes prevents you from making difficult decisions at the right time.

Example 5.10 - Cross-Cultural Conflict

If you recall, the story of News Media case study ended with a real confrontation between the board of directors based in Qatar and the employees and management based in Egypt. Eventually, the board of directors decided to lay off around 350 employees and evacuate the premises.

This case study showed a typical cross-cultural conflict between the highly assertive culture in the Gulf States and the low assertive culture in Egypt. The external consultant of the change initiative mentioned in an interview:

> "... the Egyptian management maintained that its refusal of the board of directors' decision to dismiss the bad performers was a way to maintain the organizational culture. In my view, this act by the management was a very emotional tribal attitude, that is, an emotional attachment to the tribe, whereas the board of directors viewed it as an act of insubordination."

The caring family attitude, which is normal for a low assertive culture like Egypt, was perceived as a form of corruption from the new board members, who came from a highly assertive culture. This conflict caused a great misalignment between the board of directors and the management in Egypt. Consequently, this misalignment was one of the main factors that hindered the change.

5.6   D4: UNCERTAINTY AVOIDANCE

5.6.1   Overview

This dimension deals with a society's tolerance for ambiguity.

Even though uncertainty avoidance and risk avoidance are similar to a great extent, there is a fundamental difference between them. Risk is represented as a percentage of probability that a particular event will happen. On the other hand, uncertainty has no probability attached to it. It is a situation in which anything can happen, and we have no idea about. (Hofstede, et al., 2010).

From the philosophical perspective, this dimension deals with a society's search for "Truth." High uncertainty avoidance cultures believe in an "Absolute Truth," therefore, they tend to be more religious. Low uncertainty avoidance cultures allow more discussion on religious issues. Uncertainty-accepting cultures are more tolerant of behavior and opinions that differ from their own.

5.6.2   Definition

Uncertainty avoidance is defined by Hofstede (1980) as follows:

Uncertainty avoidance is the degree to which people feel threatened by uncertainty and ambiguity and try to avoid these situations.

This dimension has an index in which each country is characterized by a score from 0 to 100. A score of 100 indicates a very high uncertainty avoidance culture.

5.6.3   Examples of Countries

The countries of the Middle East, southern Europe, and eastern Europe score high on the UAI, while Britain, Sweden, Finland, and Singapore score low.

5.6.4   Influence on the Egyptian Culture

Egypt is a strong uncertainty avoidance culture, scoring 80 in this dimension. By definition, this score means that Egyptian people feel threatened by ambiguous or unknown situations. This is true in Egypt, especially among the older generations who are generally lacking a spirit of innovation and are reluctant to change.

Egyptian people are highly concerned with regulating social behavior and have great respect for expertise. However, I do not see Egyptians as having a high regard for rules, which is supposed to be a hallmark of a high uncertainty avoiding culture. For the most part, anyone visiting Cairo for the first time will experience a loud chaotic mess. Also, Egyptians in general are never on time.

During my training sessions, I usually find some individuals who refuse the argument that Egypt is a very high uncertainty avoiding culture, especially when they see that the behaviors of the dimension are very different from their personalities and behaviors. As I explained in Chapter 4, culture can only be seen collectively and by comparison. Personality is a different issue.

> **Important Note**
>
> Culture is based on the power of many and collective measurements. It is about the trending behaviors in a society or group.

5.6.5   Power Distance and Uncertainty Avoidance

Combining the two dimensions discussed: Power Distance (PD) and Uncertainty Avoidance (UA) identify more culture types of the organization.

Figure 5-1 shows the quadruple structure of the two dimensions along with the four culture types.

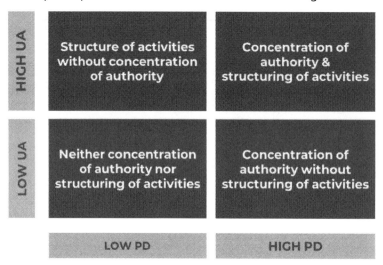

Figure 5-1. Power Distance and Uncertainty Avoidance Matrix

5.6.6   Influence in the Workplace

Table 5-5 shows the influence of uncertainty avoidance in the workplace.

Table 5-5. *Uncertainty Avoidance Behaviors in the Workplace*

Low Uncertainty Avoidance	High Uncertainty Avoidance
More changes in employers.	Fewer changes in employers.
There should be no more rules than strictly necessary.	There is an emotional need for rules in the business, even if they will not work.
Work hard only when needed.	There is an emotional need to be busy and to work hard.
More tolerance for ambiguity.	Less tolerance for ambiguity.
Less need for formalization.	More need for formalization.
Managers are more tolerant of staff criticism.	Managers are less tolerant of staff criticism.
Top managers are concerned with strategy.	Top managers are concerned with daily operations.

Low Uncertainty Avoidance	High Uncertainty Avoidance
Focus on the decision process.	Focus on the decision content.
Motivated by achievement more than security.	Motivated by security more than achievement.
More open to change and innovation.	Less open to change and innovation.

Note. Source: Hofstede, et al. (2010)

5.6.7   General Influences of Change

Below are the general influences of change:

- High uncertainty avoidance cultures do not promote innovative change initiatives.

- High uncertainty avoidance cultures require well-defined sponsorship governance with clear roles and responsibilities.

- Change should be very well structured with formal planning and clear governance to be accepted in a high uncertainty avoidance culture.

- A culture of high uncertainty avoidance will cause the change implementation to be slower. It will be the other way around in low uncertainty avoidance culture.

- In a high uncertainty avoidance culture, communication about the change should be more emotional as people are more emotional and motivated by inner nervous energy.

- High uncertainty avoidance cultures require a more detailed risk management plan.

Example 5.11 - Put Your Money in Real Estate!

In Egypt, whenever I talk to someone about investment opportunities or setting up a new business, the most frequent reply that I get is: "Put your money in real estate." People try to avoid the uncertainty of other investment areas by putting their money in real estate, which they perceive to be a safer option.

Example 5.12 - Opposition Parties!

From a political perspective, the very high uncertainty avoidance culture causes major concerns for the ruling party, resulting in specific security measures: hundreds of websites are banned; the media can only praise the ruling party, and opposition parties are the greatest supporters of the government!

On the other hand, uncertainty accepting cultures are more tolerant of different behaviors and opinions. They are more democratic and have freedom of the press.

5.7   D5: LONG-TERM ORIENTATION

5.7.1   Overview

This dimension was concluded for the Chinese Value Survey, which was based on Confucian teachings.

The main values associated with long-term orientation are:

- Thrift
- Ordering relationships by status
- Having a sense of shame
- Persistence (perseverance)

The main values associated with short-term orientation are:

- Respect for tradition
- Reciprocation of greetings and gifts
- Fulfilling social obligations
- Protecting one's reputation

Generally, long-term orientation implies investment in the future as well as the support of more entrepreneurial activities.

5.7.2   Definition

Long-term orientation is defined by Hofstede (1980) as the degree to which a society exhibits a pragmatic future-oriented perspective rather than a conventional historic or short-term point of view. This dimension has an index in which each country is characterized by a score from 0 to 100. A score of 100 indicates a very high long-term oriented culture.

5.7.3   Examples of Countries

Most East Asian countries, such as China, Japan, South Korea, and Singapore, are very long-term oriented. The USA and Sweden are short-term oriented, while Egypt is very short-term oriented.

5.7.4   Influence on the Egyptian Culture

I often find on Facebook sarcastic posts from Egyptian youth about how their families follow many of the marriage and other ritual traditions. Short-term oriented cultures like Egypt care a great deal about tradition and social obligations.

Many people like to help each other from the social obligation perspective.

Egyptian people focus on achieving quick results. Most Egyptians are normative in their thinking and

5.7.5   General Influence on Change Initiatives

Below are the general influences on change:

- ▪ Encouraging change investment in the future.

- ▪ A culture of high long-term orientation is not best motivated by direct change-based incentives.

- ▪ In a high long-term orientation culture, it is preferable to form an effective team to develop and sustain the change.

- ▪ A high long-term orientation culture is motivated by change initiatives that have long-term benefits and help achieve long-term goals.

5.7.6   Influence in the Workplace

Table 5-6 shows the influence of this dimension in the workplace.

Table 5-6. *Long-term Orientation Behaviors in the Workplace*

Short-term oriented	Long-term oriented
Main work values: freedom, rights, achievement, and thinking of oneself.	Main work values: learning, adaptability, accountability, self-discipline,
Leisure time is important.	Leisure time is not important.
Focus on profitability.	Focus on the market position.
Managers and frontline employees are in two different camps from a mental attitude perspective.	Managers and frontline employees are in the same camp.
Social difference is not desirable.	Social difference is desirable.
There are universal guidelines about what is good and evil.	What is good and evil depends more on the circumstances.
If A is true, its opposite B must be false.	If A is true, its opposite B could also be true.
Personal loyalties vary with business needs.	Investment in lifetime personal network.
Disagreement may hurt relationships.	Disagreement does not hurt.
Analytical thinking.	Synthetic thinking.

Note. Source: Hofstede, et al. (2010)

Example 5.13 - Egypt and USA National Cultures

The measurements of the national cultures of all countries are already available and can be easily obtained by searching over the internet. Table 5-7 shows the measurements of both the Egyptian and American national cultures, with Figure 5-3 showing a graphical representation of the same measurements.

Table 5-7. *Egypt's National Culture for Hofstede's 6-D Model*

	Index	Egypt	USA
1	Power distance index	70	40
2	Individualism index	25	91
3	Masculinity index	45	62
4	Uncertainty avoidance index	80	46
5	Long-term orientation index	7	26
6	Indulgence vs. restraint index	4	68

Note. Source: The Hofstede Insights *http://geert-hofstede.com/egypt.html*

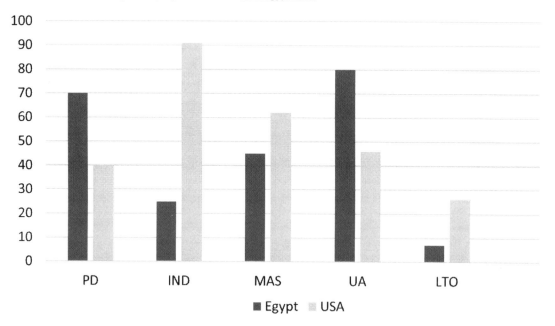

Figure 5-3. Graphical Representation of the Cultural Dimensions

Referring to our previous discussion regarding the mental image of organizations, can you identify the standard mental images for organization in both Egypt and USA?

Considering the score of both Egypt and USA, can you estimate the score of the five dimensions for both you organization and yourself.

Figure 5-2 shows the six dimensions of the model.

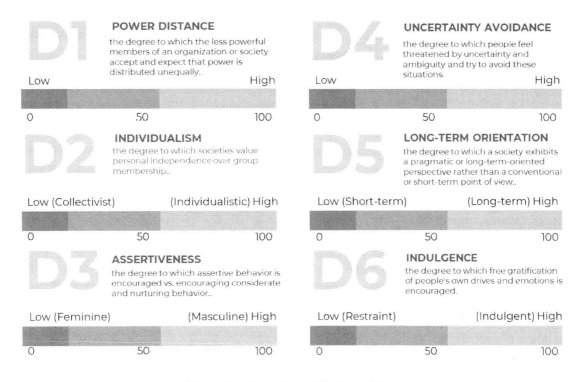

Figure 5-2. Dimensions of Hofstede Model

5.8   MENTAL IMAGES OF ORGANIZATIONS

According to Waisfisz (2015), combining the scores of the different dimensions reflects the mental image of an organization.

We already discussed an example in which reflecting the uncertainty avoidance of Egyptian organizations – a combination of large power distance, collectivism, and a strong uncertainty avoidance culture – creates a pyramid-shaped mental image of the organization.

Following are the mental images that could be formed by different combinations of the dimensions: Contest, Network, Pyramid, Family, Solar system, and Machine

Table 5-8 shows the dimensions that form these mental images.

Table 5-8. *Mental Images*

Combinations of Dimensions	Mental Image		Description
▪ Small power distance ▪ High assertiveness ▪ High individualism ▪ Low uncertainty avoidance	Contest		Autonomy, decentralization, assertiveness, and the principle of *win-it-all.*

Characteristics	Type		Description
• Small power distance • Low assertiveness • High individualism • Low uncertainty avoidance	Network		Autonomy, decentralization, consensus, jealousy, and interdependence.
• Large power distance • Low individualism • High uncertainty avoidance	Pyramid		Hierarchy, centralization, formality and procedures, and a lot of order, yet not always obvious.
• Large power distance • Low individualism • Low uncertainty avoidance	Family		Loyalty, hierarchy, simple structure, and high flexibility.
• Large power distance • High individualism • High uncertainty avoidance	Solar system		Tension between departments; autonomy; rules; and formality.
• Small power distance • High individualism • High uncertainty avoidance	Machine		Autonomy, decentralization, respect for authority, high need for structure and high need for process and standardization.

Note. Source: Waisfisz (2015)

Skill Practice 5.1 - Identify the Mental Image of Your Organization

Based on the Mental Image that was discussed in Chapter 5, identify the mental image of the organization of your project. How would this mental image influence the implementation of a new change.

The dimensions are:

- Power distance
- Assertiveness (Employee-oriented vs. Work oriented)
- Individualism (Local vs. Professional)
- Uncertainty avoidance (Flexible vs. strict)

5.9   BALANCING THE NATIONAL CULTURE

Table 5-9 shows how the national culture on change could be balanced.

Table 5-9. *Balancing the Influence of the National Culture*

Culture	Recommended strategy
Large power distance	1. Need to involve subordinates actively throughout the change process in order to get the psychological "buy-in" and ideas of those "close to the action."

Low individualistic (Collectivistic)	1. Need to build the trust. 2. Select change leader and implementers with high credibility. 3. Ensuring experience and credibility of the change leader and implementers
High uncertainty avoidance	1. Need to avoid having ambiguity about the vision of the change that may create security issue with staff. 2. Need to ensure that the use of excessive formal plans to manage the change does not create too much bureaucracy that slow down the change progress. 3. In case of reducing number of employees, a strategy of how to retain key employees should identified. Also, laying off procedures should be carefully analyzed.
Low assertiveness (Feminine)	1. Need to ensure the tendency to focus on soft factors does not compromise the need to achieve key aims and targets.
Low assertiveness (Masculine)	1. Need to ensure that staff are involved. 2. Need to make sure that people are fully aware about the reasons behind assertive decisions.
Short-term oriented	1. Need to ensure that the tendency to focus on short-term results does not hinder the long-term change goals. 2. Designing change-based performance management system.

5.10   CHAPTER IN A BOX

* The general influences of a large power distance culture on change are:
  o It is easy to authorize and initiate a change initiative.
  o It is normally not easy to complete the change smoothly.
  o Less formal planning will be required for the change.
  o There is low engagement due to a lack of commitment and ownership.
  o Subordinates are not actively involved in the change.
* The general influences of individualism on change:
  o In individualistic cultures, it is not easy to develop an effective team and sustain the change.
  o A highly individualistic culture motivates and accepts new and innovative change ideas.
  o In a low individualistic culture (collectivistic), new changes are primarily accepted based on trust rather than on rationality.
  o When using collectivistic incentives, it is better for the change to have a common mission and for at least part of the incentive to be given collectively for achieving shared goals.
  o Change should not conflict with employees' group loyalties.

- o The change communication strategy should be more rational in an individualistic culture and more emotional in a collectivistic culture.

- o In collectivistic cultures, it is necessary for a change leader to build a relationship and trust before communicating the change. In this culture, people generally acquire most of their information via interpersonal communication and make their decisions based largely on feelings and trust.

- The general influences of assertiveness on change are:

  - o A highly assertive culture normally has rapid implementation of the change.

  - o A culture of high assertiveness is best motivated by change-based incentives.

  - o A culture of high assertiveness may help increase the pace at which new changes are implemented.

  - o A culture of high assertiveness usually neglects the people side and soft factors while implementing and focusing on achieving the change's benefits. This may be detrimental to people's engagement with the change.

  - o A culture of low assertiveness may focus too much on the people side and soft factors, which may compromise the achievement of the change's benefits.

- The general influences of uncertainty avoidance on change are:

  - o High uncertainty avoidance cultures do not promote innovative change initiatives.

  - o High uncertainty avoidance cultures require well-defined sponsorship governance with clear roles and responsibilities.

  - o Change should be very well structured along with formal planning and clear governance to be accepted in a high uncertainty avoidance culture.

  - o A culture of high uncertainty avoidance will cause the change implementation to be slower. It is the other way around for low uncertainty avoidance cultures.

  - o In a high uncertainty avoidance culture, communication about the change should be more emotional as people are more emotional and are motivated by inner nervous energy.

  - o High uncertainty avoidance cultures require a more detailed risk management plan.

- The general influences of long-term orientation on change are:

  - o Encouraging change investment in the future.

  - o A culture of high long-term orientation is not best motivated by direct incentives.

  - o In a high long-term orientation culture, it is easier to form an effective team to develop and sustain the change.

  - o High long-term orientation cultures are motivated by change initiatives that have long-term benefits and help achieve long-term goals.

CHAPTER 6
INFLUENCE OF ORGANIZATIONAL CULTURE ON CHANGE

Chapter 6 - Influence of Organizational Culture on Change

6.1 OVERVIEW

As Kotter indicated, the biggest obstacle to creating change in an organization is culture. Many researchers agree that cultural aspects may hinder the change intended. However, many organizations underestimate the influence of culture on change, and not too many managers know how to change and reshape the culture in their organizations.

As we discussed in Chapter 4, any group of people that stays together for a significant amount of time will create their own unique culture specific to that group. This group culture will be influenced by the national culture of each individual within that group (for example, such things as their rational values, social rituals, religious practices, daily habits, etc.), as well as the attitudes and beliefs of the leader and key members of the group. The group culture will govern the way its members relate to and deal with each other; it will also determine how the group is viewed by people outside the group.

A group culture exists in every organization, without fail. It is this group culture that determines how its members relate to each other and to the external world. Therefore, the group culture will greatly influence the organization's image in the minds of those outside the organization.

6.2 CULTURAL LEVERS

Just like national culture, organizational culture has its own values and practices. The organizational culture is different than the national culture, but it is greatly influenced by the national culture surrounding it.

The national culture is only one factor influencing that organizational culture. Other factors include the varying influences of the founders and key managers, strategy, industry, rewards and sanctions within the company, systems, company structure, etc. Eventually, the organization will develop its own unique culture.

Core values and the culture values inside the organization could be different. The core values are the values selected by the management for strategic and/or marketing purposes. The company should work on reflecting the core values into the organizational culture. While this may be a bit confusing now, it should make sense by the end of the book.

Figure 6-1 shows our organizational culture definition that I presented in chapter 4. Organizational culture is defined as the set of values, mindsets, practices, and behaviors which are commonly shared by any group of people who together form the organization.

Figure 6-1. Simple Organizational Culture Levers

Important Note

Researchers have discovered that the values of different organizations in the same country are often similar. The differences stem mainly from varying organizational practices.

Example 6.1 - Ali, Your Order is Ready

Whenever I go to a Starbucks café in Cairo, the barista who takes my order asks for my name. This is part of the regular procedure. I tell the barista my name is Ali with a double XX, as I like to have my coffee extra extra hot (Figure 6-2). Once my coffee is ready, the barista calls out: "Ali, your order is ready!" However, if the same barista dealt with me anywhere else outside the Starbucks environment, they would never call me by my first name.

Why? Because the large power distance culture of Egypt respects status. So, while inside the café, the barista acts according to the company practices that are part of the organizational culture. However, as soon as they are outside the café environment, they would act according to their national cultural values.

Figure 6-2. Extra Extra Hot

This Starbucks example illustrates very clearly how the issue of dealing with customers in organizations is actually based on business practices, not values. No doubt business owners do not really care if they are called values or practices; their primary concern is customer satisfaction. However, it is important to understand this issue if we wish to better understand organizational culture and how to manage it.

6.3 ORGANIZATIONAL CULTURE MODELS

In an attempt to understand, measure, and assess organizational cultures, several models have been developed. Many models are all well-known and widely used to assess and measure the culture. Similar to the Hofstede Model of national culture in which six dimensions were selected to describe the society cultures, also the organizational culture models are based on selecting certain dimensions that can describe the organizational culture.

Even though I will later use the Multi-Focus Model for organizational culture in this book, I will give a brief explanation of Handy's Model which is similar to other models. Handy's Model has set two dimensions which are: Rate of change and Complexity of work process. These two dimensions identify the culture types of the organization. By looking at the two dimensions, a quadruple structure is constructed. Figure 6-3 shows the quadruple structure of the two dimensions of Handy's Model along with the four culture types.

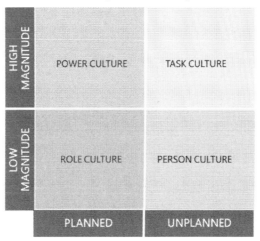

Figure 6-3. Handy's Model

The four culture types of Handy's Model are:

Power culture: This is similar to the power distance culture that we discussed in Chapter 5. It reflects a centralized top-down power and influence.

Task culture: This is a results-oriented culture that enjoys flexibility and empowerment.

Role culture: This is a bureaucratic culture run by strict procedures and defined roles.

Person culture: This is a people-oriented culture that meets individual employees' needs and expectations.

Almost all models have four culture types as shown in Figure 6-3 except the Multi-Focus as we will see later.

6.4   INTRODUCTION TO THE MULTI-FOCUS MODEL

Between 1985 to 1987, Geert Hofstede and his team developed the Hofstede Multi-Focus Model. According to Hofstede, this model was based on qualitative and quantitative studies across twenty organizations operating in different sectors. The research was based primarily on the survey used to develop Hofstede's model of national culture that was discussed in Chapter 5.

The results of the research were published in a research paper entitled "Measuring organizational cultures: A qualitative and quantitative study across twenty cases" that was written by Hofstede, Neuijen, Ohayv, and Sanders and published in Administrative Science Quarterly in 1990.

The model has the following six culture dimensions:

Dimensions 1: Means-oriented vs. goal-oriented (Organizational effectiveness)

Dimensions 2: Internally driven vs. externally driven (Customer orientation)

Dimensions 3: Flexible vs. strict (Organizational control)

Dimensions 4: Local vs. professional (Social control)

Dimensions 5: Open vs. closed (Communication effectiveness)

Dimensions 6: Employee-oriented vs. work-oriented (Management philosophy)

Figure 6-4 presents the six cultural dimensions of the Multi-Focus Model.

Figure 6-4. Cultural Dimensions of the Multi-Focus Model

Dimensions 1, 3, and 6 relate to inside the organization, while that Dimensions 2, 4, and 5 relate to the outside word. Each dimension has an index that describes the differences between organizations. By using this index, each organization is characterized by a score from 0 to 100 on this dimension. The score of each dimension can be measured by a surrey based on the description provided in Appendix C, or intuitively.

Hofstede provided an index that describes the differences between organizations. By using this index, each organization is characterized by a score from 0 to 100 on this dimension.

6.5   D1: MEANS-ORIENTED VS. GOAL-ORIENTED

This dimension contrasts "concern with means" to "concern with goals." This dimension is closely connected with the effectiveness of the organization.

The less the score is in this dimension, the more the culture is mean-oriented, which means it is mainly run by strict processes and defined roles. The more the culture is goal-oriented, the more ready it is for the change. The goal-oriented culture motivates having an inspiring leadership that presents a good deal of initiatives.

When it comes to change, this dimension plays a very important role. As shown in Figure 6-5, in a means-oriented culture, people identify more with the "how" to change than the "what" to change.

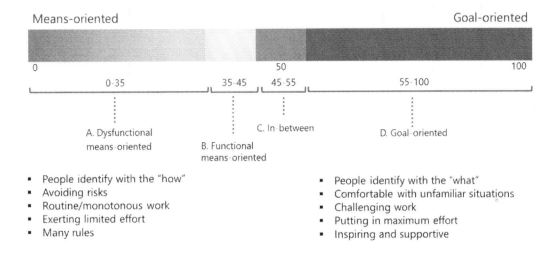

Figure 6-5. Main Behaviors of the Means-oriented vs. Goal-oriented Culture

As such, an organization with a high mean-oriented culture may not be very effective at implementing change, as people may not visualize the end result. That is why Waisfisz correlated this dimension with organizational effectiveness.   As Hofstede indicated, "avoiding risks vs. feeling comfortable with unfamiliar situations" is a key practices for this dimension.

In Appendix C at the end of the book, Table C-1 shows the behaviors of organizations based on the scores of this dimension.

It is important to remember that no single culture is good for all organizations. However, theoretically an organization should be relatively goal-oriented. The more goal-oriented an organization is, the more it accepts new ideas.

On the other hand, in organizations whose business involves substantial risk or requires a high level of quality and standards control, a mean-oriented culture tends to be far more suitable and functional. A good example of such a culture is the production unit in a pharmaceutical company. Bear in mind, however, that an extreme mean-oriented culture could create a dysfunctional environment. This is because it fosters a very bureaucratic culture in which following routine procedures are much more valued than achieving results or satisfying customers.

In a goal-oriented culture, employees are informed of the good work that they have done. They put in maximal effort and want to be more authorized by their bosses. The high goal-oriented culture motivates implementing new change initiatives especially that the mistakes are usually tolerated in such a culture. Managers help good people advance. Because people in a goal-oriented culture are keen to get things done, they encourage open communication, coordination, and knowledge sharing.

According to Hofstede, et al. (1990), a means-oriented culture correlates with the hierarchy within an organization. The more means-oriented the culture of an organization is, the more levels of hierarchy it may have. It also has a correlation with formalization and specialization. The more means-oriented an organization is, the greater the degree of formalization and specialization it will need. The more means-oriented a company is, the more mechanistic it will be.

In an organizational unit, which had in-between culture (score = 50), one of the managers commented:

> "… we are process-oriented when it comes to the daily job of each individual; however, the management is goal-oriented, setting targets and driving employees to achieve their targets for better results through a reward system and new change initiatives while providing some flexibility, but they are generally not comfortable with unfamiliar situations."

6.6   D2: INTERNALLY DRIVEN VS. EXTERNALLY DRIVEN

According to Hofstede (2014), this dimension contrasts normative vs. pragmatic; and deals with the popular notion of customer orientation.

It has the most impact on the readiness to change. It is also indicative of whether employees are normal or pragmatic. The more normative a culture is, the less people are receptive to new changes. In Figure 6-6, main behaviors are shown for this dimension.

There is no single culture that fits all organizations and all industries. It is clear that an organization that is more externally driven than its competitors will be more successful in implementing new change initiatives. However, a culture that is extremely externally driven may also be inclined to disregard or overlook business ethics.

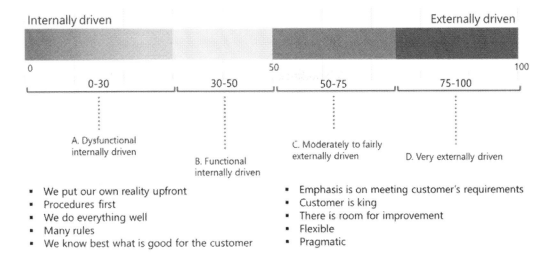

Figure 6-6. Main Behaviors of the Internally Driven vs. Externally Driven Culture

In Appendix C, Table C-2 shows behaviors of organizations based on the scores of this dimension.

In an internally driven culture, the management believes they know very well what their customers need. Depending on the context, they may be right or wrong. They may also believe that they require no ongoing improvement. In a nutshell, they do not consider the voices of their customers to be critical to their business.

Usually, a lack of competition results in an organization being less externally driven or customer-oriented and vice versa. Therefore, this dimension is also related to customer orientation. The more an organization functions under a monopoly environment, the less customer-oriented it will be and the more internally driven the culture will be. On the other hand, in an externally driven culture, the customer is king; meeting the customer's needs is extremely important and may even be prioritized over correct procedures and business ethics.

In an organizational unit, which had an externally driven culture (score = 70), the unit head commented:

> "... in my business unit, the customer comes first. Everything we do should be in the best interests of the customer. Sometimes it is OK to bend the rules and processes if the situation requires it, as customer satisfaction is a priority over applying the rules."

As we will see later when we discuss assessing the organizational change readiness in Chapter 9, the more the culture is externally driven, the more ready it is for the change.

6.6.1 More Culture Types: Results-Driven and Bureaucracy

Combining the two dimensions discussed so far: means-oriented vs. goal-oriented and internally driven vs. externally driven identify more culture types of the organization. By looking at the two dimensions, a quadruple structure is constructed. Figure 6-7 shows the quadruple structure of the two dimensions along with the four culture types and their descriptions.

As seen in Figure 6-7, a combination of extremely internally driven and means-oriented cultures create a bureaucratic culture that is at an increased risk of becoming dysfunctional. In some situations, this type of culture may also encourage corruption. Such a culture has to be managed as it does not motivate implementing new ideas and has a negative impact on the organizational change readiness.

Organizations need to have the culture of effective results-driven that is shown in top right of the matrix to be ready for transformational programs. So how do you increase the score in both dimensions in order to end up with an effective results-driven culture? This question will be answered when we reach the Tactics Themes in the ElKattan's 5-Theme Model in Chapters 11.

Figure 6-7. Combination of Internally Driven vs. Externally Driven and Means-Oriented vs. Goal-Oriented. Adapted from Constructing the Best Culture to Perform by B. Waisfisz, 2015.

Example 6.2 - Not-For-Profit Organizations

As a reflection on the News Media case study, if you look at the score of externally driven vs. internally, you will see a score of around 40. What does this mean?

This score means that the culture of News Media is somewhat internally driven. Most not-for-profit organizations like News Media are internally driven. They usually do not depend on customers to finance the operation.

News Media had an internally driven culture. As we previously explained, the more the culture of an organization is internally driven, the lower is its readiness for change. This was confirmed by a senior editor who commented:

> *"... at the outset, the organization's readiness for the change was not strong enough. That is why they resisted it so strongly."*

The question is: does such a conclusion conflict with the previous analysis that we discussed in Example 6.2, which confirmed that employees recognized the need for change?

The answer? No, it does not. Firstly, the internally driven culture was not extremely low (the score was 40). Secondly, employees may realize the need for change, but they may not be ready for or realize the urgency of the required change. This can be addressed by increasing the sense of urgency for the change, as well as expressing dissatisfaction with the current status. This requires strong and persuasive leadership.

6.7   D3: FLEXIBLE VS. STRICT

This dimension deals with the amount of internal control and discipline.

Innovative change typically requires a more flexible culture. Innovative ideas will not find good soil in strict cultures and it will therefore be difficult for them to take root and flourish. An extremely flexible culture has the potential to create a mess that results in a dysfunctional environment. In Figure 6-8, main behaviors of organizations are shown for this dimension.

According to Hofstede, a strict culture is identifiable by cost-consciousness, punctuality, and seriousness. A flexible culture has space for thinking outside the box and quick adaptability to changes.

Most organizations tend to be more restrict as organizations are built on control and authority even when involvement is a common practice. That is why manages get worried when they face resistance in a change initiative as they perceived it as a direct threat to their control.

A flexible culture has space for thinking outside the box and quick adaptability to changes. However, there is a price to pay for such a culture, which includes a loose internal structure, lack of predictability, and inconsistent control and discipline.

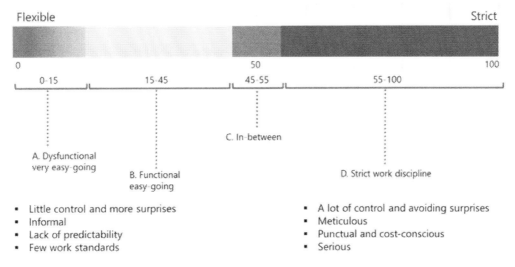

Figure 6-8. Main Behaviors of the Flexible vs. Strict Culture

In Appendix C, Table C-3 shows behaviors of organizations based on the scores of this dimension. Organizations will have sub-cultures that differ from one function to the other. For example, it is obvious that the marketing unit will want to spend as much as possible to create brand awareness, while the sub-culture of the finance department will be very different. The different units within one organization may score differently on this dimension.

Below is a comment from a senior manager in an organizational unit, which had a score of 40 in this dimension:

> *"... we have an innovative, easygoing, and flexible culture. We are quite relaxed. Some employees pay little attention to cost, which could be improved."*

6.7.1   More Culture Types

Combining the two dimensions: means-oriented vs. goal-oriented and strict vs. flexible identify more culture types of the organization. By looking at the two dimensions, a quadruple structure is constructed. Figure 6-9 shows the quadruple structure of the two dimensions along with the four culture types and their descriptions.

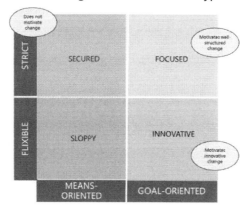

Figure 6-9. Combination of Flexible vs. Strict and Process-Oriented vs. Goal-Oriented. Adapted from Constructing the Best Culture to Perform by B. Waisfisz, 2015.

As seen in Figure 6-9, a combination of flexible and goal-oriented cultures creates an innovative culture that motivates thinking outside the box. Such culture is very healthy to have continuous improvements.

6.7.2   Relationship with National Culture

My question now is: do you think this dimension could be influenced by the dimensions of the national culture?

The answer? Yes, it is.

The higher the power distance culture, the stricter and more formal the organizational culture will be. Can you think why?

This culture is also influenced by the uncertainty avoidance culture. The higher the level of uncertainty avoidance, the less flexible the organizational culture will be.

Example 6.3 - Flexible Cultures Motivates Innovation

As a reflection on the News Media case study, News Media had a fairly (though not overly) flexible culture, which may have conflicted with the influence of the high uncertainty avoidance culture of Egypt. That is because the national culture is one of the factors that impacts the organizational culture. However, the practices of the senior management inside an organization could potentially balance out the influence of the national culture.

Also, such a flexible culture motivates having an innovative spirit that is needed to implement change. This influence was clear from the many new successful projects that the organization launched.

6.8   D4: LOCAL VS. PROFESSIONAL

This dimension contrasts organizations whose employees derive their identity from their boss and/or organization to others in which people identify with their profession.

In a local culture, people are very loyal to their boss. On the other hand, in a professional culture people identify themselves by their profession. This may lead to a high turnover of staff in professional cultures. In local cultures, people may stay in the same organization their whole life. In Figure 6-10, main behaviors are shown for this dimension.

This dimension is about social control. In a very local culture, there is a strong social expectation that employees will behave like everybody else. On the other side of the fence, employees in a professional culture will have more privacy as there are no strong social expectations around them.

This dimension could be easily assessed by the hiring criteria of organizations. Organizations that have a local culture tend to hire similar people. On the other hand, organizations that have a professional culture encourage more diversification in hiring.

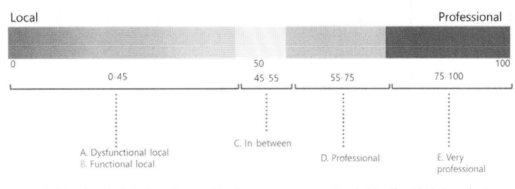

- People identify with their direct boss and/or the unit
- A critical attitude is not acceptable
- Managers want subordinates to be loyal
- A strong social expectation to be like everybody else

- People identify with their profession
- A critical attitude is essential
- Internal loyalty is not important
- There is no social expectation to be like everybody else

Figure 6-10. Main Behaviors of the Local vs. Professional Culture

In a local culture, the company cares more about the social background of a job applicant, while in a professional culture ability and aptitude for the job are the main consideration factors for hiring.

In Appendix C, Table C-4 shows behaviors of organizations based on the scores in this dimension.

Even though many people encourage diversification as it is good for enhancing and developing new ideas. However, there is no "always" when it comes to culture. For example, most Japanese companies have a local culture and they are doing extremely well.

Another example, if an organization has a conservative culture in a way that their working spaces are separate for men and women. It is obvious that people who do not have the same social background and do not accept this level of conservatism would not be a good fit for the company.

People in a professional culture are concerned about what their competitors are doing. They are long-term directed. Cooperation between different teams with different functions within the organization is also common. Therefore, this culture motivates innovation and change.

Because a critical attitude is an acceptable characteristic, employees feel comfortable critiquing new ideas, and healthy differences of opinion can be aired until an idea has been refined. However, there is always a risk that these rational disagreements could turn into heated confrontations, especially in a very high professional culture.

Below is a comment from a senior manager in a multi-national organization operating in Egypt. Their score in this dimension was 30.

> "... employees tend to identify with their managers rather than their own experience and profession. Diversity is not fully welcomed (although stated otherwise), and there is a very little interest in and lack of awareness about competitors."

6.8.1   More Culture Types

Combining the two dimensions: means-oriented vs. goal-oriented and Local vs. professional identify more culture types of the organization. By looking at the two dimensions, a quadruple structure is constructed. Figure 6-11 shows the quadruple structure of the two dimensions along with the four culture types and their descriptions.

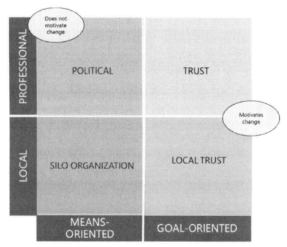

Figure 6-11. Combination of Local vs. Professional and Process-Oriented vs. Goal-Oriented. Adapted from "Constructing the Best Culture to Perform," by B. Waisfisz, 2015.

As seen in Figure 6-11, a combination of professional and goal-oriented cultures creates a trust culture that is very critical when it comes to change.

6.8.2   Relationship with National Culture

Cast your mind back to the dimensions of national culture that we discussed in Chapter 5.

The relevant dimension here is individualism vs. collectivism. Societies that are collectivistic have very tight social control over their people. Such a national culture can have an influence on making the organizational culture local.

Example 6.4 - Impact of Professional Culture on Change

Reflecting on the News Media case study, it had a fairly professional culture with a score of 60. As we have learned, employees in such a culture have a critical attitude and expect their leaders to be very credible and experienced. Unfortunately, the person who was assigned from the board to lead the change at News Media was neither experienced nor credible, which created a real conflict with the team. This was explained by a key manager, who said:

"... this leader had experience neither in how to manage changes nor in how to lead such an organization. Credibility is built upon accumulated experience in relevant areas. However, in the case that we are discussing right now, the change leader had no such accumulated experience."

It is clear that the experience and credibility of the change leader was insufficient to build trust in the change amongst the employees. It has since been proven that this lack of experience and credibility was one of the main reasons for the failure of this change.

Reflecting on the News Media case study, the organization had a very open culture with a score of 12. As such, there was excellent communication between the employees and their managers – that is, the employees were involved in every decision made by the managers.

An open culture such as this is very resistant to secretive change. The vision of the change was secretive, vague, and not transparent, which cultivated a strong resistance to it among the employees.

It was inevitable that failing to involve employees in such a high open culture would create resistance. This was confirmed by the marketing manager, who said:

"... the employees used to be involved in every decision made by their managers. Therefore, these employees showed a great deal of resistance to this change for which the decisions were made at the top level and in which they were not involved."

The question is, how did such a conflict happen?

This conflict happened was a result of the large power distance of the board, who were based in one of the Arabic countries in the Gulf area.

The influence of the very high open organizational culture was in direct conflict with the influence of the large power distance culture and its related style of management.

6.9   D5: OPEN SYSTEM VS. CLOSED SYSTEM

This dimension is about the communication climate. It relates to the approachability and accessibility of an organization. The more closed the culture is, the more secretive the organization becomes. Because of this, newcomers often have difficulty understanding what is going on around them and it takes considerable time and effort for them to fit into the organization.

In Figure 6-12, main behaviors of organizations are shown for this dimension.

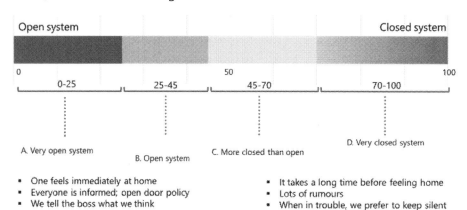

Figure 6-12. Main Behaviors of the Open vs. Closed Culture

The change leader who initiates a change in an open culture should be aware that employees resist secretive or non-transparent initiatives; also, they expect to be involved about the change.

In Appendix C, Table C-5 shows the expected behaviors inside the organizations based on the scores of this dimension. Also, Chapter 6 has more description about this dimensions.

On the other hand, in an open culture communication is easier and more effective. Employees can easily access and talk to their managers about anything that is on their mind, even in threatening situations that may impact the whole organization.

Below is a comment from a senior manager in a multi-national organization. Their score in this dimension was 70.

> *"... new employees sometimes do not feel at ease when entering into the company's culture. Employees usually do not tell their managers if they feel threatened."*

Example 6.5 - Impact of a Very Open Culture

Reflecting on the News Media case study, the organization had a very open culture with a score of 12. As such, there was excellent communication between the employees and their managers – that is, the employees were involved in every decision made by the managers.

An open culture such as this is very resistant to secretive change. The vision of the change was secretive, vague, and not transparent, which cultivated a strong resistance to it among the employees.

It was inevitable that failing to involve employees in such a high open culture would create resistance. This was confirmed by the marketing manager, who said:

> *"... the employees used to be involved in every decision made by their managers. Therefore, these employees showed a great deal of resistance to this change for which the decisions were made at the top level and in which they were not involved."*

The question is, how did such a conflict happen?

Example 6.5 - Impact of a Very Open Culture

This conflict happened was a result of the large power distance of the board, who were based in one of the Arabic countries in the Gulf area.

The influence of the very high open organizational culture was in direct conflict with the influence of the large power distance culture and its related style of management.

6.9.1   Relationship with National Culture

The higher the power distance, the more closed the organization is as the top management do not tend to involve their subordinates and do not share most of the information with them. Also, the more the national culture is avoiding uncertainty, the more influence for the organizations to be more closed.

6.10   D6: EMPLOYEE-ORIENTED VS. WORK-ORIENTED

This dimension contrasts a concern for people to a concern for completing the job.

The name of this dimension is self-explanatory. In a very high work-oriented culture, a great deal of pressure is placed on employees because jobs must be completed to a schedule, regardless of their workload and stress levels. Management believes that without such pressure nothing would get done.

In a very high work-oriented culture, the organization's interest in work is much higher than its interest in employees' personal problems. In Appendix C, Table C-6 shows the expected behaviors inside the organizations based on the scores of this dimension.

In Figure 6-13, main behaviors of organizations are shown for this dimension.

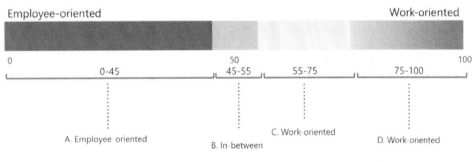

Figure 6-13. Main Behaviors of the Employee-Oriented vs. Work-Oriented Culture

Appendix C shows the expected behaviors inside the organizations based on the scores of the six dimensions. Also, Chapter 6 has more description about these dimensions.

A combination of high work-oriented culture with a high process-oriented culture, results in a high rate of employee burnout.

I have always been a very employee-oriented manager with a consultative leadership style. As such, I would not think about starting to implement any change before getting the buy-in from most employees. I also tend to consider the personal situations of the employees. However, there are many situations where you really need to have a bit of work-oriented culture to get the job done.

Being employee-oriented may cause too much focus to be placed on the well-being of employees, which may compromise the achievement of the change's key aims and targets. However, being employee-oriented will result in less anxiety and grumbling about the new changes.

Below is a comment from a senior manager whose unit scored 20 in this dimension.

> "... in our unit, employees always come first. A democratic leadership style is common, and employees are often consulted before making decisions."

6.10.1   Relation with National Culture

This dimension is influenced by the assertiveness cultural dimension (masculinity vs. femininity) that we discussed in Chapter 5. The higher the assertiveness culture, the more work-oriented the organization will be.

Example 6.6 - Quality Control

As a reflection on the News Media case study, Figure 6-14 shows the culture measurements of the News Media case study, which were measured using a survey developed by Hofstede Insight. With a score of about 70, News Media was classed as reasonably goal-oriented. Working in the media industry influences the culture towards being more goal-oriented, as news needs to be gathered and published quickly in what is generally a fast-paced environment. At News Media, there was always conflict between the operations unit and the quality control unit that was applying the ISO standards on the organization. ISO involves a lot of procedures that need to be followed and complied with. People in a goal-oriented culture do not normally like or pay attention to standard processes such as the ISO standards.

In an attempt to empower the quality control unit, the chairman decided that the unit would report directly to him. Even with this increased power and autonomy, the manager of the quality control unit continued to complain about the constant conflict arising from the operations unit failing to follow the proper procedures.

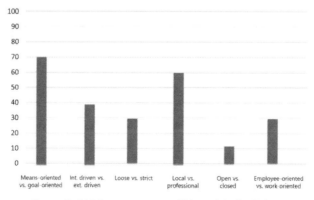

Figure 6-14. Measurements of News Media Culture

> The more goal-oriented a culture is, the more people realize the need for continual change, as evidenced by the experiences of several key personnel. Recalling the case study, the director of the marketing unit said:
>
> > *"... at the beginning, the employees welcomed the change and were fully engaged; they were looking forward to turning into a huge profitable organization similar or identical to the BBC."*
>
> And the head of the project management unit commented:
>
> > *"... during the five years that I spent there, the organization was changing; new projects, divisions, and offices were established."*

It is also related to the power distance in which decisions are centralized at senior management, who are usually responsible for imposing new changes. In addition, little attention is paid to the personal issues of employees, this usually results in silent resistance from inside the organization.

6.11   INFLUENCE ON CHANGE IMPLEMENTATION

Table 6-1 shows the general influence of cultural dimensions on change.

Table 6-1. *Influence of the Cultural Dimensions on Change Implementation*

	Dimension	Influence on change implementation
1	Means-oriented vs. goal-oriented	The more goal-oriented the culture is, the more people realize the need for an organization to continuously change.
2	Internally driven vs. externally driven	The more internally driven the culture is, the less will be the willingness to change.
3	Flexible vs. strict	The more loose or flexible the culture is, the more it motivates new and innovative ideas and change.
4	Local vs. professional	The more professional the culture is, the more employees expect to be involved with the change. It also reflects how visible the resistance will be. The more professional the culture is, the safer the employees feel to express their resistance without facing negative consequences.
		The more local the culture is, the more likely it is that any negative opinions will not be voiced; however, the resistance does not disappear, but becomes negativity and rumors, which quickly affect the rest of the colleagues.
5	Open vs. closed	The more open the culture is, the more employees expect to be involved and the more they will resist secretive and non-transparent change initiatives.
6	Employee-oriented vs. work-oriented	The more work-oriented the culture is, the less consideration there will be for the people side of the change.

Example 6.7 - Cross-Culture Conflicts

News Media had an employee-oriented culture with a score of 30. The management and employees of such a culture resisted some of the quick, unjustifiable, and assertive decisions that were made by the board. The change consultant commented on this by saying:

Example 6.7 - Cross-Culture Conflicts

"... the management maintained that its refusal to dismiss the bad performers was a way to preserve the organization's culture. In my viewpoint, this act by the management was a very emotional tribal attitude, that is, an emotional attachment to the tribe, whereas the board viewed it as an act of corruption and a cover up."

It is obvious that this employee-oriented culture was influenced by the feminine or the low assertiveness national culture of Egypt. Because the board did not care about the well-being of the employees and took aggressive action against the employees and key managers, there was great resistance to any change. This was one of the main reasons for the failure of the intended change. This cross-culture conflict happened as the culture in the Gulf area is much more assertive than the culture in Egypt, where the company was operating.

6.12 CHAPTER IN A BOX

This chapter took a close look at the Hofstede Multi-Focus Model and the influence of the culture on an organization's business behavior.

- Many organizational culture models are used to define and measure organizational culture. We discussed in this chapter: The Hofstede Multi-Focus Model and Handy's Model.

- The Multi-Focus Model has the following six dimensions:
  - Means-oriented vs. Goal-oriented
  - Internally driven vs. Externally driven
  - Flexible vs. Strict
  - Local vs. Professional
  - Open vs. Closed
  - Employee-oriented vs. Work-oriented.

CHAPTER 7
ELKATTAN'S 5-THEME MODEL

Chapter 7 – ElKattan's 5-Theme Model for Change Management

7.1   OVERVIEW

Now that we have reviewed - in the first six chapters- the concepts of change, change management, and culture, you should be ready to align your understanding with ElKattan's Model.

In this chapter, I will provide a general description of ElKattan's 5-Theme Model for Change Management. In the following five chapters, we will navigate through the model and explore its practical and structured approach.

My objective in developing this model was to address the gaps that I found in the other change management models, and to establish a complete framework that covers all areas of change management, providing managers with a new framework that enables them to achieve the desired change goals in a practical manner. The model is structured to ensure:

* A well-defined change vision is developed.

* An effective sponsorship governance is established.

* Proper preparation and readiness of the stakeholders and organization for the proposed change.

* The right theme, narratives, and messages are developed.

* The requisite level of awareness, competence, and engagement of the change community is secured.

* Formulation of the change management strategy and tactics.

* Proper integration between change management and project management plans.

* Identification and realization of the intended change outcomes and benefits.

* Institutionalization and integration of the new change within the organization's culture.

7.2   RESEARCH METHODOLOGY

After encountering upper management resistance to a change initiative as a company CEO, while simultaneously preparing for my doctorate in 2012, it became clear to me that the ideal topic for my research would be the question of what makes people resist change.

From 2012 to 2016, qualitative research was conducted under the supervision and mentorship of Swiss Management Center University, with the support of ITIM International, which trades as Hofstede Insights in Finland and Netherlands.

The main research question was: "What are the specific change management practices that have a significant positive impact on the success of the change initiatives?"

After completing the quantitative and qualitative surveys with more than 150 participants in two different case studies. I collected and coded the change management issues, and categorized them according to the following:

1. Change vision

2. Change sponsorship

3. Assessing the current state

4. Managing stakeholders

5. Managing culture

6. Managing organizational alignment

7. Managing communication

8. Strategy

9. Tactics

10. Change planning

11. Change appraising

Afterward, I designed the model by reflecting the four areas: (Managing stakeholders, Managing culture, Managing organizational alignment, and Managing communication) into four work streams:

1. Stakeholder management

2. Culture management

3. Organizational alignment

4. Communication management

And I reflected the remaining areas into what I called the five themes of the model:

1. Vision and sponsorship theme

2. Assessment theme

3. Strategizing theme

4. Tactics theme

5. Planning and appraising theme

This model, along with its five themes and four work streams, was a product of that research intertwined with my own experiences in numerous projects; the intention being to have a comprehensive framework on the topic of change management that would be of real value to senior managers and change leaders.

Figure 7-1 shows the relationship between the five themes.

Figure 7-1. The Relationship between the Five Themes

After concluding the research and development on the model, I introduced the model in my doctoral dissertation in 2016. In 2017, ElKattan's 5-Theme Model was then published in a paper in the Arabian Journal of Business and Management Review, under the title: The Five Themes of Change Management.

After nearly three years of writing, editing, and reviewing, the most recent version of the model is now being published here. Appendix D provides further details about the research methodology used.

7.3 THE MODEL'S THEMES AND COMPONENTS

Table 7-1 below provides the description of the five themes, along with the objective in each case.

Table 7-1. *Description of ElKattan's 5-Theme Model*

Vision and Sponsorship Theme	The objective of this theme is to understand the problem and what the risks are of not changing, identify how the world will be different after the change has been implemented, and develop the sponsorship governance and change management methodology.
Assessment Theme	The objective this theme is to assess the current state from the perspectives of: the stakeholder, culture, organizational alignment, and communication, in order to enable development of the appropriate change management strategy and tactics.
Strategizing Theme	The objective of this theme is to develop the strategy or the assumptions that it is presumed, if used, will make the change happen.
Tactics Theme	The objective of this theme is to identify the change management tactics that will help achieve the change management strategy.
Planning and Appraising	The objective of this theme is to appraise the value of the change, finalize the Go/No-Go decision, and develop a consolidated change management plan of all the work streams.

Theme	

Each theme has four change management components. The components in each theme are generally sequential, but it is not necessary to follow the same order. They can also be practiced in a cyclical fashion throughout the change journey.

Figure 7-2 shows the names of the four components of each one of the five themes. For example, the Assessment theme has the components: (1) Assessing stakeholder readiness, (2) Assessing culture, (3) Assessing organizational alignment, and (4) Assessing communication.

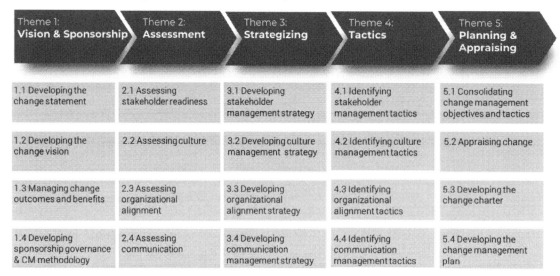

Figure 7-2. The Model's Themes and Components

Some change management models - as explained in Appendix A - have predefined steps to manage a change. However, there is not a single prescribed approach that must be followed for all changes. The approach must be tailored according to the problem, the objective, the context, the change size, etc. Selecting the right components from ElKattan's Model is a way to tailor the model based on the variables of a given situation.

Important Note

This model's components are a complete manifesto to enable managers to lead a change initiative and realize its benefits. However, some change initiatives may require the implementation of only some of the components, while others may require the implementation of all the components.

7.4   THE MODEL'S FOUR WORK STREAMS

A core concept of ElKattan's Model for Change Management is its change management work streams, making the model comprehensive, unique, and balanced.

Each work stream directs a critical perspective related to the change. The model's work streams are: (1) Stakeholder management, (2) Culture management, (3) Organizational alignment, (4) Communication management. They are characterized in this way in order to make the model balanced by addressing within each stream the different areas that may impact the change implementation.

The three components in each row in Figure 7-3 represent the tactics identification stage in each work stream. The three components are from the three themes: assessment, strategizing, and tactics. For example, the culture work stream has its own dedicated components: One component to assess the culture, one to develop the culture management strategy, and the last one to identify the culture management tactics.

The components of each work stream should be linked together and executed consecutively.

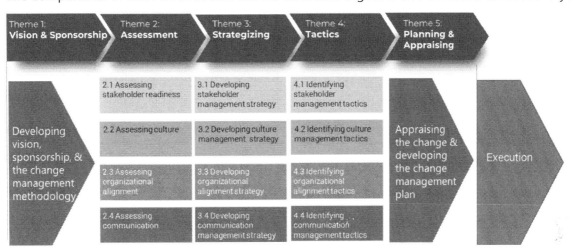

Figure 7-3. Components of the Work Streams

Before starting the implementation of any work stream it is assumed that the change vision and change management methodology have already been developed and the sponsorship has been established.

Below is a brief description of the four work streams:

Stakeholder management work stream. A process that ensures that the stakeholders are always aware, competent, and engaged by going through the steps of assessing the stakeholder readiness to formulate the stakeholder management strategy and tactics that are integrated in the change management plan and finally implemented.

Culture management work stream. A process that ensures that the change values, along with their behaviors and mindsets, are well-guided to motivate the implementation of the change by going through the steps of assessing the culture to formulate the culture management strategy and tactics that are integrated in the change management plan and finally implemented.

Organizational alignment work stream. A process that ensures that the organizational strategy, capabilities, and capacity are aligned to enable and sustain the change by going through the steps of assessing the organizational elements to formulate the organizational alignment strategy and tactics that are integrated in the change management plan and finally implemented.

Communication management work stream. A process that ensures the communicating of the right messages by going through the steps of assessing the communication to formulate the communication management strategy and tactics that are integrated in the change management plan and finally implemented.

The four work steams are shown in Figure 7-4.

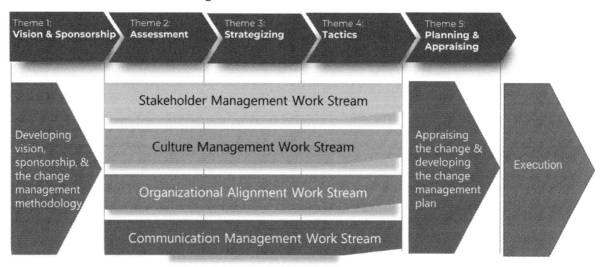

Figure 7-4. Work Streams in ElKattan's Model

There is another work stream that is embedded within the explicit components of the model, which is the outcome/benefit management work stream.

7.5   THE MODEL'S CHANGE LIFE CYCLE

The model has a three-phase change life cycle (Readiness-Transition-Sustaining and Realizing Benefits). Figure 7-5 shows the three phases.

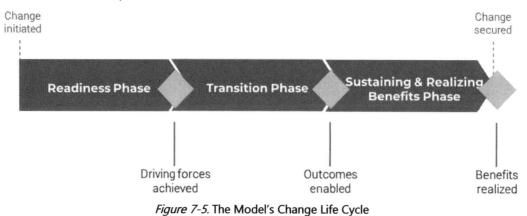

Figure 7-5. The Model's Change Life Cycle

Below is a description of the three phases:

7.5.1   Readiness Phase (R)

The Readiness phase has a number of sub-phases that the change leadership should go through to come up with the change management plan, and to assure that the desired readiness to the change is established.

In the first sub-phase, the procedure is undertaken by means of establishing change sponsorship, developing the change vision and the change management methodology that will be applied.

In the second sub-phase, assessing the current state is to be conducted from the various perspectives of: the stakeholder, culture, organizational alignment, and communication.

In the third sub-phase, the change management strategy is to be formulated based on the assessment of the current state.

In the fourth sub-phase, the change management tactical activities are to be identified in such a way as to achieve the change management strategy.

In the fifth sub-phase, the change is appraised, and the change management plan is developed.

And in the last phase, the leadership team should ensure the right awareness and readiness and that the vision is well-communicated and there is a high degree of dissatisfaction in respect of the current state. The implementation of the change should not start unless the change driving forces - that I discussed in Chapter 2 - are achieved.

Figure 7-6 shows the readiness sub-phases. The first five sub-phases in Figure 7-6 represent the five themes of the model.

The milestone that marks the end of this phase is achievement of the change driving forces.

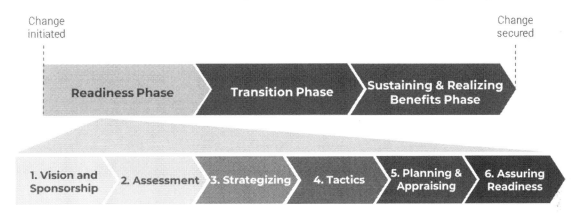

Figure 7-6. The Sub-Phases of the Readiness Phase

7.5.2   Transition Phase (T)

In this phase, the change starts to happen. Through the Transition phase, the team implements the technical solution as well as the change management tactics to ensure that the right performance and engagement are gained.

It is good practice to conduct a survey before or during the phase to get feedback from the stakeholders about their expectations and requirement from the change initiative.

During this phase, the projects' outputs are to be delivered according to the project management plan, and once the outputs are delivered, the change management team should start monitoring the achievement of the change outcomes.

It is critical, in this phase, to have the right awareness, to develop the competence, and to support stakeholders in adapting to the new workplace environment.

The milestone that marks the end of this phase is having the outcomes enabled.

7.5.3   Sustaining and Realizing Benefits Phase (S)

In this phase, the real change happens, which can be generally observed in achieving the outcomes and realizing the change benefits. Therefore, a measurement plan for the outcomes and benefits should be designed to keep tracking of the progress and recommend the right tactics if needed.

It is good practice to conduct a satisfaction survey in this phase to get feedback and keep track of the progress. The change leadership team must ensure that the new changes are sustained and embedded into the operations and culture.

The milestone that marks the end of this phase is realization of the benefits.

7.6   THE BIG PICTURE

Figure 7-7 shows the full picture of ElKattan's 5-Theme Model. It may seem a bit confusing at first, but it will become clear as we go through it.

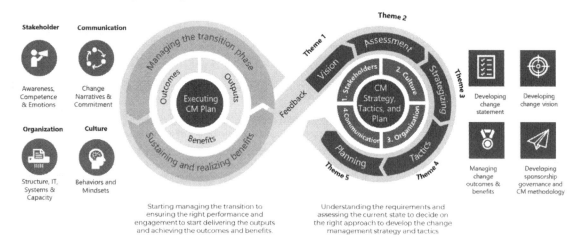

Figure 7-7. Big Picture of ElKattan's Model

Let us start with the right-hand side. The four blue boxes to the right are the four components of the vision and sponsorship theme that should be implemented at the beginning of the change.

And the remaining four themes: Assessment, Strategizing, Tactics, and Planning and Appraising are implemented in the Readiness phase for the four work streams and ending up with the change management strategy, tactics, and plan.

On the left-hand side, we execute the change management plan and start managing the Transition phase. During this phase, we deliver the project's outputs that will help enable our change outcomes.

Next, we move to the Sustaining and Realizing Benefits phase in which we ensure that the change is sustained and that the outcomes are achieved and the benefits are realized.

As change comes with uncertainty, you should keep getting feedback on a regular basis to update your change management plan accordingly. It is an iterative process that should be happening all the time.

In the next five chapters, I will provide various tools, templates, and examples that will aid in explaining the model.

7.7 INSIGHTS FROM THE PRACTICE

Below are some important comments that readers should be aware of before delving further into our model.

* Regardless of which change management model is chosen, in many situations the success of the change may be solely dependent on the leadership style and the charisma, persuasion techniques, and talents of the leaders.

* Change can be implemented in three different ways:

  o The first way is by imposing the change through a leader who uses the power of their own personality, their relationships, and their authority to implement the change and require, and even force, people to abide by it.

  o The second way is by managing the change through leaders and strong key managers within the organization. Most of the time, this type of change is planned and managed in closed rooms, utilizing tactics such as one-way communication, and changing the rules and processes of the company.

  o The third way depends primarily on mobilizing and engaging the whole change community. Theoretically, the first two ways will have a high probability of failure; however, they may work satisfactorily in some cultures and/or circumstances.

* Change management is a combination of art and science. It should be remembered that although the art component is an important factor in the equation, it is not widely addressed in this model.

* There is no single recipe for effective change management. Change practices need to be tailored to reflect the context, culture, complexity of the change, investment, and strategic planning of the organization.

* A separate discipline can be created inside the organization to manage the change. This can be affected by establishing a change management office. Change management can also be coordinated and/or integrated with other organizational functions, such as the project management office, the strategic planning unit, or the HR unit.

7.8 DEVELOPING CHANGE MANAGEMENT COMPETENCE

After years of practicing, applying, training, and dealing with different types of learners in the world of change management, I have recognized some of the reasons why people have experienced success in change management and why others have been unable to apply its principles.

So, let us begin with two central tips on how to achieve the maximum benefit from the next five chapters of this book.

Tip #1: Mastering four ways of thinking

As we venture further on our change management journey together, once you (1.) understand well the point that is being discussed, you are encouraged to (2.) critique the information that I presented. Then, (3.) reflect on your real cases with the goal of, (4.) influencing your workplace environment with what you have learned in order to make a positive contribution within your organization.

Figure 7-8 shows the four modes of developing a competence: understand, critique, reflect, and influence.

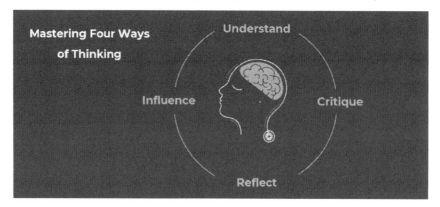

Figure 7-8. Understand, Critique, Reflect, and Influence

Tip #2: Achieving the three elements of change management competence (Attitude, Skills, and Knowledge)

The first element is positive attitude. This book, along with its case studies, enables the reader to appreciate the importance of using change management. Once you have realized this importance and achieved the goal of adopting a willingness to learn and build your competence, it will be easier to grasp the second element: skill.

Throughout the book, there will be skill practice assignments engineered to help you enhance your skill. Additionally, the book is designed to consider reflection and skill practices as a part of achieving successful outcomes.

Recalling the skiing story in Chapter 1, you will never know how to ski – or ride a bicycle – by merely possessing the right knowledge and attitude; to learn how to ski and ride a bicycle, you must practice. You must also expect to fall down while learning and to accept this as part of the process. Falling down is a significant part of the overall learning process.

This book is full of knowledge about change management. Through reading the book's content and its case studies, you will reach the last element: knowledge.

7.9   CHAPTER IN A BOX

- The model consists of the following five themes: (1) Vision and Sponsorship, (2) Assessment, (3) Strategizing, (4) Tactics, and (5) Planning and Appraising.

- The model has the following four work streams: (1) Stakeholder management, (2) Culture management, (3) Organizational alignment, and (4) Communication management.

- The change model's life cycle has the following three phases: (1) Readiness (R), (2) Transition (T), (3) Sustaining and Realizing Benefits (S).

Figure 7-9 shows the three phases of the model.

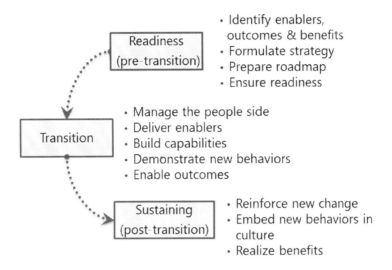

Figure 7-9. The Model's Three Phases

- The tips for maximizing the benefit you get from the book:

   ○ Understanding, critiquing, reflecting, and influencing.

   ○ Achieving the three elements of change management competence: attitude, skills, and knowledge.

CHAPTER 8
VISION AND SPONSORSHIP THEME

Chapter 8 - Vision and Sponsorship Theme

8.1   OVERVIEW

The process of applying the change management must begin by developing a vision and establishing a powerful leadership team through well-defined governance. If you have already read the News Media case study in Chapter 3, you may have recognized how critical the vision and the leadership role are to change.

Developing the change vision and sponsorship are two of the most crucial steps in change management. And implementation of the change initiative should not start until the change is clear and well-communicated vision to all stakeholders.

Figure 8-1, which I call The Big Picture, presents the link and relationship between the essential change management elements that we will be addressing in this and the next four chapters. Hopefully, by going through this big picture, our story will be a bit clear before we start delving into the details of the model.

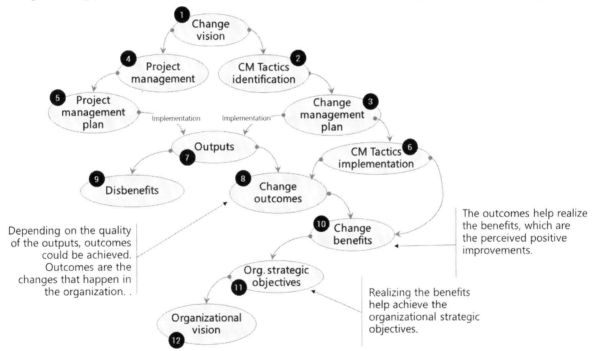

Figure 8-1. The Big Picture. Adapted from MSP, 2012

Now, let us go through the big picture from top to down to see what happens during the implementation of a change initiative.

First, we start by developing the (1) Change vision, which we will do in this chapter, and while developing the vision, we identify the (7) Change outputs, the (8) Change outcomes, and the (10) the Change benefits. We should also identify the link between the (10) Change benefits and the (11) Organizational strategic objectives that are formulated to achieve the (12) Organizational vision.

Once the (1) Change vision is developed, we will need to have the (2) CM Tactics identification, which requires conducting an assessment for the current state (Chapter 9), developing the change management strategizing (Chapter 10), and identification the tactics (Chapter 11) to end up having the (3) Change management plan, which we will do in Chapter 12.

As we know, any change initiative includes at least one project, so we will need to have the (4) Project management process to identify the scope and define the work breakdown structure to develop the (5) Project management plan. It is important to align and/or integrate the (3) Change management plan with the (5) Project management plan.

Based on the quality of the outputs that are mainly the results of implementing the (5) Project management plan as well as the quality of the (6) CM Tactics implementation, we get the (8) Change Outcomes. Outcomes are the changes that take place in the organization. Hence, with the (7) Outputs and the (8) Change outcomes, we realize the (10) Change Benefits. Remember that change is all about realizing benefits.

On the other hand, the (7) Outputs may cause some (9) Disbenefits to the stakeholders, which will thus need resistance management.

And as I indicted earlier, the (10) Change benefits help achieve our (11) Organizational strategic objectives, and ultimately, realize the (12) Organizational vision.

Note that the (12) Organizational vision is not the (1) Change vision; the (12) Organizational vision answers the question: "What does our business want to achieve or become in the long term period?" By the end of this chapter, you will have built a good understanding of the elements of the change vision.

Having the full picture clear, next, we will start our journey with ElKattan's Model for Change Management in which we will see how to develop the change vision and form sponsorship governance.

So, what is "sponsorship governance"?

By sponsorship governance, I mean to have a framework that guides establishing the change governance structure, selecting the sponsors along with their roles and responsibilities, defining shared norms, shared values, shared strategy, shared story, and deciding on the structure of meetings among the sponsorship committee.

8.2   OBJECTIVE

The objective of this theme is to understand the problem along with the risk of not changing, identify how the world will be different after the change has been implemented, and form the right change sponsorship governance. Figure 8-2 shows the four components that need to be completed to develop the change vision and sponsorship.

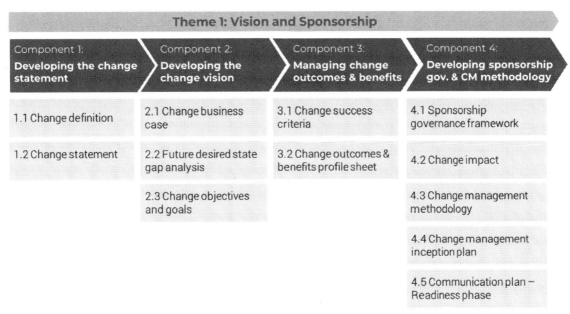

Figure 8-2. Components and Deliverables of the Vision and Sponsorship Theme

The first component is: Developing the change statement. The change statement is considered the DNA of the change initiative, as we will see later; it gets everyone aligned in a very simple way.

The second component is: Developing the change vision. By the end of this component, we should have a clear description of the future desired state.

The third component is: Managing change outcome and benefits, and its main objective is to know how to track and measure the change outcomes and the benefits.

The last component is: Developing sponsorship governance and change management methodology. In this component, we form the sponsorship committee and its governance framework along with the change management methodology that will be applied. As shown in Figure 8-2, each component has its own change management deliverables.

I will include here the summary of the components and deliverables that are shown in Figure 8-2 so that you have the choice of focusing, skimming, or skipping whatever you want based on what is of most relevance to your case.

COMPONENT 1: DEVELOPING CHANGE STATEMENT

The objective of the change statement component is to define what to change, why to change, theory of change, what to achieve, when, and how.

Deliverable 1.1: Change Definition

The objective of the change definition is to provide a quick understanding of the change from the perspective of the key individuals and to raise their readiness regarding the change implementation.

Deliverable 1.2: Change Statement

The objective of the change statement is to get everyone aligned by outlining a simple description of the change in a general way.

COMPONENT 2: DEVELOPING CHANGE VISION

The objective of this component is to gain an understanding of the change journey, and to have a clear comparison between the current state and the future state upon successful implementation of the change.

Deliverable 2.1: Change Business Case

The objective of this deliverable is to determine the reason for the change and the risks of not changing as well as the outcomes and benefits of the change.

Deliverable 2.2: Future Desired State Gap Analysis

The objective of this deliverable is to have a comparison between the current and future state as well as the challenges that may hinder moving to the future desired state.

Deliverable 2.3: Change Objectives and Goals

The objective of this deliverable is to identify the objectives and goals of the change initiative, which are classified into the change outputs, outcomes, and benefits.

COMPONENT 3: MANAGING CHANGE OUTCOMES AND BENEFITS

The objective of this component is to determine the basis of the outcomes and benefits with regard to measurement and tracking.

Deliverable 3.1: Change Success Criteria

The objective of having the change success criteria is to provide tangible and measurable objectives and goals that indicate the progress toward the adoption of the future desired state.

Deliverable 3.2: Change Outcome/Benefit Profile Sheet

The objective of this deliverable is to have a comprehensive profile sheet for the identified outcomes and benefits. Before developing the profile sheet, an alignment with the performance management system is required.

COMPONENT 4: DEVELOPING SPONSORSHIP GOVERNANCE AND CM METHODOLOGY

The objective of this component is to develop the sponsorship governance as well as the change management methodology and communication plan of the readiness phase.

Deliverable 4.1: Sponsorship Governance Framework

The objective of this deliverable is to identify the change sponsors and teams and to establish the roles, governance structure responsibilities, accountability, shared norms, and shared values among the change committees.

Deliverable 4.2: Change Impact

The objective of this deliverable is to understand the impact of the change on the organization.

Deliverable 4.3: Change Management Methodology

The objective of this deliverable is to decide on the structured approach that will be applied.

Deliverable 4.4: Change Management Inception Plan

The objective of this deliverable is to have a plan for the deliverables and the data collection methods defined in the change management methodology to end up having the change management plan.

Deliverable 4.5: Communication Plan – Readiness Phase

The objective of this deliverable is to develop the first communication plan to start communicating the vision and establish sufficient readiness for the change.

Next, I will introduce our third case study: Polytechnique University. It is a fictional case study that will be used to provide samples of the deliverables of some components.

8.3   POLYTECHNIQUE UNIVERSITY CASE STUDY

8.3.1   Overview

"... many of the students literally sleep in the classes. They are so disengaged from the instructors, especially those who sit in the back. On the other hand, the instructors are only concerned to get through what they want to say in front of a bunch of such boring power point slides."

These are sentiments expressed by one of the students at Polytechnique University (PU). Another student sarcastically wrote on the university Facebook page: "*... the power points slides are well recited!*" It was meant as if the session goes on as a sort of religious recitation.

Polytechnique University, located in the Middle East, is small university providing engineering and computer science degrees. The two faculties have 30 programs that include more than 2,000 students. The programs offer both bachelor's and master's degrees in different fields.

Both engineering and computer science have been identified as among the most critical levels for improving the value of human resources in the country, and helping youth, both male and female, play a productive and meaningful role in the country's development.

8.3.2   The Transformational Program

The university's management decided to launch a student-centered transformational program as an initiative to achieve their strategic goals of enhancing the education system and creating a campus-wide learning culture. The goals of the new change were to enhance the learning process and improve the graduate skills to meet international standards. The program also aimed to establish partnerships with international entities to improve course content, methods of teaching and capabilities of the instructors and program directors.

One executive commented:

"... even though the idea of the program is great and will positively benefit almost all of our community to a

great extent, upon announcing the new program, we had a great resistance from many of our stakeholders. I think the reason is that people do not want to change what they used to do. I believe if we run the program, it will have a total failure and will not be able to deliver the anticipated outcomes."

It was obvious that many of the faculty members were not engaged; did not understand the need and impact of the change, or their role in the program's success. This particular executive's comment made it clear that the critical issues subject to triggering failure of the change were primarily related to the people-side of change – engagement and mindset – which is one of the basic objectives of change management.

8.3.3   The Change Impact

This transformational program was projected to impact the 30 academic programs within the two faculties, extending for at least three years; affecting not only the instructors and students, but also impacting employees at all levels. Furthermore, the program was expected to impact external stakeholders partnering with the university, such as part-time instructors, international universities, and executive training providers.

The stakes were high for the anticipated impact of the program, thus, management believed that all stakeholders should be positively engaged at all levels, understanding the need for and impact of the program, as well as their role in its implementation.

8.3.4   Why Change Management?

Another program director said:

"... as we have bad experiences in previous initiatives, before we start the implementation, we just decided to add the change management element to the program in order to avoid all the mistakes that may cause the program to fail."

The program's management requested that a change management consultant join the program's leadership. They believed that change management would help align all stakeholders and create the appropriate awareness, in turn, further aiding in achieving the program's goals and benefits.

Concerning the addition of a change management component to the program, one program director commented:

"... we want to have the change management to assure having a focused capability building and knowledge transfer by involving stakeholders throughout, and provide them with training and coaching. We need to do the proper communication and resistance management, but we do not know how, and from which point we should start?"

8.4   COMPONENT 1: DEVELOPING CHANGE STATEMENT

8.4.1   Overview

In this component, we begin to explore how to develop the change vision. As a first step, we will introduce the change definition as a brief description of the change before we set out to write the main deliverable of the change statement component, or the change DNA. I will also introduce the concepts of theory of change and nested outcomes while explaining the change statement.

8.4.2 Objective

The objective of the change statement component is to define what to change, why to change, theory of change. In addition to what to achieve, when, and how.

Figure 8-3 shows the two deliverables of this component.

Figure 8-3. Deliverables of Developing the Change Statement Component

From now through the end of the chapter, I will be explaining all the deliverables of the four components. Now, let us start with the first deliverable: The change definition.

8.4.3 Deliverable 1.1: Change Definition

The objective of the change definition is to provide a quick understanding of the change from the perspective of the key individuals and to raise their readiness regarding the change implementation. Change definition presents a brief description of the change which is necessary to have before writing the change statement.

There should be a unified change definition, so, we can either receive feedback from all the individuals and then get them combined together or conduct a meeting to come up with a unified change definition. And in developing this definition, each key individual should answer each one of the questions below:

1. What specific problem will the change initiative solve?
2. What are we changing? And how?
3. Who are the impacted stakeholders?
4. Can people create a power that can cause resistance to the change?
5. What should be the short and long-term goals?
6. Why are you interested in accepting a leadership role for this project?

The above questions are shown in more detail in Table 8-1.

Table 8-1. *Change Definition*

The change problem	What is the main specific problem that needs to be solved by the change? How do the employees experience this problem on a day-to-day basis?
The solution	What are we changing? What specific solution do you believe is required to solve the problem? Are there different alternatives for the suggested change? What are the technical solutions?
Impacted stakeholders	Who are the people who will be affected and need to change the way they work? How many? How powerful are they? Where do they work? Which units? What disbenefits they may experience? Are they within a specific managerial level, or at all levels? What other characteristics are important to know about the people who will be impacted?
The power	In what ways can you see people using resources or coming together to create a power that can cause resistance to the change?
Quick wins and goals	What specific quick wins can the organization focus on achieving? What long-term goals can be achieved by implementing the change?
Personal story	Why are you interested in accepting a leadership role for this project?

After combining all the answers to these questions, as a change leader, you will be ready to start crafting the change statement that I will discuss next.

At this point, I suggest that you hold back and think of any change initiative you have in mind, give it some reflection, and try to write down its change definition.

8.4.4   Deliverable 1.2: Change Statement

8.4.4.1   Overview

The change statement is a good starting point for the change management. In fact, it could be considered the DNA of our change initiative. While the structure of the statement is simple, developing it is not an easy task. It requires time and experience.

An organization's change statement is often confused with the vision statement. This can be particularly confusing, especially when dealing with a transformational change; however, the two types of statements are fundamentally different. The organizational vision is typically derived from the mission, which drives the organization's business strategy. The organizational vision statement typically has an inspiring, long-term goal that is achievable within a specific time frame. On the other hand, the change statement has a different structure, as set out below:

1. We are changing *(what to change?)*

2. To pursue *(why change – motivating long-term goal)*

3. By *(how – theory of change)*

4. Our next milestone to achieve *(immediate outcome)*

5. By the end of *(when)*

6. We will execute the following *(change management tactics)*

The structure of the change statement was adapted from the organizing statement given in the Leading Change course taught by Marshall Ganz[1]. A comparison between the change statement and the organizational vision statement is provided in Table 8-2.

Table 8-2. *Comparison Between Organizational Vision Statement and Change Statement*

Organizational vision statement	Defines the long-term goal of the organization that should be achieved in a certain time horizon. It answers the question: *Where do we want to go?* and is used to set out a 'picture' of the organization in the future. A vision statement provides inspiration and the basis for the strategic planning (Kaplan & Norton, 2004).
Example	To be (long term goal) the regional leader in in providing online engineering services for (niche market) the medium engineering companies in Egypt in (time horizon) five years.
Change statement	The change statement includes: what to change, why to change, theory of change, what to achieve, when, and how.
Example	Example of the Polytechnique case study change statement could be: We are changing (what to change) the content and the way the instructors teach to make the learning process more interactive to pursue (why change – motivating long-term goal) a wonderful and international learning experience and culture. By (how - theory of change) changing the mindset of the staff to accept a student-centered approach rather than the traditional content-centered approach. Our next milestone to achieve (immediate outcome) is to establish a dedicated committee as a leadership team and to announce adapting a student-centered learning methodology by the end of (when) May 15.

8.4.4.2 Objective

The objective of the change statement is to get everyone aligned by outlining a simple description of the change in a general way. It is advisable to limit the change statement to a maximum of 100 words.

---

[1] Marshall Ganz (born 14 March 1943), is the Senior Lecturer in Leadership, Organizing, and Civil Society at the Kennedy School of Government at Harvard University. He is credited with devising the successful grassroots organization model and training for Barack Obama's successful 2008 presidential campaign. Ganz is also the author of the Harvard Business Press publication, *Leading Change - Leadership, Organization, and Social Movements.*

8.4.4.3   Change statement structure

Since the change statement is our real starting point, its elements do not have to be extremely well defined at the beginning; just write it as best you can, as you will keep revisiting it until it has been perfected.

Even though there are many other elements that are not mentioned in the change statement, it is the core of the change initiative (or its DNA) that makes the program clear to everyone in a very simple way.

Unlike the organizational vision statement, the change statement gets updated throughout the process. When the change outcome in the statement is achieved, we update it to reflect another outcome with its own date. The change statement has six elements that can be split into three parts. Below is a description of the elements of the change statement:

Part I:

1. We are changing *(what to change)*

This is what we aim to change in the organization to achieve a specific goal. This element could be written for the change statement of the change initiative in the Polytechnique case study as follows: "*We are changing (what to change) the content and the way the instructors teach to make the learning process more interactive.*"

2. To pursue *(why change – motivating long-term goal)*

This is a big and broad motivating long-term goal that should reflect the end result of our change. It should be selected in a way that emotionally links most of the stakeholders to the change. It can be an ultimate major change benefit or an organizational strategic objective.

This element could be written for the change statement of the change initiative in the Polytechnique case study as follows: "to pursue (why change – motivating long-term goal) a wonderful and international learning experience and culture."

Part II:

3. By *(how - theory of change)*

The objective of the theory of change is to agree on the most important assumption that is most likely to make the change successful.

The theory of change is what we believe -if done- will make the change happen. For example, we may have an assumption that if we have 100% involvement of all employees, the resistance will disappear and the change will be successful. This assumption is referred to as the "theory of change."

In order to develop the assumption of the theory of change, we need to understand the context and the change dynamics. Therefore, Once the change problem and challenges are clearly defined, we should answer following questions: (1) Why has the change problem not been resolved?, (2) Who has the power and/or the resources but may not be supporting the change?, (3) Who is unsatisfied with the current state?, and (4) Why do we anticipate harmful resistance?

Once the above questions have been answered, we start thinking about the assumption that will make the change successful. For example, the assumption may be that if we have 100% involvement and commitment from all employees, the resistance will disappear and the change will be successful; we will refer to this assumption as the "theory of change." We will start addressing the theory of change concept in this chapter while developing the change statement.

Some people may think the theory of change is about making people fully aware of the problem. Others may think it is about having a different mindset, others may think it is all about putting some pressure on certain people or by exchanging power.

The theory of change could be done intuitively or as a conclusion of our assessment and analysis. Since, we have not yet started our assessment, we can just try to have the assumption based on our experience and understanding of the context.

There may be more than one assumption (theory of change). However, only one theory of change is required in the change statement to highlight the main hypothesis.

The theory of change could be related to: increasing awareness, building capacity, assuring competence, involving and engaging the stakeholders, using different sources of power, pressuring some stakeholders, changing the culture, etc. As it is an assumption, it needs to be constantly validated. If it does not work as expected, it must be changed and/or modified. To come up with our theory of change, we follow the structure shown in Table 8-3.

Table 8-3. *Theory of Change Structure – Polytechnique University Case Study*

If we do/use:	Change the mindset of the staff.
Then the result will be:	The staff will accept having a student-centered approach rather than the traditional content-centered approach.
Because:	They will highly appreciate both the personal and students benefits that they will gain upon reshaping the culture.

4. Our next milestone to achieve *(immediate outcome)*

As we know, the outcomes are the change results achieved based on the quality of the outputs. Outcomes reflect that a change is really happening on the ground. The outcomes should be concrete, specific, visible, and measurable.

The change statement could have the ultimate change outcome. However, in the case of having nested outcomes, the change statement could have an immediate outcome rather than the ultimate one. Next, we will discuss in more detail the concept of nested outcomes.

This element could be written for the change statement of the change initiative in the Polytechnique case study as follows: "Our next milestone to achieve (immediate outcome) is to establish a dedicated committee as a leadership team and to announce adapting a student-centered learning methodology."

Nested outcomes

Nested outcome means that the ultimate change outcome could be achieved by achieving several sub-outcomes (enabling outcomes) that could happen in a shorter period of time. In this case, the change statement would include the immediate outcome. Once this sub-outcome is achieved, the change statement needs to be updated with the next sub-outcome planned to be achieved.

A workshop could be conducted to brainstorm as many possible outcomes that could help achieve the ultimate outcome.

Why do we have the immediate outcome in the change statement?

Because these immediate outcomes could be considered the quick wins of the change. Achieving quick wins is essential to increase engagement and buy-in. Quick win proves the concept and get more people on board. In addition, it helps the team focuses on a short-term goal to achieve while having the end result in mind.

The concept of the nested outcomes can be represented in a pyramid shape. In Figure 8-4, you can see the ultimate change outcome at the top of the pyramid, along with its sub-outcomes, which is called by Marshall Ganz at Harvard Kennedy School as nested outcomes.

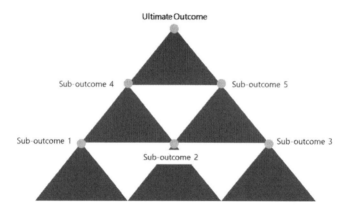

Figure 8-4. Outcomes Pyramid Chart. Adapted from by Marshall Ganz Leading Change Course

Does the change statement have to have a sub-outcome?

No. The change statement could have the ultimate change outcome. However, for a transformational change, it is better to have an immediate outcome rather than the ultimate one.

Later in this chapter, we will discuss in more detail how to identify the outcomes of a change initiative. As shown in Figure 8-5, the immediate outcome in the change statement could be identified by analyzing the required effort and resources vs. impact. The analysis will identify four types of outcomes:

1. Quick wins outcomes

2. Critical outcomes

3. On-going outcomes

4. Least important outcomes

The four types of outcomes help achieve the ultimate change outcome. However, theoretically the quick wins outcomes are recommended to be selected in the beginning.

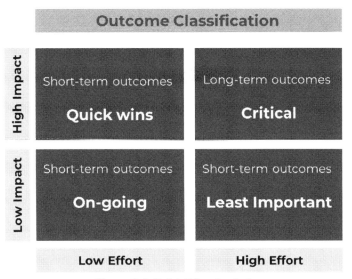

Figure 8-5. Quick Wins Analysis

5. By the end of *(when)*

This is the date by which the immediate change management goal that is written in the statement will be achieved.

Part III:

6. We will execute the following *(change management tactics)*

These are mainly tactics that will help achieve the immediate outcome. The tactics should be based on the theory of change and able to increase the change readiness and engagement.

Make sure that tactics are not written as activities from the project management perspective. Check Example 8.1 for sample change management tactics that can be used in a change statement.

Example 8.1 - Change Statement

This is an example of a change statement that was written for the Polytechnique change initiative.

We are changing (what to change) the content and the way the instructors teach to make the learning process more interactive to pursue (why change – motivating long-term goal) a wonderful and international learning experience and culture. By (how - theory of change) changing the mindset of the staff to accept a student-centered approach rather than the traditional content-centered approach. Our next milestone to achieve (immediate outcome) is to establish a dedicated committee as a leadership team and to announce adapting a student-centered learning methodology by the end of (when) May 15.

We will do the following (tactics):

- Provide extensive orientation and training about modern teaching approaches with emphasis on the student-centered approach.

- Launch a digital marketing campaign regarding the modern teaching approaches.

- Change the criteria of the course evaluation according to the objective of the change..

Skill Practice 8.1 - Write your Change Statement

Think of a change you would like to implement in your organization and write its change statement.

Here are some questions to guide you: What is the problem that triggered the change? What makes your idea a change and not a project? How will the world be different if you solve the problem? What will be required to implement the change? What kind of activities do you need to do to ensure a successful change? What are the strategic change management goals? Can you think of a quick win? What tactics will you use to achieve the change management goals?"

| Theme 1: Vision & Sponsorship | Component 1: Developing the change statement | 1.2 Change Statement |

We are changing (what to change) .... to pursue (why change - motivating

long-term goal)...

by (how - theory of change) ....

.... Our next milestone to achieve (immediate

outcome) .... by the end of (when) ....

We will execute the following (change management tactics):

....

....

8.5 COMPONENT 2: DEVELOPING THE CHANGE VISION

8.5.1 Overview

Every change must start with a compelling story. It does not have to be complete from the beginning, but it should be rational enough to convince people to begin delving into it.

The vision of the change primarily addresses the *why*, which is crucial to establishing sufficient readiness for the change. If a change does not have a well-defined vision, there will be no reference for making the decisions, and effort may go in different or even opposing directions. It may also be difficult to determine where the change should end. Developing a clear change vision is critically important. Without a solid vision, discrepancies may cause unnecessary frustration, resulting in disengagement.

The change vision is a way to identify the gaps between current and future expectations. However, change is full of uncertainties and risks that cannot be fully anticipated. The future – no matter what you do – is endlessly unpredictable.

Important Note

There is a misconception that any change initiative should begin with modifications to the organization's structure. Firstly, this will depend on the required alignment with change and secondly, aligning with the transformational elements is more essential.

Each deliverable of this component puts different pieces to the full picture. Table 8-4 has the deliverables that are required to have a unified vision. We already discussed the change definition and the change statement.

Table 8-4. *Deliverables that make up the full vision*

Component	Deliverable
1. Developing the change statement	Change definition
	The change statement
2. Developing the change vision	Change Business case
	Future desired state gap analysis
	Change objectives and goals
3. Managing the change outcomes and benefits	Change success criteria
	Change outcome/benefit profile sheet

8.5.2   Objective

The objective of this component is to gain an understanding of the change journey, and to have a clear comparison between the current state and the future state upon successful implementation of the change.

As shown in Figure 8-6, this components has three deliverables: the change business case, future desired state gap analysis, and change objectives and goals. Each deliverable puts different pieces into the full picture

Figure 8-6. Deliverables of Developing the Change Vision Component

Important Note

Organizational change is typically a response to external environmental pressure rather than internal issues. Therefore, responding to external drivers leads a longer life span.

8.5.3   Deliverable 2.1: Change Business Case

The objective of this deliverable is to determine the root cause of the problems and the risks of not changing as well as the outcomes and benefits of the change.

The business case include the following items: (1) Problem of the change, (2) What are we changing?, (3) Impacted stakeholders, (4) Root causes of the problems, (5) Risks of not changing, (6) Change outcomes, and (7) Change benefits. Below, we will discuss how to develop these items of the business case.

8.5.3.1   Change Problem

The first item is the change problem. It is important to start with specifying the problems that the change is supposed to solve. Remember that we already started thinking about our problem while developing the change definition. Here you list the top three problems that the change initiative will solve. Of course you can have more or less but I recommend starting with three.

To clearly identify the problem of the change, at least the following question are to be answered: What are the specific problems the change initiative is supposed to solve? Why hasn't the problem been solved so far? How do the stakeholders experience these problems in the long term as well as in the day-to-day operations?

8.5.3.2   What to change?

The second item is what we are all interested in; it is our solution or what are we changing? Notice that this element is linked to Part 1 of the Change Statement. However, here you can write more details.

To know what we are changing, at least the following question are to be answered: What specific change do you believe is required to solve the problem? Which aspects could be ultimately affected by the change (business model, culture, systems, IT, or people)? What are the different alternatives for the technical solutions? Is the change part of other changes happening in the organization??

8.5.3.3   Impacted stakeholders

The third item has a list of the stakeholders who will be impacted by the change initiative. The list should not go too broad or too narrow. Also, you can identify the most impacted stakeholder group.

To identify the impacted stakeholders, at least the following question are to be answered: Who are the stakeholders who will be impacted by the change? How many? Are they within a specific managerial level, or all levels? What characteristics are important to know about them?

8.5.3.4   Root causes

Our fourth element in the change business case is the root cause or the reason why the problem exists. I will use a tool to help identify the root causes as well as the risks of not changing.

To identify the root cause, you first define the problem, which is usually a symptom, so you need to ask what are the reasons behind this problem? By answering this question, you may find the root cause of the problem, and then you repeat the same question again until you find root cause of the deeper problems.

8.5.3.5   Risk of not changing

Next, we have the risk of not changing, which is important to explain why the change is required. To identify the risks of not changing, you ask what are the consequences that might happen if we do not solve the problem in the short term period, and then you repeat again until you find consequences in the long-term period.

Figure 8-7 shows the root causes and risks of not changing for the Polytechnique University case study using the problem map analysis tool.

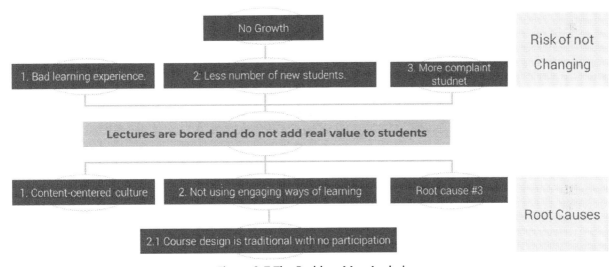

Figure 8-7. The Problem Map Analysis

Example 8.2 - Change Business Case

Figure 8-8 shows an example of the change business case for the Polytechnique University case study.

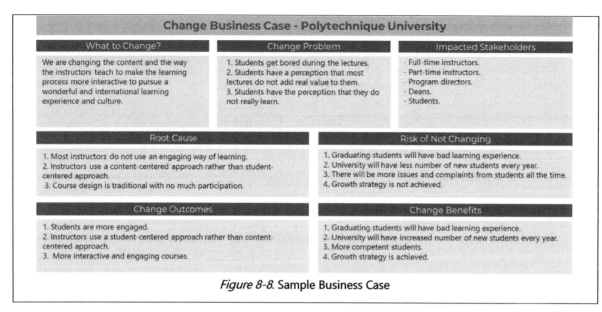

Figure 8-8. Sample Business Case

8.5.3.6   Change outcomes

The outcomes are the results in operations archived by a change after a transition period based on the quality of the projects' outputs

To get the outcomes, we link them with the root causes. This means the outcomes should be the result of managing the root causes. For example, if one of root causes in the Polytechnique case study is having a content-based culture, them the associated outcome is having a student-centered outcome.

8.5.3.7   Change benefits

The benefits are the gains from a change through outputs and resulted outcomes that contribute toward achieving the strategic objective.

The benefits should be the opposite of the risks of not changing. For example, if one of root causes in our case study is: Less number of new students, then the associated benefit will be: Increased number of new students. Figure 8-9 shows all the elements of the change business case along with the relationship between the root cause and change outcome as well as risk of not changing and change benefit.

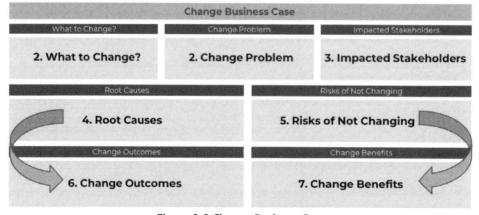

Figure 8-9. Change Business Case

Figure 8-10 shows the relationship between the root cause and change outcome as well as risk of not changing and change benefit for the Polytechnique University case study.

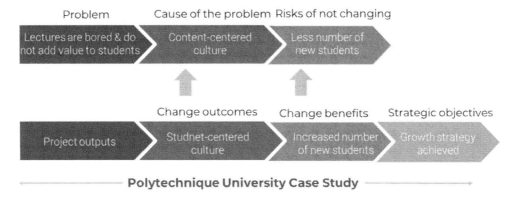

Figure 8-10. Relationship Between the Root Cause, Outcome, Risk of Not Changing and Benefit

---

Skill Practice 8.2 - Developing the Business Case

Develop the business case of the change that you identified in Skill Practice 8.1.

8.5.4 Deliverable 2.2: Future Desired State Gap Analysis

The objective of this deliverable is to have a comparison between the current and future state as well as the challenges that may hinder moving to the future desired state.

In this deliverable, and to understand the change journey, we will have a clear comparison between the current state and the future state and then do a gap analysis to identify the challenges that may hinder moving the organization to the future desired state.

As both the current state and the future desired state must be related only to the change initiative. We can represent the current state by the root causes identified in the change business case, while the future desired state could be represented by the associated change outcomes. You can also have the risks of not changing versus the benefits.

As shown in Figure 8-11, we get from the business case both the current state and future desired state. We put them in a table to do a gap analysis to identify the challenges that may hinder us going forward.

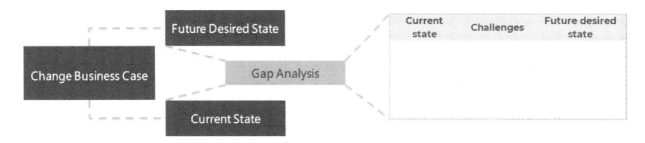

Figure 8-11. Future Desired State Gap Analysis

The root cause/outcome are to be categorized according to three perspectives: (1) Stakeholders management, (2) Culture management, and (3) Organizational alignment (business model, structure, IT, systems, capacity, etc.). A workshop can be conducted to identify the challenges related to every root cause that may hinder achieving the outcome.

Table 8-5 has a sample of the current state and future desired state for the Polytechnique University case study.

Table 8-5. *Future Desired State Gap Analysis Template*

Current state (Root causes)	Perspective	Future desired state (Outcome/Benefit)	Challenges	Recommendations
Content-centered culture	Culture management	Student-centered culture		
Not using engaging ways of learning	Stakeholder management	Students are more engaged.		
Course design is traditional	Organizational alignment	Interactive and engaging course design		

8.5.5 Deliverable 2.3: Change Objectives and Goals

8.5.5.1 Objective

The objective of this deliverable is to identify the objectives and goals of the change initiative, which are classified into the change outputs, outcomes, and benefits.

Having finalized the previous two documents: the change business case as well as the future desired state, we can go one step further by concluding the objectives and goals of the change initiative.

To identify the objectives and goals, I will use a very interesting tool called the change logic map. As shown in Figure 8-12, this map has six columns and can be read from left to right or from right to left.

If you want to read it from the strategic thinking perspective: you go from left to right as follows:

- The strategic drivers drive selecting the organizational strategic objective. Many tools are used in strategic management to identify these drivers.

- The strategic objectives are achieved by realizing the benefits. By the way, it is important to have this link because the lack of a clear link between the change benefits and the strategic objectives is one of the reasons for not getting people aligned and motivated with the change.

- The benefits are realized through the change outcomes.

- The outcomes are achieved based on the quality of the outputs.

- And finally, we need some sort of inputs and enablers to support delivering the outputs. The inputs and enablers could be required number of staff budget, or certain training programs.

If you want to read it from the implementation perspective: you go from right to left.

Figure 8-12 shows the Change Logic Map for a hypothetical innovation change initiative that has an objective of having a higher innovative culture inside the organization.

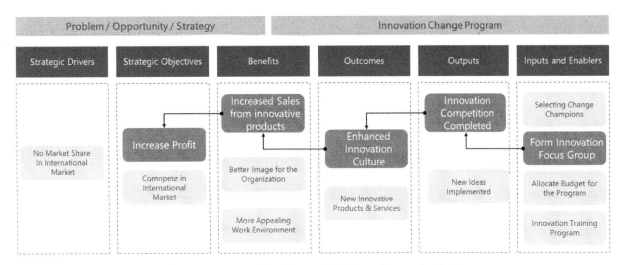

Figure 8-12. Innovation Change initiative - Change Logic Map

The arrows in Figure 8-12 Identify the cause-and-effect relationship between certain five items in the change logic map. The cause-and-effect relationship is essential in drawing the full picture.

Let me explain what I mean by cause-and-effect relationship, using the example in Figure 8-12.

Starting from first item on the right side, the map states that we need to form an Innovation Focus Group as an input to plan for an innovation competition.

The competition as an output will help achieve having a higher innovative culture. Having a higher innovative culture as an outcome will help having new sales from new innovative products. Finally the new innovative products will help achieve the strategic objective: increase profit.

The change logic map is a great tool to align between the strategic objectives, the change benefits, outcomes, outputs, and enablers. It is a snapshot of the initial thinking of the program.

Identifying the right benefits is very important because they are the bridge between the change and the strategic objectives.

Important Note

The most important aspect of any change initiative is the identification of its end benefits, which help achieve the strategic objectives. However, getting there is not easy!

8.6   COMPONENT 3: MANAGING THE CHANGE OUTCOMES AND BENEFITS

8.6.1   Overview

Change management is all about realizing the benefits. It is very important to understand how the change outcomes and benefits contribute to the achievement of the organization's strategic objectives.

Measuring the outcomes and benefits are some of the most difficult and controversial issues in change management. It is very important to select the right measures to be used for measurement. Two measures for each outcome and benefit are recommended.

The change activities should continue until the outcomes are achieved and the intended benefits are realized.

Important Note

It is worth mentioning that there could be an overlapping and/or duplication of benefits and strategic objectives. Therefore, before identifying the benefits, it is important to understand the strategy very well and exercise caution while defining the relationships between all elements.

8.6.2   Objective

The objective of this component is to determine the basis of the outcomes and benefits with regard to measurement and tracking.

The objective of this component is achieved by developing the deliverables shown in Figure 8-13.

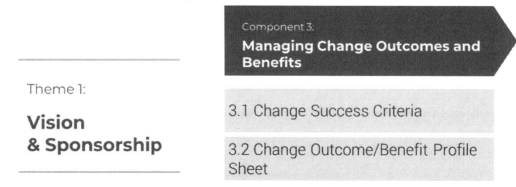

Figure 8-13. Deliverables of Managing the Change Outcomes and Benefits Component

8.6.3   Deliverable 3.1: Change Success Criteria

The objective of having the change success criteria is to provide tangible and measurable objectives and goals that indicate the progress toward the adoption of the future desired state. This will enable us to track the results (outcomes and benefits) rather than only tracking the change process and activities.

Without having measures and targets for the outcomes and benefits, they may remain as only passive statements. Also, not aligning with the organizational performance management system may distract the efforts in random directions.

In order to track the success of the change, outcomes and the benefits must be measured. Without being measured, they are nothing more than the good intentions of the change leaders. Outcomes are related to operations and they are non-financial while the benefits can be either financial or non-financial. Practically speaking, intangible objectives are a bit difficult to be measured. Therefore, measuring could also be done using a qualitative method (such as stories, open ended questions, and interviews) to give a complete picture of how they have been realized.

The objectives can be measured quantitatively, qualitatively, and by time (QQT). In this section, we will have samples of quantified measures. Before quantifying, we need to select the measures that will be quantified.

Important Note

Benefits-led change management is designed to realize the benefits rather than justify the change idea and its selected solution. This is a principle in benefits management that is referred to as "Start with the end in mind."

At least one measure should be selected for each outcome or benefit, and it is preferable to have both lagging measures and leading measures. The leading measure is an intermediate measure that helps achieve the lagging one.

Table 8-6 shows samples quantification for the innovation change initiative presented in the change logic map in Figure 8-12.

Table 8-6. *Change Quantification - Change Innovation Program -*

Element	Description	Measure	Target
Objectives	Increase profit	% Profit margin	15%
	Compete in international market	% Market share in Africa	5%
Change Benefits	Increased sales from new innovative products	$ Total sales	$1M
		% ROI per product	> 30%
	Better image for the organization	% Customer perception	80%
	More appealing work environment	% Employee engagement index regarding innovation	80%
		# Employee net promoter score	15
Change	Enhanced innovative culture	% Innovation culture scan	75%

Element	Description	Measure	Target
Outcomes	New innovative products and services	# New innovative products	5
		% Products that generated value in the market	90%
Change Outputs	Innovation competition program	# Innovation ideas evaluated	>100
	New ideas implemented	# Innovation ideas funded	>10
		# Innovation ideas implemented	>5
Change Inputs and Enablers	Selecting change champions	# Innovation champion in each area	>3
	Form innovation focus groups	# Staff in each focus group	5
	Allocate budget for the program	$ Program budget	$100K
	Innovation training program	$ Training budget	$10K
		% Employees trained	75%

Quantifying the outcomes and the benefits is not an easy task and requires adequate experience. Many factors can impact the selection of an accurate forecast for the targets. People may also tend to overestimate their forecasting because they are excited about the idea or to ensure the project is approved.

As a rule, you should not really trust your forecast if it is not based on historical data. Therefore, it is very important to collect as much historical data as possible.

It is recommended that the outcomes and the benefits be quantified by conducting a workshop for senior managers and related stakeholders involved in the change. For each benefit, agree what measures will be used to measure the benefit. Afterwards, participants should be asked to quantify these measures and explain their rationale. The good thing about this technique is that everyone is engaged by sharing their knowledge and experience while explaining their rationale. The greater the number of knowledgeable and experienced people involved, the better the forecast and the validation will be. Intuition is always a good tool to employ in this activity. Participants can also be asked to think of the most optimistic and pessimistic estimates in order to obtain a more realistic picture.

Before starting the workshop, ensure the participants:

- understand the current performance
- have reviewed past performance
- start with a baseline with which to compare

Upon finalizing the estimate, participants should be asked to give their confidence rating for the prediction. This will provide an idea of how reliable the estimates are. All assumptions made by the participants while doing the forecasting must be clearly documented.

8.6.4 Deliverable 3.2: Change Outcome/Benefit Profile Sheet

The objective of this deliverable is to have a comprehensive profile sheet for the identified outcomes and benefits. Before developing the profile sheet, an alignment with the performance management system is required.

The profile sheet should be developed and finalized before or during the implementation of the project. Before developing the profile sheet, you should have a baseline of the current performance as well as the planned target. It is essential to know approximately when the measurement will begin and its frequency. It is also necessary to determine when and how it will be measured, who is responsible for measuring it. Table 8-7 presents a sample of the Outcome/Benefit Profile Sheet that is written for the benefit: "More appealing work environment" that presented in Table 8-6.

Table 8-7. Outcome/*Benefit Profile Sheet Template*

Change benefit: More appealing innovative work environment	
Description:	Having an appealing innovative work environment is an important aspect. This will increase employees satisfaction and attracts good people.
Owner:	Sponsorship committee
Measurement	
Measure:	% Employee Engagement Index
Description:	The measure is about the engagement level of employees with innovation in their work activities and responsibilities.
Baseline:	25%
Target:	75%
Scale of improvement:	200%
Measurement process	
Time to full realization:	One year
Measurement start date:	January
Measurement frequency:	Every six months
How to measure:	Survey
Measurement responsibility:	HR
Measurement cost:	10 days
Impacted stakeholders	
Stakeholder 1	

Stakeholder 2
Assumptions
Assumption 1
Assumption 2
Risks
Risk 1

Skill Practice 8.3 - Developing the Change Logic Map.

Develop your program's change logic map along with a profile sheet for the change outcomes and benefits.

Example 8.3 - Culture Change Initiative

Reflecting on the Global Trans case study that was introduced in Chapter 1, below is an example of its change logic map.

Global Trans had a strategic objective as: Continuously improve skills through learning experiences. Therefore, they planned to implement the change initiative: "Culture change toward a more knowledge sharing and learning organization" in order to achieve the objective. Figure 8-14 shows the change logic map of this example.

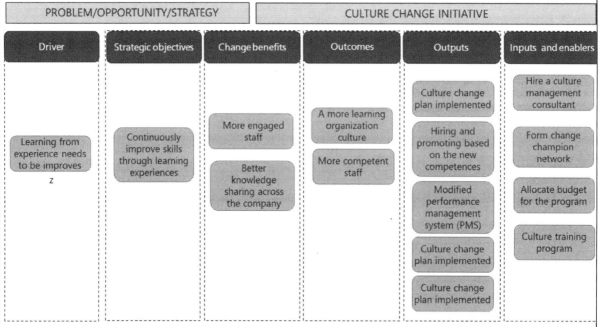

Figure 8-14. Culture Change Initiative - Change Logic Map Example

Table 8-8 shows samples quantification for the outcomes and benefits shown in Figure 8-14.

Example 8.3 - Culture Change Initiative

Table 8-8. *Culture Change Initiative - Sample Quantification*

Element	Description	Measure	Target
Initiative: Culture change toward a more knowledge sharing and learning organization			
Strategic Objective	Continuously improve skills through learning experiences	% Employee benefited from knowledge sharing	70%
		% Meeting required skills	80%
Change Benefits	More engaged staff	% Employee engagement	85%
	Better knowledge sharing across the company	# Knowledge sharing evaluation score	75
Change Outcomes	A more learning organization culture	# Score of learning organization culture	75
	More competent staff	% Competence assessment score	90%
Projects Outputs	Culture change plan implemented	# Ontime plan implemented	3 months
	Hiring and promoting based on the new competences	% Awareness of new process	80%
	Modified performance management system (PMS)	# Ontime change implemented	1 month
		% Employees affected by new PMS	50%
	New list of related competences introduced to staff	% Awareness of new related competences	70%
	Form change sponsorship group representing all areas	# Functions represented in sponsorship committee	90%
Inputs and Enablers	Hire a culture management consultant	# Ontime hiring	1 month
	Form change champion network	# champion per function	2
	Allocate budget for the program	$ Program budget	$50K
	Culture training program	$ Training budget	$10K

8.7 COMPONENT 4: DEVELOPING SPONSORSHIP GOVERNANCE AND CHANGE MANAGEMENT METHODOLOGY

8.7.1 Overview

As Kotter indicated, a transformational change cannot be led by an individual. It needs to have an official group of responsible senior managers at its helm. This group of senior managers can have different names. However, I will refer to this group as the sponsorship committee. The members of this committee (change sponsors) must be committed and accept accountability to support the change. Commitment to make the change a reality should not stop at the doors of the sponsors; they should also delegate their authority to other senior managers whenever possible. If the sponsorship committee is to succeed, they must have a shared story, a shared purpose, shared values, and a shared strategy.

8.7.2 Objective

The objective of this component is to develop the sponsorship governance as well as the change management methodology and communication plan of the readiness phase.

The objective is achieved by developing the deliverables shown in Figure 8-15.

Figure 8-15. Deliverables of Developing Sponsorship Governance and CM Methodology Component

8.7.3 Deliverable 4.1: Sponsorship Governance Framework

8.7.3.1 Objective

The objective of this deliverable is to identify the change sponsors and teams and to establish the roles, governance structure responsibilities, accountability, shared norms, and shared values among the change committees.

The governance framework should be clear, aligned, and well-defined. It should also include escalation processes and the decision-making process.

It is important that the sponsors agree about the change purpose that was discussed earlier in the change statement. They will also be responsible for strategizing to achieve the change goals and pursue the purpose.

8.7.3.2   Change sponsors

A change sponsor can be defined as an individual who is accepting accountability for enabling others rationally, technically, and emotionally to achieve the change goals under conditions of uncertainty.

According to eight different research studies that were conducted by Prosci from 1998 to 2016 on the greatest contributors to the success of transformational projects, sponsorship was the number one contributor. The more a change lacks the right sponsorship, the more conflicts and obstacles it will experience.

As previously indicated, having different sponsors avoids the risks associated with having a single person leading the change. Normally, in organizations with a large power distance culture (refer to Chapter 5 for more details), the change is led by a few senior managers with minimal involvement from the rest of the stakeholders.

It is essential that the sponsors include people who have both a high level of power and will be highly impacted by the change, provided they are competent and powerful enough to lead and remove the obstacles. The sponsors must have the relevant experience, as well as personal and professional credibility.

Important Note

According to many research studies conducted by Prosci, it has been determined that effective sponsorship is the number 1 contributor to change success.

Once the sponsors have been selected, the next step is to get them aligned. It is enormously difficult to achieve a transformational change if the sponsors are not fully aligned.

Sponsors must be qualified according to the following criteria:

* Commitment to participate and be active and visible throughout the change implementation.
* Ability to effectively communicate the change vision.
* Powerful enough to provide support and remove obstacles.
* Capable of evaluating and making strategic decisions.

8.7.3.3   Change governance structure

The objective of change governance structure is to define the change hierarchy that identifies the line of authority and relationships between the different entities participating in the change.

Figure 8-16 presents a sample of a change governance structure. The change management role can be assigned to a change management office, a senior manager, an HR unit, a committee, or a dedicated change team.

In a transformation program, a change management office (CM Office) can be established to be responsible for the change at both the organizational and individual levels.

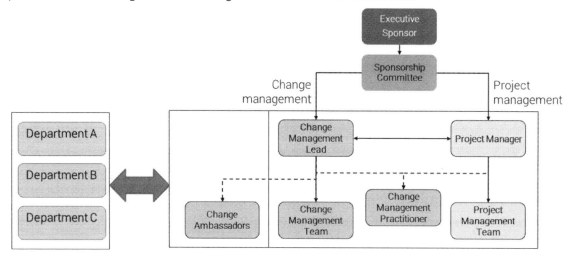

Figure 8-16. Change Governance Structure Sample

8.7.3.4   Roles

Each member of the sponsorship committee should be assigned at least one role. Following are examples of roles that may be considered:

- **Change Initiator/Owner**: A strategic planner or the person who proposed the idea and/or the solution.

- **Change Sponsor:** A senior individual who can secure the budget, support the implementation, remove obstacles, and lead the whole change initiative. This role related to the change is different and separate from the role of a manager. A sponsor is accountable for formulating the change management strategy and tactics.

- **Change Management Practitioner (Consultant):** An internal or external individual who is responsible for setting the change management approach as well as coordinating and tracking the change management process. This person is not accountable for the change management strategies and tactics.

- **Change Management Lead:** An individual who is accountable for the change management deliverables, plan, and implementation. This individual has direct control on the change management team, change management practitioner, and change ambassadors.

- **Change Management Team:** A group of individuals who facilitate the change management activities. They ensure that all activities are completed, and communication is delivered using a variety of ways.

- **Project Manager**: The individual responsible for managing the project and ensuring that it meets its objectives as far as quality, scope, and time.

- **Project Management Team**: A group of individuals who are responsible for implementing the projects according to their scope and timeline to achieve the change goals.

- **Outcome/Benefit Owner**: This role is accountable for achieving the outcomes or realizing the benefits.

- **Outcome/Benefit Manager**: This role is responsible for measuring the outcome or the benefit and reports to the outcome/benefit owner.

Important Note

There is no single structure that fits all change initiatives. However, the smaller the change, the simpler the structure should be.

8.7.3.5 Responsibilities

Sponsors need to have a solid understanding of their responsibilities. They must be committed to a supportive attitude and be ready to deal with uncertainties. Responsibilities may differ depending on the role. Below is a sample of general responsibilities that can be assigned to a sponsorship committee:

- Developing and communicating the vision.

- Formulating the change strategy.

- Selecting the change management tactics.

- Appointing change management lead and the project managers.

- Approving milestones.

- Securing the project's budget.

- Assuring that all the stakeholders are aligned.

- Developing and executing the sponsorship roadmap.

8.7.3.6 Shared norms

It is very important that the shared norms are defined by the sponsors themselves. The norms should govern all the rules and practices that define how they work and deal with each other.

8.7.3.7 Shared values

Having shared values is the key to genuine alignment. Unfortunately, people usually underestimate their importance. Below are some values that is desirable to have in common among the change team:

- We value using the power of engagement and commitment more than the power of authority.

- We value two-way communication more than one-way communication.

- We value a bottom-up approach more than a top-down approach when making decisions related to the impacted stakeholders.

* We value iterative implementation and planning more than complete upfront planning.

8.7.3.8   Shared strategy

This refers to the strategy that should be agreed upon by all the sponsors to adopt. So far, the only strategy we have discussed is the theory of change that drives the selection of the change management tactics. The change management strategy will be discussed in more detail in Chapter 10.

8.7.3.9   Shared story

This is the narrative that all the sponsors should use to run counter to the current narrative that does not support the new change. This will be discussed in more detail while addressing the communication management work stream.

Table 8-9 below presents a sample governance framework based on the previous discussion.

Table 8-9. *Sample Governance Framework*

	Name	Role in organization	Role in committee
Names and Roles			
1	Name	Head of committee	Executive sponsor
2	Name	CEO	Sponsor, Change owner
3	Name	Marketing manager	Sponsor, Change initiator
4	Name	Project manager	Project manager
Responsibilities			
<ul><li>Communicating the vision.</li><li>Selecting the change champions.</li><li>Supervising the assessment.</li><li>Formulating the change strategy and tactics.</li><li>Selecting projects and appointing project managers.</li><li>Approving milestones.</li><li>Securing the project's budget.</li></ul>			
Shared norms			
<ul><li>...</li><li>...</li></ul>			
Shared values			
<ul><li>...</li><li>...</li></ul>			
Shared strategy			

Shared story

Structure of meetings

- **Frequency of meetings**: Every two weeks in the main building.
- **Decision making process**: Voting.
- **Meeting rules**
- ...
- ...
- ...

Involvement roles

	S1	S2	S3	S4	S5	S6	S7
Deliverable #1							
Deliverable #2							
Deliverable #3							

1. Approve　　**2. Accountable** (Decide/Approve)　　**3. Responsible** (Decide/Implement)

4. Participate (Implementation and taking decisions)　　**5. Inform before and after** (To be consulted for feedback)　　**6. Inform after** (completion/taking decisions)

8.7.3.10　Structure of Meetings

Finally, sponsors should agree on how they schedule and arrange their change initiative related meetings.

I will provide in Chapter 11 when discussing the communication tactics general tips about the sponsorship launching meeting as well as how the change sponsors communicate with each other and with the stakeholders. If the sponsors do not meet and communicate with each other in the most suitable way, the change will, most probably, fail.

8.7.3.11　Involvement roles

Finally, sponsors should be assigned one or more of the involvement roles that are shown in Table 8-9 for the different tactics and deliverables.

8.7.4　Deliverable 4.2: Change Impact

The objective of this deliverable is to understand the impact of the change on the organization.

Assessing the impact of the change on the organization as an important step to do before developing the change management methodology. The impact assessment can be conducted through surveys or interviews. Either way, we should have the same structure.

We will assess the change impact on three perspectives: (1) Organizational, (2) Culture, and (3) Stakeholder. Notice that the three perspectives are aligned with the three work streams of ElKattan's Model: organizational alignment, culture management, and stakeholder management.

Figure 8-17 show the elements that will be assessed in our change impact assessment framework.

There are some elements in the figure that could be called transformational elements as a high degree on impact on them would probably cause a transformation change. These elements are: (1) Strategy and business mode, (2) Values and mindsets, and (3) Leadership.

Normally, the change is considered to be transformational when the impact score is more than 60%, provided that one of the first three transformational elements has a score of more than 50% as well.

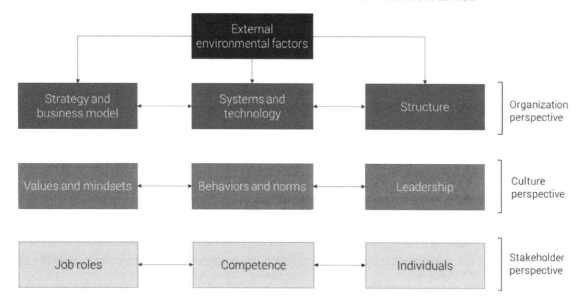

Figure 8-17. Change Impact Elements

8.7.5   Deliverable 4.3: Change Management Methodology

The objective of this deliverable is to decide on the structured approach that will be applied.

The change management methodology is the structured approach that will be used to have the change management strategy, tactics, and plan. The approach should include: the change life cycle, components, deliverables, assessments, and how and the data will be collected and analyzed.

Before developing the methodology, sponsors need to understand the impact of the change on the organization. Supposedly, the more the impact on the organization, the more change management practices to be applied.

Based on the change impact and vision, sponsors decide on the change management components and deliverables to be implemented.

Table 8-10 shows a template of the proposed deliverables of the readiness phase.

Table 8-10. *Change Management Deliverables - Readiness Phase*

Deliverable name	Objective	Comments
Stakeholder management work stream		
Deliverable 1		
Deliverable 2		
Culture management work stream		
Deliverable 1		
Deliverable 2		
Organizational alignment work stream		
Deliverable 1		
Deliverable 2		
Communication management work stream		
Deliverable 1		
Deliverable 2		
Planning and appraising theme		
Deliverable 1		
Deliverable 2		

It is good practice to collect the data and conduct the assessments using a mixed methods approach. The mixed-method approach includes both quantitative methods (such as questionnaires and surveys) and qualitative methods (such as interviews, focus groups, and workshops). The quantitative methods involve larger number of people and help in understanding certain patterns within the organization. On the other hand, the qualitative methods help in gaining a deeper understanding.

Table 8-11 shows a template of the proposed methods for the data collection.

Table 8-11. *Data Collection Methods*

Method	Objective	Frequency	Target stakeholders
Quantitative methods			
Survey 1			

Method	Objective	Frequency	Target stakeholders
Survey 2			
Qualitative methods			
Focus group			
In depth interview 1			
In depth interview 2			
Workshop 1			

8.7.6   Deliverable 4.4: Change Management Inception Plan

The objective of this deliverable is to have a plan for the deliverables and the data collection methods defined in the change management methodology to end up having the change management plan.

Figure 8-18 shows the three phases of the model's change life cycle: (1) Readiness, (2) Transition, and (3) Sustaining and realizing benefits.

The readiness phase has six sub-phases where the first five represents the five themes of the model. The last one is the assuring readiness phase in which we ensure that the vision is well-communicated and there a high degree of dissatisfaction of the current state.

The inception plan covers the activities related to the assessment theme, strategizing theme, tactics theme, and planning and appraising theme. It has five main milestones as follows: (1) Kick-off meeting, (2) Current state assessment completed, (3) Change management strategy approved, and (4) Change management tactics approved, and (5) Change management plan developed.

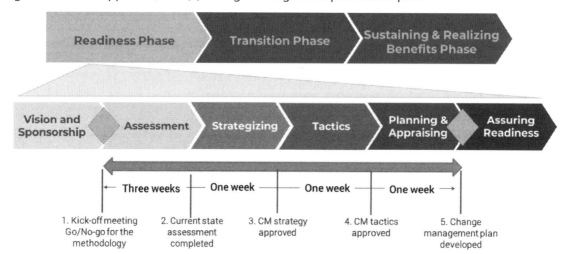

Figure 8-18. Change Management Inception Roadmap

Table 8-12 shows a template for the inception plan.

Table 8-12. *Change Management Inception Plan*

Deliverable name	Start date	Duration	Responsible	Involved stakeholders
1. Kick-off meeting				
Kick-off meeting				
2. Assessment				
Assessment kick-off meeting				
Deliverable 1				
Deliverable 2				
3. Strategizing				
Strategizing kick-off meeting				
Deliverable 1				
4. Tactics				
Tactics kick-off meeting				
Deliverable 1				
Deliverable 2				
5. Planning and appraising				
Deliverable 1				
Presenting change management plan				

8.7.7 Deliverable 4.5: Communication Plan – Readiness Phase

8.7.7.1 Overview

Communication is one of the most important aspects in change management. It can be achieved through different ways, such as arranging events or conducting meetings or workshops for the target stakeholders, conducting the campaign internally or externally, developing an identity for the change initiative along with brochures and/or videos, posting news in internal portals or on social media, and providing open communication channels for employees to discuss their concerns and problems.

Communication should be designed to ensure having a well-communicated vision, to address the capabilities required to start the first steps of implementation, and to Increase the dissatisfaction with the current state.

Communication must be proceeded throughout the implementation of the implementation of the change initiative, and reach all the stakeholders. Repeating the key messages along with as much information as possible is a good practice.

Communication must have a relatively compete information because people deal with incomplete information just as they do with an incomplete picture. When people see the shape shown in Figure 8-19, the brain automatically starts processing by completing the shape, and recognizes it is an incomplete circle. Similarly, people psychologically complete any incomplete information, which helps the creation of rumors about the change. Missing information is why rumors spread during change initiatives.

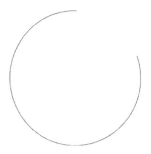

Figure 8-19. Incomplete Shape

Therefore, it is strongly recommended that the key messages be constantly repeated, along with as much detailed information as possible, with an emphasis on what seems to be not clearly understood.

8.7.7.2   Objective

The objective of this deliverable is to develop the first communication plan to start communicating the vision and establish sufficient readiness for the change.

8.7.6.1   Communication plan elements

Each activity in the communication plan should have these elements: (1) Activity name, (2) Communication aspects, (3) Target stakeholders and their numbers, (4) Message senders, (5) Time and place, (6) Frequency, (7) Method of delivery, and (8) Channel, as shown in Figure 8-23.

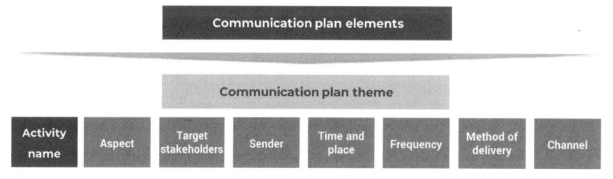

Figure 8-20. Elements of the Communication Plan

The communication plan could be designed on four different levels: (1) The leadership, (2) The management, (3) The change ambassadors, and (4) The staff. Next, I will give more details regarding the communication plan elements.

(1) Activity name

A very brief name for the activity.

(2) Communication aspects

The communication aspects are the subjects that will be addressed within each activity. The communication plan should mainly address the "why" to establish a sufficient readiness, so that the stakeholders will be willing to support during the readiness phase. The communication aspects can have any of the elements that we have previously included in the vision deliverables: change statement, change business case, future desired state gap analysis, or the change objectives and goals.

Over the duration period of the plan implementation, the communication messages should be addressing the why, what, who, and when, with special emphasis on the risks associated with not changing and its impact on the individual-level, such as the change in workload, job roles, day-to-day operations, conflicts between programs, etc. Also, it is important to introduce the change sponsors with casting light on the one who will be the contact person for feedback and suggestions.

(3) Target stakeholders and their numbers

Target stakeholders represent anyone who will be communicated by this event. Communicated messages should be crafted for each stakeholder segment, while taking their perceived loss into consideration.

(4) Message sender

Each activity in the plan should have a message sender from among the change sponsors. According to Hiatt (2006), it is recommended that top managers communicate the big picture and issues related to business and strategies, but not how the change will personally impact the employees, as this should be undertaken by direct managers.

(5) Time and place

When will the event be launched, and where will it be held - if it is a physical event.

(6) Frequency

Frequency indicates how many times the same event should be repeated.

(7) Method of delivery

It is advisable to consider different methods of delivering the content of the communication plan perspectives. Ways of delivery can include graphics, videos, presentation, messages, and infographics.

(8) Communication channels

The communication channels can be achieved through social media platforms (Facebook, Twitter, Instagram, etc.), physical meetings, online meetings, SMS, brochures, frequently asked questions (FAQ), workshops, e-mails, events, internal portals, newsletters, or the organization's website.

Table 8-13 shows a template of the communication plan with one communication activity.

Table 8-13. *Communication Plan Template*

Activity name	Communication aspect	Target stakeholder	Message sender	Time & place	Frequency	Method	Channel
Communication plan theme: "You can make a difference"							
General assembly	- Change vision. - Lessons learned from previous change initiatives. - Objectives of assessments.	- All staff (200)	- CEO	Jan 1, Main meeting room	Once	Presentation	Event
Activity 2							

8.8 CHAPTER IN A BOX

A summary of the vision and sponsorship theme is shown in Table 8-14.

Table 8-14. *Summary of the Vision and Sponsorship Theme*

Theme objective	The objective of this theme is to understand the problem along with the risk of not changing, identify how the world will be different after the change has been implemented, and form the right change sponsorship governance.			
Theme components	1. Developing the change statement	2. Developing the change vision	3. Managing the change benefits	4. Developing sponsorship governance and CM methodology
Component objective	The objective of the change statement component is to define what to change, why to change, theory of change, what to achieve, when, and how.	The objective of this component is to gain an understanding of the change journey, and to have a clear comparison between the current state and the future state upon successful implementation of the change.	The objective of this component is to determine the basis of the outcomes and benefits with regard to measurement and tracking.	The objective of this component is to develop the sponsorship governance as well as the change management methodology and communication plan of the readiness phase.
Deliverables	▪ Change definition ▪ Change statement	▪ Business case ▪ Future desired state gap analysis ▪ Change objectives and goals	▪ Change success criteria ▪ Change outcome/benefit profile sheet	▪ Sponsorship governance framework ▪ Change impact ▪ Change management methodology ▪ Change management Inception plan ▪ Communication plan – Readiness phase

CHAPTER 9
ASSESSMENT THEME

Chapter 9 - Assessment Theme

9.1   OVERVIEW

In this theme, we will assess stakeholders, culture, organizational alignment, and communication. These four aspects represent our four work streams, which were introduced in Chapter 7.

For the stakeholder assessment, we will use ElKattan's ACE Model to assess the stakeholder readiness with the change in order to enhance the engagement with the change to ensure smooth implementation. We will also assess the sponsors performance to ensure having the right sponsorship is in place to lead the change.

For the culture assessment, we will use ElKattan's Style Framework for Culture Readiness. These styles are based on both the Hofstede Model and the Hofstede Multi-Focus Model, which were described in detail in Chapters 5 and 6.

For the organizational alignment readiness, we will use ElKattan's Organizational Alignment Framework to make sure the organization is prepared and ready for the change.

Finally, we also assess the current communication channels and narratives inside the organization to determine using the effective channels and to craft the right change narrative.

9.2   OBJECTIVE

The objective of the assessment theme is to assess the current state from the stakeholder, culture, organizational alignment, and communication perspectives, in order to enable developing the appropriate change management strategy and tactics. This objective is achieved by the components and their deliverables presented in Figure 9-1.

Theme 2: Assessment			
Component 1: **Assessing stakeholder readiness**	**Component 2:** **Assessing culture**	**Component 3:** **Assessing organizational alignment**	**Component 4:** **Assessing communication**
1.1 Stakeholders influence analysis	2.1 Culture readiness assessment	3.1 Organizational elements assessment	4.1 Channel assessment
1.2 Stakeholder register and map	2.2 Value assessment	3.2 Resource analysis	4.2 Stakeholder narratives assessment
1.3 Stakeholder readiness assessment	2.3 Decision-making assessment	3.3 Risk analysis	4.3 Communication climate assessment
1.4 Change energy index	2.4 Leadership assessment		
1.5 Sponsorship assessment			

Figure 9-1. Components and Deliverables of the Assessment Theme

I will include here the summary of the components and deliverables that are shown in Figure 9-1 so that you have the choice of focusing, skimming, or skipping whatever you want based on what is of most relevance to your case.

COMPONENT 1: ASSESSING STAKEHOLDER READINESS

The objective of this component is to identify how much the stakeholders are prepared and ready for the change along with the issues that may drive them to either support or resist the change.

Deliverable 1.1: Stakeholder Influence Analysis

The objective of this analysis is to identify the influence of the stakeholders on the change initiative based on their power and interest in the change.

Deliverable 1.2: Stakeholder Register and Map

The objective of this deliverable is to list and/or visualize the change stakeholders according to their resistance category, and influence on the change.

Deliverable 1.3: Stakeholder Readiness Assessment (ACE Assessment)

The objective of this deliverable is to anticipate the stakeholder readiness to change to identify the gaps that need to be given more attention.

Deliverable 1.4: Change Energy Index

The objective of this deliverable is to identify the level of energy associated with the change implementation.

Deliverable 1.5: Sponsorship Assessment

The objective of this deliverable is to assess the sponsorship governance and the sponsors performance to ensure the right actions are taken.

COMPONENT 2: ASSESSING CULTURE

The objective of this component is to identify the culture elements that may hider or motivate the change implementation and to ensure having the right change values and core values in place.

Deliverable 2.1: Culture Readiness Assessment

The objective of this deliverable is to identify the degree to which the culture motivates or hinders the implementation of any change.

Deliverable 2.2: Value Assessment

The objective of this deliverable is to identify and assess the values that are directly linked to the realization of the change outcomes and benefits.

Deliverable 2.3: Decision-Making Assessment

The objective of this deliverable is to identify how the decisions are being taken inside the organization to ensure the right alignment with the change goals.

Deliverable 2.4: Leadership Assessment

The objective this deliverable is to identify to what degree the organization's leaders follow the required behaviors and mindsets of the change.

COMPONENT 3: ASSESSING ORGANIZATIONAL ALIGNMENT

The objective of this component is to assess the readiness of the organizational elements, the required resources, and risks of the change.

Deliverable 3.1: Organizational Alignment Assessment

The objective of this deliverable is to determine to what level the organizational elements are ready and aligned with the change goals.

Deliverable 3.2: Resource Analysis

The objective of this analysis is to identify the existing and missing resources required by the change and who can provide these resources.

Deliverable 3.3: Risk Analysis

The objective of this analysis is to identify the anticipated risks that may hinder the implementation of the change.

COMPONENT 4: ASSESSING COMMUNICATION

The objective of this component is to assess the internal communication and identify the stakeholder narratives regarding the change.

Deliverable 4.1: Channel Assessment

The objective of this deliverable is to assess the effectiveness of the organization's communication channels that are used to deliver the messages to the stakeholders.

Deliverable 4.2: Stakeholder Narratives Assessment

The objective of this deliverable is to identify the change stories that are being narrated by the impacted stakeholders themselves.

Deliverable 4.3: Communication Climate Assessment

The objective of this deliverable is to identify to effectiveness of the internal communication climate.

9.3 COMPONENT 1: ASSESSING STAKEHOLDER READINESS

9.3.1 Overview

According to Hiatt (2006), an organizational change cannot be successfully implemented unless it is managed at the individual level.

"Stakeholders" includes three main groups of people: the leadership team, who are the decision makers and have ownership interest; the implementation team, who are involved in implementation or transforming inputs into outputs; and the impacted people, who are required to make a change in the way they work, their behaviors, and/or their mindset. Figure 9-2 shows the three groups and how they intersect.

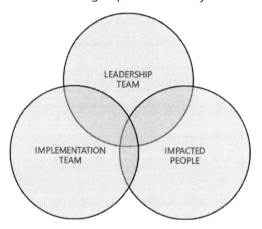

Figure 9-2. **Main Stakeholder Groups**

In change management, stakeholders is defined as the individuals or groups who may influence, be impacted, or perceive themselves to be impacted by the change. Therefore, the first two questions that we should have clear answer to are: "Who are the people who will influence the change?" "Who are the people who will be impacted by the change?" Once this is clearly defined, we should start anticipating who may support or oppose the change.

Change should be managed on the individual level as everyone will be impacted differently and will have their own personal factors that will lead them to either support or resist the change. Everyone will have their own perception and inner world regarding the change.

From the individual perspective, change management practices should assure that impacted employees are provided with all appropriate information, support, and motivation to help them move to the new desired state.

9.3.2   Objective

The objective of this component is to identify how much the stakeholders are prepared and ready for the change along with the issues that may drive them to either support or resist the change. Identifying the issues is our main goal from this component as based on these issues, we will develop our change management strategy to bring the maximum number of people on board with the change.

This component is achieved by developing up to five deliverables, depending on the context and change size. The five deliverables are shown in Figure 9-3.

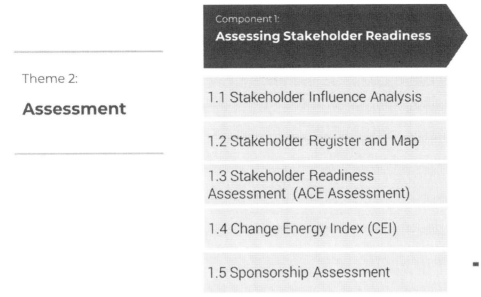

Figure 9-3. Deliverables of Assessing Stakeholders Component

9.3.3 Deliverable 1.1: Stakeholder Influence Analysis

9.3.3.1 Objective

The objective of this analysis is to identify the influence of the stakeholders on the change initiative based on their power and interest in the change. Influence is relational; If person A and B have the same power; when person A is more interested in the change than person B is, then person A has higher influence.

Before we start the analysis, we need to understand what power is, and how it differs from authority.

9.3.3.2 What is power?

One of the definitions of power is *the ability to achieve what you want*. The more capable you are in achieving what you want, the more powerful you are. In contrast with the society change initiatives, organizational change initiatives are decided by those stakeholders who have the authority to make decisions.

The question is: why do some managers fail to manage change initiatives when they have full power in organizations?

The answer is that some managers use only the power from their rank authority.

Authority is only one resource that can be turned into a form of power; there are other resources that can also be turned into power.

One example that we can all relate to, a three-month-old baby could be as powerful as their father; perhaps even more powerful. A baby can turn one simple resource that they have – crying – into power to achieve what they want.

In organizations, employees have their own resources that can be turned into power that works with or against the change. Basically, if all employees unite, they will have what is called "power with," which can sometimes be stronger than the power of those who have high-ranking authority. One strategy that some people employ is to keep the information to themselves to develop a source of power by having other people always interested in what they have.

The important thing to remember is that power is not only about having authority.

During the implementation of a change, we do not want to rely solely on the power of our authority. If we do so, our capabilities to lead the change will be limited. If we lead the change in a way that encourages ownership among the staff, motivation, and commitment, we will end up having a great source of power which is even more effective than the power of authority. Of course, in some cultures and situations, authority and cohesive power may be the only, or the most effective, way to change things.

Some researchers claim that power is not static and is always moving in some directions depending on how people utilize their resources. Sources of power can be classified as formal and informal as follows:

1. Formal:

- **Authority**: Power that is based on rank authority that can impose actions, reward people, control funding, etc.
- **Process**: Power that is based on following procedures and quality standards.

2. Informal:

- **Information and expertise**: Power that is based on control of information and having special skills.
- **Relationships with executives**: Power that is based on strong ties with top management.
- **Network**: Power that is based on an individual's influence and network.
- **Norms**: Power that is based on how people relate to each other inside the organization.
- **Dependency**: Power that is based on being the center of many dependent activities.
- **Scarce resources**: Power that is based on providing scarce resources.
- **Solidarity**: Power that is based on the agreement of some stakeholders to act collaboratively.
- **Charisma**: Power that is based on an individual's personality and interpersonal style.

9.3.3.3   Power distribution

Before assessing the influence on the change, we need to understand the power distribution in the organization. We need to know who holds the required resources that could help achieve the change objectives and goals? Therefore, we need to ask the following questions:

- Who has the required formal and informal resources that we need for the change?
    - What are these resources?
    - Do they have a stake in solving the change problem?
    - What are their interests in the change?

* Whose interests might oppose the implementation of the change and why?

Once we have a clear answers to the above questions, we can start identifying the power distributed inside the organization. Understanding the distribution of power through different lenses will enable us to choose the most effective strategies to make the change we wish to achieve.

Michael Jarrett in his article "Organizational politics can be an asset to strategy execution," -published by Instead- stated that: "... Identifying the types of political behaviors in your organization is the first step to using it for positive change."

The question is: why am I talking politics now?

To answer this question, let me go through the definition of the organizational politics.

By definition, organizational politics is using one's power, based on the available resources, to influence decisions in order to achieve a certain personal agenda or organizational outcome (Draft, 2012).

To summarize, different resources can be turned into power; and using this power as stated in the definition is the organizational politics.

Jarret stated that power can be classified based on two dimensions: (1) Formality (formal/informal), and (2) Level of activity (organizational level/individual level). The two dimensions form the four quadrants presented in Figure 9-4.

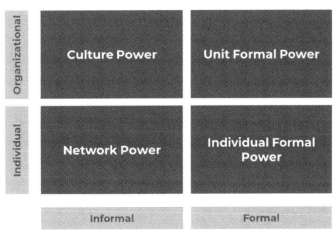

Figure 9-4. Classifications of Organizational Power

According to Jarret, power inside organizations can be classified as follows:

* **Network power**
  Network power is based on individual influence and networks. It is important for the leadership team to attract individuals who have the network power as ambassadors or champions for the change, as they have a high level of influence on the people around them.
* **Individual formal power**
  Individual formal power is based on the power that is driven from the formal authority of the position. This is also called "rock power." Usually, the financial director has this type of power.

- **Culture power**

  The culture power is based on the mix of norms, behaviors, dominant mindset, practices, beliefs, and shared values inside the organization. The change will face great resistance if it is accompanied by a conflict with the organizational culture.

- **Unit formal power**

  The unit power depends on many factors. It could be based on their formal source of authority or the processes that can be controlled by the unit such quality control. Also, the dependency and scarce resources that I mentioned earlier can increase the power of the units.

Usually, one of the four types will be dominant, with the most impact and influence on the decisions related to the change. It is good practice to quantify the power of the four types relative to each. Assuming that the total power inside the organization is 100, give a number for each type providing that the total is 100. While assigning a number for each type, try to provide specific examples and evidence. Assuming that the individual formal power inside the organization has a score of 50 out of 100, then, consider this as 100% and distribute this percentage among key individuals.

9.3.3.4   Power vs. Interest analysis

Once we have a clear picture about the power distribution, we can assess the stakeholder influence by doing a power/interest analysis by mapping the stakeholders in terms of their power vs. interest in the change.

As shown in Figure 9-5, the stakeholder influence could be classified into five categories: (1) Very high (A+), (2) High (A), (3) Medium (B), (4) Low (C), and (5) Very low (C-) based on the combination of the rating of the power and interest.

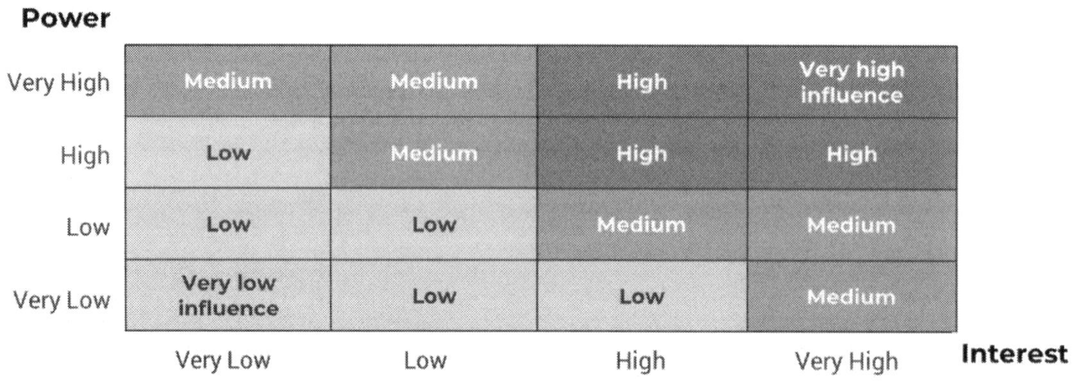

Power

	Very Low	Low	High	Very High
Very High	Medium	Medium	High	Very high influence
High	Low	Medium	High	High
Low	Low	Low	Medium	Medium
Very Low	Very low influence	Low	Low	Medium
	Very Low	Low	High	Very High → **Interest**

Figure 9-5. Stakeholder Power vs. Interest Analysis

Note that people may have the interest to support or oppose the change. Therefore, an A influence can be also a high influence to support or to oppose the change.

Table 9-1 has a template that can be used for the stakeholder influence analysis.

Table 9-1. *Stakeholders Influence Analysis*

	Position	Power	Interest	Influence rating	Comment
Organizational dominant power: Individual formal power Evidence:					
Stakeholder 1	Financial director	High	High	High (A)	
Stakeholder 2	Library manager	High	Low	Medium (B)	
Stakeholder 3	Unit manager	Low	Low	Low (C)	

9.3.4   Deliverable 1.2: Stakeholder Register and Map

The objective of this deliverable is to list and/or visualize the change stakeholders according to their resistance category, and influence on the change.

In order to complete this deliverable, we need to identify both the resistance category and influence on change for every stakeholder (group or individual). As we already discussed the influence on the change in the previous deliverable, we will discuss next how to define the stakeholder resistance category.

9.3.4.1   Stakeholder resistance analysis

Stakeholder resistance category can be identified by analyzing the perceived gain and Degree of change for every stakeholder. As shown in Table 9-2, we identify the perceived gain by analyzing the benefits minus the disbenefits for the stakeholders.

Table 9-2. *Stakeholder Resistance Analysis*

Program description:	
Stakeholder Name:	
<What change the stakeholder has to do?>	**Perceived benefits from the change**
	1.
	2.
Degree of change	**Perceived disbenefits from the change**
<Low /High >	1.
Perceived gain (perceived benefits minus perceived disbenefits)	2.
<Low/High>	3.

Once the above analysis has been done, the stakeholders can generally be categorized by analyzing the degree of change that the stakeholders will do versus the gain that they perceive, which is the difference between the perceived benefits and the perceived disbenefits. Figure 9-6 shows four resistance categories that are created by combining the two elements: (1) Perceived gain and (2) Degree of change.

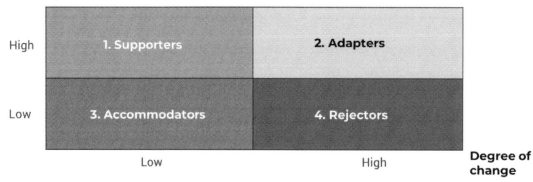

Perceived gain

	Low	High
High	1. Supporters	2. Adapters
Low	3. Accommodators	4. Rejectors

Degree of change

Figure 9-6. Stakeholder Resistance Categories

Once the above analysis has been done, the stakeholders can generally be categorized as follows.

- **The supporters.** Those people totally accept the change. They reject all the element of current state and support moving forward to the future desired state. As shown in Figure 9-6, theoretically, they have high perceived gain and low degree of change.

  They usually have a fair awareness of the change initiative and trust the leadership team. They are willing to participate, change, and act.

- **The adapters.** Those people are more toward accepting the change. They reject some of the elements of current state and support moving forward to most of the elements of the future desired state. As shown in Figure 9-6, theoretically, they have high perceived gain and high degree of change.

- **The accommodators**. Those people are more toward rejecting the change. They want to keep most of the elements of current state and accept some of the elements of the future desired state. As shown in Figure 9-6, theoretically, they have low perceived gain and low degree of change.

- **The rejectors.** Those people totally reject the change. They reject all the elements of the future desired state and want to keep the current state as is. As shown in Figure 9-6, theoretically, they have low perceived gain and high degree of change.

It is important for the change leaders to avoid generalization or stereotyping. Having some stakeholders categorized as rejectors, does not mean they will resist the change. This is just a hypothetical categorization based on the degree of change and the perceived gain.

9.3.4.2   Stakeholder needs and interests

How the stakeholders perceive the benefits depends on their personal needs and interest.

Interests and needs could influence why people support or resist a change. Why? Because they drive people's choices. For example, if we impose on people a change that have many proposed benefits but will conflict with their interests, they may not act in favor of the change and may not share their resources needed by the change.

And what is the relationship between the needs and interests?

The personal needs will formulate the personal values, and will drive the interests. For example, stakeholders who keen to satisfy their basic needs, they will be interested to have financial rewards and incentives as a sort of benefits from the change.

Senior stakeholders may need to boost their status and self-esteem; therefore they will be interested in the change if it will help them get higher position.

Other stakeholders may need to have achievement; they will be interested in doing challenging projects or getting new and quick results out of the change.

If the stakeholders have a shared need of developing their capabilities; this will then be translated into interest in the change if it will provide more training or development.

How do we know the stakeholders' needs and interests?

Interviews and group meetings could be a good source to identify shared needs and interests. Once we know the shared needs and interests, we should answer for the following important questions:

- o Does the change conflict with the shared needs and interests by any mean?
- o Are the stakeholders' interests at risk from the change?

Learning how to realize the needs along with their associated interests and how to address them in the change communication messages and narratives is critical in change management.

Table 9-3 has a template for this deliverable.

Table 9-3. *Shared Values and Interests*

Stakeholder	Need/Interest	Method of identification	Change conflict (Yes/No)	Are the interests at risk?	Importance to address

9.3.4.3   Stakeholder change register

As we have both the stakeholder influence and resistance category, we can finalize the stakeholder change register and map. Table 9-4 shows a template that can be used for the stakeholder change register.

Table 9-4. *Stakeholder Change Register*

	Potential Resistance category	Influence on change	Comments
Stakeholder 1	Supporter	A	
Stakeholder 2	Adapter	C	
Stakeholder 3	accommodators	B	
Stakeholder 4	Rejector	A	

9.3.4.4   Stakeholders map

The stakeholder map -shown in Figure 9-7- displays the stakeholders color-coded based on their influence and resistance categories. The map can be done for individuals and/or units.

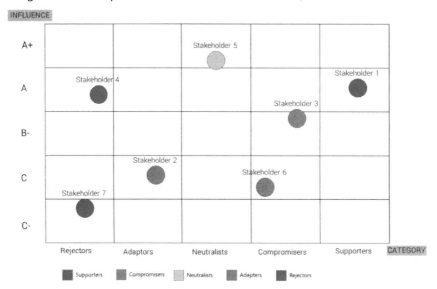

Figure 9-7. Stakeholders Map

The organizational structure can also be presented with the same color codes with writing next to each unit the letter that represents its influence on the change. Both the stakeholders map and the color-coded organizational structure should be kept confidential and not shared with all stakeholders, as people may be offended if they realize they have already been labeled and added to a certain category.

So far, we went through four main categories of the stakeholders: (1) Supporters, (2) Adapters, (3) Accommodators, and (4) Rejectors. Next, I will present more categories that need to be considered while managing a change.

9.3.4.5   Change sponsors

Change sponsors are powerful key stakeholders together lead the change and remove the obstacles along the way. The main responsibility of sponsors is to enable and engage others to accept the change in spite of its uncertainties.

Typically, they should have enough power and influence to implement the change, as well as an interest in the outcome. They should also be in a position to provide financial and non-financial resources to the program.

9.3.4.6   Change ambassadors (champions)

The ambassadors are those individuals who can be empowered by the leadership team to accept the responsibility of engaging others to act for the benefit of the change in spite of uncertainty and perceived loss. The ambassadors team is not about position and rank. Anyone can be on this team as long as they are committed to accepting the responsibilities.

The ambassadors are usually led by the change manager. However, as shown in Figure 9-16, they may need to have a structure. They can be grouped in such a way that each ambassador focuses on a special area of the change and communicates to a certain group of employees.

Figure 9-16. Ambassadors Structure

9.3.4.7   Neutralists

The neutralists are not really with or against the idea. They perceive no benefit or loss for themselves. Therefore, they do not really care if the change happens or not. They may also have their own plans. However, they would not mind supporting the change if they are pushed and asked to support it.

Neutralists may be aware of the change, but they are not motivated to take any initiative toward achieving it. If these people are ignored, they may develop some resistance to the change. This group needs to be motivated to join the supporters group, if possible. They should not be left out.

9.3.4.8   Apathetic

The apathetic group include people who are exhausted from the many programs that have been previously implemented. They are frustrated and have no more energy whatsoever to support any new programs. They will not help, not because they do not like the idea, but because of their lack of energy.

If these people agree to join and support, they will add no power or benefit whatsoever. The right approach needs to be taken to restore their energy. It would be a great step forward if they could at least be moved into the neutralists group.

Some people may be of the mistaken belief that they are resisting. However, it is primarily about a lack of energy. Managing this apathetic group could be more difficult than managing typical change resistance. Why? Because resisting people have energy that can be mobilized in a way that restores their enthusiasm, while apathetic people have no energy to be mobilized in the first place.

> **Important Note**
>
> Managing apathetic people is more difficult than managing opposition and resistance to change. Resistance denotes energy, while apathetic people have no energy whatsoever.

9.3.4.9   Incompetence resistors

This group of stakeholders may resist or be disengaged, as they are not confident in themselves or the organization's capabilities. This group needs to be technically developed by providing the right training and/or coaching. They can be emotionally reached with the slogan: "*You can make a difference.*"

Some stakeholders in this group could have a victim mentality. They would assume that one the main purposes of the change is to get rid of them. These people could end up leaving the organization.

9.3.4.10   Rational resistors

Some people, while aware of the vision of the change, are not convinced with the rationale behind it. This group may be able to help develop the change idea. If they are convinced, they may be moved to join the supporters.

The people in this group may have their own reasons for believing that the organization is addressing the wrong problem. The right amount of rational resistance is healthy and important to the change. Those who have rational resistance can help redefine the vision and develop the solution. However, if they are not properly managed, they may eventually oppose the change.

This group of stakeholders is mainly interested in facts and logic. They need to be made fully aware of what triggered the change and all the information that was the basis of the decision with regard to such things as analysis, financial aspects, and statistics. They need to understand the risks of not changing, especially on the individual level. Transformational programs need to have healthy discrepancy among people to improve the vision and solutions. Therefore, having the right level of rational resistance is helpful.

9.3.4.11   Emotional resistors

Some stakeholders may refuse to support the change because it is against their personal interests, needs, or benefits. They may also have some personal issues or trust problems with the leadership team. In any case, they are unlikely to openly mention their real motive for resistance. These people may also have political concerns. Some of the strategies that can be used to manage such emotional resistance are negotiation, accommodators, reassurance, and building trust.

9.3.4.12   Political resistance

While classifying our stakeholders, we also need to understand the organizational politics.

Playing politics is normal and exists everywhere. In general, organizational politics can play a good or bad role inside the organization. Bad or dysfunctional organizational politics will not only cause the change to fail, but can also negatively affect the whole organization. On the other hand, good organizational politics may not only help the change move forward, but some transformational programs may not be successful if politics is not well utilized. Therefore, it is important to identify who is playing organizational politics. This group could also include those who have other programs currently running that may share the same resources. Depending on the strategy used to deal with them, this group may resist or collaborate with the change initiative.

Resistance could happen when the change initiative disturbs -intentionally or unintentionally the political equilibrium inside the organization. Trade-off and/or reassurance could be a good strategy dealing with political and power conflict.

9.3.4.13   Confronting stakeholders

As previously described, stakeholders in the confrontation group have both rational resistance and emotional resistance. For example, they perceive a great loss to themselves and at the same time they have another logical reason for opposing the idea.

If the stakeholders in this state are not properly managed, they will aggressively resist the change. They will always, either openly or behind the scenes, criticize the change. They will only point to the negative issues. This group of stakeholders needs to be negotiated with to manage their emotional resistance first. Addressing only their rational issues will pointlessly consume a lot of time and effort.

A good strategy dealing with the confrontation group could be: "getting them out of the way."

9.3.5   Deliverable 1.3: Stakeholder Readiness Assessment (ACE Assessment)

The objective of this assessment is to identify the issues that impact the readiness to change to identify the gaps that need to be given more attention.

We will use ElKattan's ACE Model for this assessment, which is made up of four layers; each layer consists of a number of elements, which impact the stakeholders' participation in any change initiative. These layers are as follows:

Layer 1: Assumptions and Beliefs

This layer is the deepest one, which is not easy to reach. It has two main elements that greatly affect the participation and engagement toward the change: Assumptions and Beliefs toward the change.

Layer 2: Awareness, Competence, and Engagement

This layer has three elements that represent the methodology of the model: Awareness (A), Competence (C), and Engagement (E).

Layer 3: Rationale and Emotions

This layer has two elements that have the highest impact on the stakeholders' behaviors toward the change initiative: Rationale and Emotions.

Layer 4: Intention to Behave and Behaviors

This layer has two elements related to behaviors: Intention to behave toward the change and actual behaviors. Figure 9-8 shows the layers and elements of ElKattan's ACE Model.

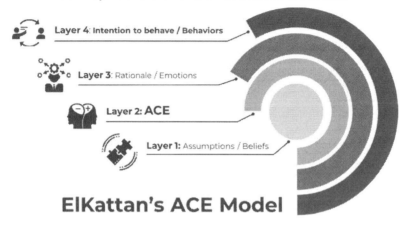

Figure 9-8. ACE Model Layers and Elements

Layer 1 has two elements representing the stakeholders' assumptions and beliefs toward the change. The elements of layer 1 are translated into the three elements in Layer 2: Awareness (A), Competence (C), and Engagement (E). The name of the model comes from these three elements. Hypothetically speaking, these three ACE elements are processed by the stakeholders to become their rationale and emotions toward the change initiative, which exist in layer 3. The way we feel (emotions) and think (rationale) will affect our behaviors, which exists in the last layer. Next, I will explain all the element of the ACE Model in more detail.

> **Important Note**
>
> As Kruger indicated, 90% of resistance is due to soft factors that are intangible and related to culture and emotions.

9.3.5.1   Layer 1: Assumptions / Beliefs toward the change

Assumptions and beliefs toward the change represent the stakeholder perceived idea about the change. They are also the root causes of the status of the elements in layer 2 (Awareness, Competence, and Engagement).

These elements could be the root causes that can be managed directly by enhancing communication, providing training, increasing trust, etc. They could also be deep drivers that cannot be easily managed such as conflict brought about by some personality traits, organizational culture, deep structure, etc.

The drivers that are identified in this layer are the basis of the ACE readiness assessment, and categorized according to awareness, competence, and engagement.

The drivers identified for the awareness are: (1) Clarity of vision, (2) Need for change, (3) Change benefits, (4) Risks of not changing, (5) Expectations, and (6) Sponsorship.

These six drivers are used to construct the awareness survey presented in Appendix E, Table E-1.

The drivers identified for the competence are: (1) Knowledge, (2) Skills, and (3) Attitude. Table E-2 shows the survey used to measure competence based on these three drivers.

9.3.5.2   Layer 2: Awareness (A) / Competence (C) / Engagement (E)

The ACE model assumes that the assumptions and beliefs toward the change are translated into three elements: Awareness (A), Competence (C), and Engagement (E). The name of the model comes from these three elements. Assessing the three elements: Awareness (A), Competence (C), and Engagement (E), will indicate the stakeholder readiness to change. Low readiness to change does not necessarily mean a high resistance to the change. If we want to assess the resistance, we will need to assess the other three elements: Rationale, Emotions, and Behaviors.

The ACE survey that is provided in Appendix E quantifies the readiness and identifies the negative issues affecting the readiness to change. In addition to the survey, assessment can be carried out through conducting workshops or interviews.

When I was thinking about the three elements in layer 2: Awareness, Competence, and Engagement, I first considered calling them "KSA," which stands for Knowledge, Skills, and Attitude. Then I considered, "What, How, and Why" or "Thinking, Acting, and Feeling." At a later stage, I thought about calling them, "Communication, Capabilities, and Motivation." Finally, I chose Awareness, Competence, and Engagement and named the model based on their initials.

The word "competence" was selected in preference to "how," "capabilities," "acting," or "skills," as competence implies beyond having merely the right skills. Competence is defined as the knowledge, skills, and attitudes (KSA), needed to undertake a job or role effectively. It includes one's attitude toward learning or applying a certain skill.

The word "awareness" was selected over "communication," as it encompasses having effective communication. Table 9-5 shows a comparison between the different names of the elements of layer 2.

Table 9-5. *Different Names of Awareness, Competence, and Engagement*

Selected names	Option 1	Option 2	Option 3	Option 4
Awareness	Knowledge	What	Communication	Thinking
Competence	Skills	How	Capabilities	Acting
Engagement	Attitude	Why	Motivation	Feeling

The comparison in the above table provides another layer of depth of layer 2 in the model. Figure 9-9 shows that these elements define the individual readiness to change.

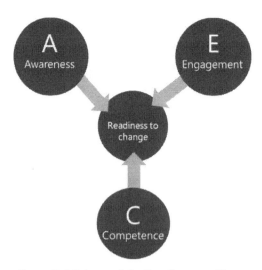

Figure 9-9. Drivers of the Readiness to Change

Increasing the readiness to change is the ultimate aim of change management practices during the readiness phase. Readiness to change means that stakeholders are rationally, technically, and emotionally engaged.

To guarantee that individuals are willing to act and provide support for the benefit of change, high scores in these three elements are essential. The assessment provides preventive analysis to anticipate areas of resistance, and serves as an intervention tool to be used.

9.3.5.3   Awareness (A)

Awareness is very important to ensure people are informed about the reasoning behind the change. It also provides them with the opportunity to voice their wishes and concerns.

By assessing the "A" (Awareness), problems and gaps are identified in terms of why, what, when, where, and how. Any lack of awareness can then be addressed through communication and awareness coaching.

9.3.5.4   Competence (C)

The competence element indicates the fit of the current staff regarding the requirements of the new change. In other words, how much development will be required?

Competence is the combination of three elements needed to perform a task effectively; knowledge, skills, and attitude (KSA). To ensure people have the right knowledge and skills to work within a given project, measuring competence is crucial.

By assessing the "C" (Competence), any gap in competence that may preclude implementation of the change is identified and assessed. It answers the questions: Is the problem related to skills or lack of knowledge? Is it related to attitudes that prevent others from practicing their skills? Any lack of competence can then be addressed through mentoring and competence coaching.

We have two types of competences: behavioral competences and technical competences.

Behavioral competences. A collection of common desired behaviors required by the change across all functions. From the change management perspective, the below behavioral competences are recommended:

- Results-driven

- Knowledge sharing

- Building trust

- Motivation

Technical competences. A collection of generic or function specific knowledge and skills required for excellent implementation of the change initiative. From the change management perspective, the below technical competences are recommended:

- Change management

- Strategic management

Competences could be different for the leadership role than the non-leadership role. Also, they could be different based on the scope of the different functions. Therefore, you may need to assess the change specific competences as well.

The competence assessment should provide what we call the change competence map, as shown in Figure 9-10. This map could be done on the individual, unit, or the organizational levels.

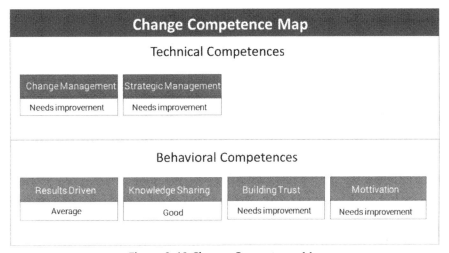

Figure 9-10. Change Competence Map

9.3.5.5 Engagement (E)

By assessing the "E" (Engagement), any lack of motivation is examined, such as: What is impeding full participation in the change? Why are participants unwilling to commit to the risks involved in the change?

Assessing engagement is one of the most difficult assessments. For example, one critical aspect that greatly influences engagement is self-interest, which plays a critical role in accepting or opposing change. As can be expected, assessing such an issue is very subjective. On the other hand, people should not be blamed for having self-interest toward any change. This can be summed up in the common thought of: "How will this impact me?"

The methodology of the ACE model in assessing the engagement is to assess the change inhibitor emotions, which are discussed in the third layer of the ACE model. These emotions are: (1) Complacency, (2) Loss, (3) Apathy, (4) Fear, (5) Self-doubt, (6) Distrust, and (7) Isolation.

9.3.5.6   Assessing Awareness, Competence, and Engagement - Readiness to change

The ACE assessment can be based on a self-assessment, using a survey or an interview. If both methods are used, there should be an agreement on the final score, thereafter, it is considered as the baseline.

Table 9-6 provides a sample of the ACE Assessment Report.

Table 9-6. *ACE Assessment Report*

	Assessment (baseline)	Desired	Gap (Yes/No)	Issues
Awareness	80%	100%	Yes	
Competence	64%	80%	Yes	
Engagement	81%	80%	No	
Comments				

Figure 9-11 shows a graph representation of the assessment.

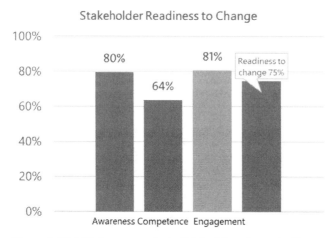

Figure 9-11. ACE Assessment - Individual Readiness to Change

9.3.5.7   Layer 3: Rationale toward the change / Emotions toward the change

Hypothetically speaking, the three ACE elements are processed by the stakeholders to become their rationale and emotions toward the change initiative.

The rationale and emotions form people's perception about the change. Usually, people resist how they perceive the change and not the change itself. A description of all the elements of the model will be provided later in this chapter.

Different behaviors are supposed to take place based on the status of the rationale and emotions toward the change. Hypothetically speaking, rationale, emotions, and behaviors toward the change -as shown in Figure 9-12- will indicate the type of resistance.

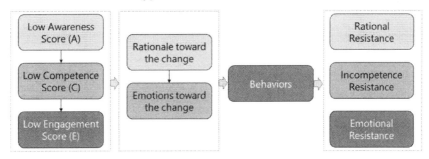

Figure 9-12. Relationship Between Elements of the ACE Model and Resistance

9.3.5.8   Emotions toward the change

Emotions are simply how we feel about the change.

When it comes to change, emotions are the key to success. Why?

Because emotions drive choices and actions, when people are emotionally engaged, they accept the project and become willing to not only change but also actively provide it their support. Also, because resistance to change is mainly an emotional process, a change leader who is able to manage emotions will be able to avoid a negative spirit and toxic environment. The leadership team should manage the change in a way that positively mobilizes feelings. Also, it is good practice to assess the stakeholders' emotions throughout the change implementation.

Any change touches people's feelings. Therefore, once the change initiative has been announced, stakeholders' emotions are divided into two main categories toward either accepting or rejecting the change:

- **Change inhibitor emotions.** The emotions of this category are: (1) Complacency, (2) Loss, (3) Apathy, (4) Fear, (5) Self-doubt, (6) Distrust, and (7) Isolation.

- **Change enabler emotions.** The emotions of this category are: (1) Urgency, (2) Dissatisfaction, (3) Being energized, (4) Hope, (5) Self-efficacy, (6) Trust, and (7) Solidarity.

As shown in Figure 9-13, the emotions are identified in each category in a way that every two emotions are paired together. For example, A complacency emotion should be mobilized to be replaced with the urgency emotions and so on.

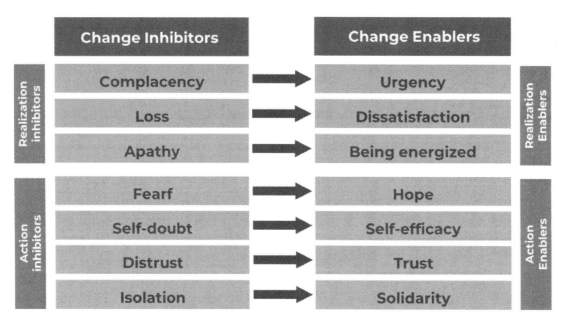

Figure 9-13. Emotional Inhibitors and Enablers

The first three emotions in the change inhibitors category are called "Realization inhibitors" as they may prevent people from responding or accepting a change in the first place, while the remaining four emotions are called "Action inhibitors" which may prevent people from doing actions even if they respond to the change. On the other hand, the first three emotions in the change enablers category are called "Realization enablers" as they may motivate people to respond or accept a change, while the remaining four are called "Action enablers" which may encourage people to act once they respond to the change

It is important to realize that emotions from both categories may exist at the same time; yet, both can be genuine.

9.3.5.9   Rationale toward the change

Rationale is simply how we think about the change. It is the logical basis for the expected behaviors and actions toward the change. The rationale could be related to particular facts or experiences.

The ideas are categorized into three categories: Self, Us, and Now. The "self" category is about how the individual thinks of himself; for example, *I am not competent for this change.* The "us" category is about how the individual thinks of the organization in general, for example, the organization is not competent for this change. The "now" category is about how the individual thinks of the external environment will impact the results of the change.

9.3.5.10   Layer 4: Intention to behave toward the change / Behaviors

Behaviors are simply what we do and act toward the change. The two elements: rationale and emotions toward the change will determine how the stakeholders will behave.

Monitoring behaviors will help change leadership identify when resistance is taking place. Resistance can take many forms and is manifested through various behaviors. Behavioral resistance may fade and resurface in other forms. Following are examples of the most common behaviors of change resistance:

1. **Compliance behavior**. This is the most difficult resistance to deal with because it is not readily apparent. Sometimes compliance is not seen as resistance because work is still getting done. However, complete compliance can also be attributed as a reason for a change to fail (recall the example of Zero resistance discussed in Chapter 2).

Those who resist using this compliance behavior may express their concerns more destructively, away from direct supervisors. Gauging levels of energy and enthusiasm may indicate whether or not the behavior is a form of resistance.

2. **Silence behavior.** It is common in Egypt to hear the saying, "Silence is a sign of acceptance. Change leaders should think twice before believing such a concept. Silence does not translate to consent when introducing a transformational program that comes with its own set of benefits, disbenefits, and uncertainties.

Silence can be a challenging resistance style to deal with, requiring keen awareness of silent employees who may be concealing their disposition, while thinking, "I will always keep my ideas and feelings about the change to myself, and will not let you argue with me about them."

Change leadership should have the skill to support silent individuals in expressing their resistance directly.

3. **Avoiding behavior**. Avoidance is a resistance style that can appear, in some aspects, similar to silence behavior. For example, the resistant employee does not attend related sessions, changes the subject, or makes excuses for preoccupation with other tasks, etc.

4. **Denial behavior.** This behavior can be detected when people are observed to be speaking and acting as if the change will not occur; "nothing will change" or "this is the same as the previous ones," etc. This behavior is demonstrative of apathy or a complete rejection of the change.

5. **Attack behavior.** The most obvious of the five resistance behaviors – attack behavior – should not be confused with the healthy rational of opposing particular ideas. This behavior can be identified through angry words and aggressive reactions. Change leadership should have the skill of not taking such an attack personally, or as it is intended toward their experience and credibility.

This layer has two different elements related to behaviors, which I will discuss next.

9.3.5.11 Intention to behave

The intention to behave element implies the potential behavior, which is the result of the rational and emotional attitudes toward the change.

What we think (rationale) affects how we feel (emotions) and act (intention to behave), and what we feel affects how we think and act.

9.3.5.12 Behaviors

Normally, stakeholder's behaviors that we observe are the same as their intention to behave. However, the behaviors may not reflect the intention to behave, depending on other external forces that the stakeholder may be experiencing.

We should be aware that behaviors affect how we feel and think. This is an important concept to know; if we impose a certain behavior on people to adopt, this behavior may then affect how they think and feel. Figure 9-14 shows the relationship between the ACE three elements, rationale, emotions, intention to behave, and behaviors.

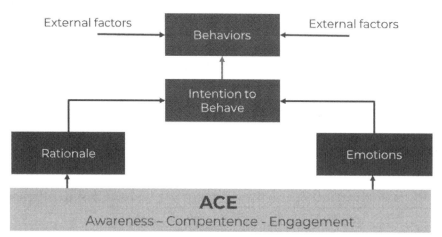

Figure 9-14. Relationships Between the ACE Elements

9.3.5.13 Assessing Rationale, Emotions, and Behaviors - Resistance to change

In order to assess the rationale, emotions, and behaviors during the implementation of the change, we need to monitor participants by using a monitoring sheet. In this monitoring sheet, we catalog the three elements for each situation related to the change. Table 9-7 shows a template of the monitoring sheet.

Table 9-7. *ACE Monitoring Sheet*

Situation	Emotions	Degree of emotions (1-100)	Ideas about the change	Behaviors
Situation 1				
Situation 2				
Comments:				

9.3.6 Deliverable 1.4: Change Energy Index (CEI)

The objective of this deliverable is to identify the level of energy associated with the change implementation. The change energy is measured using an index called the Change Energy Index (CEI). We will use a tool called ElKattan's Change Energy Meter to calculate this index.

After understanding the stakeholder readiness to change using our ACE Model and identifying the issues that will drive our stakeholder management strategy, let us go one step further by identifying what we call the change energy index, which is a new concept I am introducing in this book.

Understanding the level of Energy related to the change will help formulate the right change management strategy. This level of energy is measured using an index called the Change Energy Index (CEI), which I will explain next.

9.3.6.1   ElKattan's Change Energy Meter

The change energy tool is just another way to visualize the emotions toward the change.

Do you recall the change emotions that we were explained in the previous deliverable?

The change emotions in the ACE Model are categorized to inhibitor emotions and enabler emotions as presented in Figure 9-13. Next, let us see how we use these emotions to get the change energy index.

In the scale of the Change Energy Tool that is presented in Figure 9-15, the left side has the positive energy toward the change. I assume it is clear that the enabler emotions will be on the same side.

The middle area has the little energy or no energy at all, while the left side will have the negative energy. Let us switch to the change inhibitor emotions, which will be on the right side in which we have the negative energy.

We assume that when the negative energy toward the change is more than the positive energy, it will be very difficult to achieve a successful change.

But how can we quantity the negative and positive energy toward the change?

The quantification can be done by the ACE assessment as the criteria of the engagement survey should be based on the emotions that we have in the Change Energy Meter.

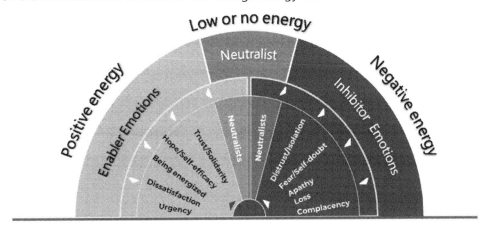

ElKattan's Change Energy Meter

Figure 9-15. ElKattan's Change Energy Meter

The question is: how to calculate the Change Energy Index (CEI)?

The CEI is calculated as the percentage of positive energy minus the percentage of the negative energy. And we ignore the neutralists, who will have average rating in the assessment.

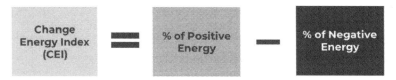

It is obvious that the higher the CEI we have, the closer we are to achieving the change objectives. To stat the implementation, you need to have at least an index that is greater than 15%. And what if we have an index with a minus sign?

Skill Practice 9.1 - Identify the Stakeholders Energy Structure
Identify the stakeholders energy structure of your project.

9.3.7   Deliverable 1.5: Sponsorship Assessment

The objective of this deliverable is to assess the sponsorship governance and the sponsors performance to ensure the right actions are taken.

Kotter indicated that successful transformation programs rely 70% to 90% on leadership. Moreover, it is extremely difficult to put a transformational program on the right track by forcing people to accept it and react positively.

According to eight different research studies conducted by Prosci from 1998 to 2016 on the greatest contributors to the success of transformational projects, sponsorship is the number one contributor to success. The more a change lacks the right sponsorship, the more conflicts and obstacles it will have.

According to different researchers, change sponsors who lead change initiatives typically make the following common mistakes:

1.   Not being active and visible throughout the implementation.

2.   Do not have effective 2-way communication.

3.   Not being accessible nor powerful enough to provide support and remove obstacles.

4.   Neglecting the management of the people side.

Table 9-8 below has some general criteria that can be used for assessing the sponsorship based on the common sponsorship mistakes. Figure 9-17 shows the results of the assessment.

Table 9-8. *Sponsors Assessment Sample*

Criteria	Rating 1 (very low) - 5 (very high)
Total score: 45%	
1. Commitment to being active and visible	Score: 75%

Criteria	Rating 1 (very low) - 5 (very high)
1.1 Regularly attended project status meetings.	2
1.2 Had face-to-face meetings with frontline supervisors.	5
1.3 Regularly attended committee meetings.	5
1.4 Was active, visible, and present at all special events (kick-off, training, etc.).	4
2. Effective 2-way communication	Score: 25%
2.1 Listened to and addressed the concerns of subordinates and peers.	2
2.2 Communicated effectively in different ways throughout the implementation.	2
2.3 Had consistency between the communicated message of the change and actions (walk the talk).	2
3. Accessibility and power	Score: 44%
3.1 Was always accessible to provide support.	2
3.2 Had a high degree of control over the people being impacted by the change.	2
3.3 Had a high degree of control over the systems being impacted by the change.	5
3.4 Was powerful enough to make strategic decisions and remove obstacles.	2
4. Management of the people side	Score: 38%
4.1 Was able to motivate and engage his team with the new change.	3
4.2 Was able to link the team performance appraisal with the change objectives.	3

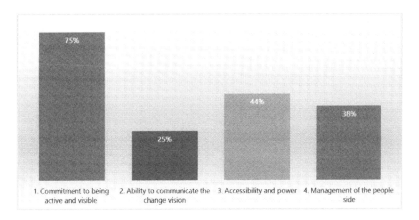

Figure 9-17. Sponsors Assessment

Evaluation of the sponsors could also be prepared based on their responsibilities. Such an evaluation should be communicated to all sponsors so they are aware of what is expected of them.

Table 9-9 shows a sample survey that can be used for the sponsorship governance assessment. It is advisable to design a questionnaire that fits the specific context. Each question receives a rating from 1 to

5, where a rating of 1 is lowest and a rating of 5 is highest.

Table 9-9. *Governance Framework Assessment Sample*

	Criteria	Rate (1 - 5)	Comments
1	Does the program have an effective governance structure?		
2	Does the sponsorship team involve stakeholders from all impacted units?		
3	Are accountability and responsibilities clear?		
4	Are the roles clearly assigned to sponsors?		
5	Is there an effective balance of power (not too much centralization)?		
6	Are the governance rules set and followed?		
7	Are the minutes of meetings taken regularly and well recorded?		
8	Does the governance have an efficient decision-making process?		

9.4   COMPONENT 2: ASSESSING CULTURE

9.4.1   Overview

The organizational culture has a direct impact on how resistance manifests. For example, in an open organizational culture, the resistance will be visible, as employees talk with their boss about everything without any inhibitions. Conversely, in a closed organizational culture, most of the resistance will be passive and/or hidden, as most employees never tell their boss what they really think. Culture assessment is one of the most important steps in successfully managing change resistance.

Strategy and culture are the two main organizational elements that govern transformational changes in organizations. The strategy explains the change goals from a logical perspective, while the culture expresses the change from a values perspective. In order to have a successful and motivating change, the three elements; strategy, culture, and change must be aligned.

The difficulty in assessing the culture lies in the fact that the real values are largely unspoken and invisible. It can only be observed through behaviors, practices, and shared norms.

A good way to shoot yourself in the foot while leading a transformational change is to ignore the behaviors and mindsets of the people involved. It is important to allocate some time to troubleshoot the existing culture to understand these behaviors and mindsets. This could be done intuitively or by conducting a survey from one of the organizational culture models.

Understanding the culture will also give us an understanding of how the people inside the organization will deal with or resist the change.

Important Note

Culture is magically transferred to the newcomers of any group, slipping into their minds and hearts and directing most of their practices and behaviors.

Changing the culture with regard to behaviors and mindset is essential in change management. However, it can be difficult to change in a relatively short time, especially if it is a threat to traditional norms and long-time ways of doing things.

According to Alas and Vadi (2014), when employees seek information about a change, they mainly focus on aspects related to their values, behaviors, and mindsets. Therefore, understanding the culture would help identify the most appropriate strategy and tactics to be applied to successfully achieve the change.

9.4.2   Objective

The objective of this component is to identify the culture elements that may hider or motivate the change implementation and to ensure having the right change values and core values in place.

By the end of this component, you should have answers to the following questions:

- What cultural elements do we anticipate to conflict with the change?

- What are the dominant behaviors and mindsets with respect to the change initiative?

- How do people interact and relate to each other?

- What is the willingness to change from the culture perspective?

Changing behaviors and mindsets is one of the biggest challenges in change management. Many of the sources of change resistance are related to culture. Many cultural issues have the potential to impact the implementation of a change, such bureaucracy, complacency, anxiety, mistrust uncertainty avoidance, and power distance, leadership style, etc. The list is very long! Developing this component will help us determine the cultural source of resistance before starting our challenging culture change journey.

The objective is achieved by developing the deliverables that are shown in Figure 9-18.

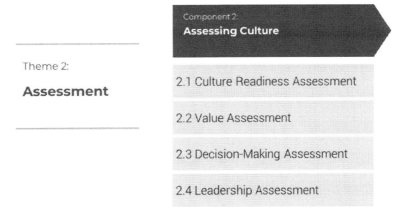

Figure 9-18. Deliverables of the Assessing Culture Component

9.4.3   Deliverable 2.1: Culture Readiness Assessment

The objective of this deliverable is to identify the degree to which the culture motivates or hinders the implementation of any change.

To assess the culture readiness, we will use ElKattan's Style Framework for Culture Readiness. In this framework, eight values are selected that I called culture readiness styles, which I will refer to as styles. These styles are: (1) Bureaucracy vs. results, (2) Complacency vs. urgency, (3) Anxiety vs. safety, (4) Silos vs. knowledge sharing, (5) Mistrust vs. trust, (6) Uncertainty avoidance vs uncertainty acceptance style, (7) Power distance, and (8) Innovation.

There are other values that could be inheriting the implementation of the change such as: Communication, Competition, Conflict, Control, Cooperation, Efficiency, Inspirational leadership, Loyalty, Motivation to work hard, Playing political, and Inward looking.

Important Note

During the transition period of the change, it is more effective to offer rewards that are behavior-based rather than skill-based.

Following is a description of the eight culture styles:

1. Bureaucracy vs. results style. This cultural style is related to the degree people inside the organization are results-oriented vs. excessively process-oriented.

S1: Bureaucracy vs. Results

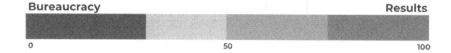

Organizations leaning more toward a results-driven culture tend to be inclined to embrace change. The results culture style occurs when combining the first two dimensions of the Multi-Focus Model (means-oriented vs. goal-oriented and internally driven vs. externally driven). Higher scores in these two dimensions are demonstrative of a results culture style or forward-leaning tendency toward a willingness to change.

On the other hand, as seen in Chapter 6, having both a means-oriented and internally driven culture produces a bureaucratic culture, resulting in exceptional challenges in implementing change, particularly if urgent changes are required. Thus, an excessively bureaucratic organization will normally face resistance to change. Counterbalancing a bureaucratic culture is achieved by supporting a goal-oriented and externally driven culture.

2. Complacency vs. urgency style. This culture style reflects the amount of energy within the organization and the degree to which personnel may or may not believe in the necessity and/or room for improvement or change.

S2: Complacency vs Urgency

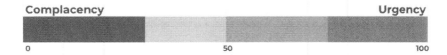

Complacency occurs when the perception exists that there is little room for improvement, necessitating the establishment of a sense of urgency to achieve engagement in the change initiative. Complacency is one of the main obstacles to have a successful implementation of any change initiative; elevated levels of complacency directly correlate to personnel reluctance in accepting or participating in change initiatives.

Complacency as a culture appears in an organization for many reasons, including, but not limited to, discrepancies in competition, poorly defined delivery deadlines, a lack of follow-up by management, or simply due to a highly internally driven culture; an example of which might be found within governmental entities. Complacency can be identified by the way people work and respond to requests.

Sources of complacency may or may not include the following:

- Setting targets that can be easily achieved.

- A lack of performance feedback.

- Focusing on narrow goals.

- Excessively positive and cheerful speaking of management.

- Lack of discussion with employees about problems, opportunities, or potential crises.

Balancing cultural complacency may require the introduction of practices that encourage a higher level of work-oriented culture within the organization.

Complacency vs. urgency style can be identified by the following:

- Identifying if employees are making their utmost effort or not.

- Identifying if employees feel threatened by competition.

- Identifying if employees are inclined toward striving to be or remaining ahead of competitors.

A strong sense of urgency can decrease complacency. This can be accomplished by continuously communicating the risks of being complacent toward change on both the part of the organization and the individual.

The culture of complacency is primarily related to the internally driven culture dimension. However, a balance may be achieved by creating a more goal-oriented, professional, open, and work-oriented culture.

3. **Anxiety vs. safety style**. This culture style reflects the degree to which those working within the

organization feel either secure or insecure.

S3: Anxiety vs Safety

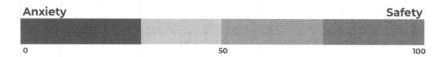

Normally, people value the need for security and are risk-conscious, preferring to feel themselves in a safe and protected environment; thus, some may also feel less motivated to engage in change that comes with elevated risk or ambiguity. Such a change may create a culture style of anxiety (jeopardy), fear of the unknown or being forced to step outside their comfort zone. The mere idea of change may cause and/or increase anxiety, or a sense of being in jeopardy within the organization; thus, higher anxiety levels within a culture produce increased resistance to change.

The employee-oriented vs. work-oriented dimension that was discussed in Chapter 6 has a genuine impact on this particular style indicative to the degree in which the organization is sincerely concerned for those striving to excel in their work. An employee's sense of safety is directly correlated to the level of employee-orientation within the organization.

Counterbalancing an excessively anxiety culture is achieved by establishing a goal-oriented, open, and employee-oriented culture.

4. Silos vs. knowledge sharing style. This culture style measures the level of varying units within the organization in their ability to coordinate and share information.

S4: Silos vs Knowledge sharing

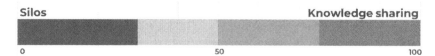

A silos style occurs when departments or management fail to share information, demonstrating a lack of common interests and goals. The silo mentality is believed to divisively impact operations by reducing employee morale and may contribute to the overall failure of a company, its products, and/or culture.

> **Important Note**
>
> Each culture dimension has its advantages and disadvantages and that reshaping of the culture should be done in consideration of the context, strategy, and overall scope of the organization.

A knowledge sharing style will maintain a sufficient eagerness-to-learn culture, enabling an organization to continuously evolve and improve.

Establishing an organizational knowledge sharing culture and experience is crucial to influencing willingness to change. Generally, organizations that encourage knowledge sharing will have increased levels of creativity and success in implementing change.

People who work in a knowledge sharing culture style enjoy having access to new technology and systems; they are more open-minded, consistently come up with new ideas, and are willing to explore modernized options and alternatives.

Establishment of a balanced knowledge sharing style would require increased employee goal-orientation, less rigidity, and establishing increased level of professional and open culture.

5. **Mistrust vs. trust style**. This culture style indicates the level of trust and/or mistrust among individuals and within the hierarchy. Trust is crucial in the acceptance of change, particularly within collectivistic cultures.

S5: Mistrust vs Trust

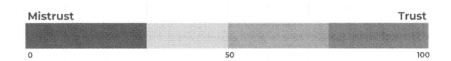

A combination of goal-oriented, professional, open, and employee-oriented culture creates a culture of trust between employees and the hieratical levels.

6. **Uncertainty avoidance vs uncertainty acceptance style**. This culture style indicates to what level the people inside the organization feel threatened by uncertainty and ambiguity and try to avoid these situations.

S6: Uncertainty avoidance vs Uncertainty acceptance

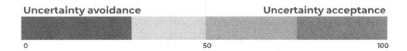

This style is primarily related to the uncertainty avoidance national culture dimension that was discussed in Chapter 5.

This culture style indicates to what level new ideas and change initiatives are suggested and implemented inside the organization. This style is directly related to innovation and intrapreneurship culture inside the organization.

To have an uncertainty acceptance culture, the organization needs to have a goal-oriented, flexible, professional, and employee-oriented culture.

7. **Power distance style**. This culture style reflects the degree that an organization is managed using a centralized and top-down power and influence and is primarily related to the power distance dimension discussed in Chapter 5.

S7: Power distance

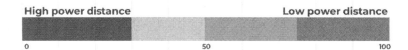

Excessive power distance produces an elevated authoritarian management style within the organization and is recognizable in the placement of emphasis on control and dominance. People do what they are told to do; their primary concern being to maintain a personal advantage. An elevated authoritarian style of management within a culture will result in a visible decrease in the willingness to participate in change.

Counterbalancing the power distance style is achieved by establishing an increasingly goal-oriented, flexible, professional, open, and employee-oriented culture.

8. **Innovation**. This culture style reflects the degree that an organization culture motivates developing new idea and activities.

S8: Innovation

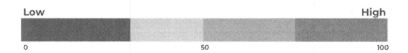

Culture Change Readiness Index (CCRI)

The Culture Change Readiness Index (CCRI) identifies the degree to which the culture motivates or hinders the implementation of any change. It combines the rating of the culture styles in one index that has a scale from -100 to +100. Figure 9-19 provide an example of the Culture Change Readiness Index (CCRI).

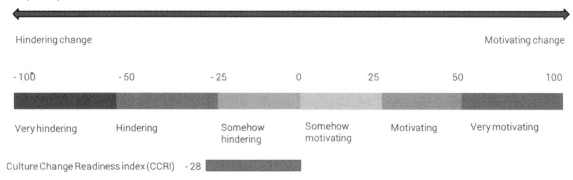

Figure 9-19. ElKattan's Style Framework for Culture Readiness

9.4.4   Deliverable 2.2: Value Assessment

The objective of this deliverable is to identify and assess the values that are directly linked to the realization of the change outcomes and benefits. I will refer to these values as the change values.

As discussed in the culture overview that I presented, a value is the sense of broad feelings and emotional tendency in a certain dimension. Most of the time, values are hidden and can only be observed through behaviors and actions.

The values are reflected into the surrounding mindsets and behaviors.

As shown in Figure 9-20, in our change management methodology, we consider three types of values that overlap with each other: (1) Change values, (2) Organizational core values, and (3) Organizational culture values.

The core values are typically suggested by top management to help achieve the strategy, while the change values are typically identified by the change leadership to help achieve the change goals.

On the other hand, the culture values are identified by using one the organizational culture models. This can be done by the organizational culture models such as the Multi-Focus Model that I presented in Chapter 6 and ElKattan's Style Framework that I used to assess the culture readiness.

The change values could be part of the organizational core values and could be totally different; and the change values and the core values could also be part of the organizational culture values and they could be different.

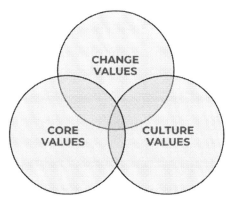

Figure 9-20. Change Values, Core Values, and Culture Values

Therefore, assessing the culture values could be a good step to do before suggesting the change values along with their behaviors and mindsets. The change values (as well as the core values) could be translated in the form of culture practices, not culture values.

The following steps are to be done to deliver the value assessment deliverable:

1. Identifying the change values related to the change goals.

2. Define the set of mindsets and behaviors related to each value.

3. Assess the change values by rating the behaviors and mindsets as: very low, low, in-between, high, or very high.

Before identifying the change values, you may need to conduct interviews or workshops to get answers for the following questions:

▪   What existing culture elements (values, mindsets, or behaviors) that may not allow stakeholders to work in ways that support the change?

- What existing culture elements conflict with the new behaviors and etiquette required by the change?

- What existing culture elements may hinder the realization of the outcomes and benefits of the change?

Example 9.1 - Activity-based Workplace

Going from a traditional workplace to an activity-based workplace where places are unassigned and shared between all employees has become a common change initiative in recent years.

Working in such a workplace requires shift in the employees mindsets and behaviors. Such a shift is critical to make sure that the change benefits (such as improved workflow, collaboration, and production) are realized. The change in the culture is also required to overcome the perceived disadvantages such as: lack of privacy, lack of concentration, lack of autonomy, distraction, lack of leadership, etc. Below are some highlights of the main required shift in the culture:

- As everyone used to have their own workspace, a mindset shift is required from 'my office' to 'our office' and from 'my space to 'our space.'

- As everyone is required to work anywhere, a change in behavior is required from 'work at my own desk' to 'work wherever is available.'

- As office space used to be allocated based on status, hierarchy, and authority, a shift in mindset is required from status-based allocation to needs-based allocation.

- More flexibility is required so that employees can make decisions on what workspace best fits their specific needs.

- As there are no assigned offices, reliance on paper should be greatly reduced.

Table 9-10 below shows the identified values, mindsets, and behaviors for the open space environment. A culture of belonging, mindfulness, continuous improvement, and small power distance. Upon finalizing the description of the values along with their set of behaviors and mindsets, they were assessed by the stakeholders to identify to what degree they exist in the current culture.

Table 9-10. *Open Workspace Culture*

Value	Description	Mindset	Behavior
Belonging *"We belong to our workplace"*	This value reflects the extent to which employees feel the space identity.	- It is 'our space' not 'my space' and its 'our office' not 'my office'. - Space is perfectly designed to accommodate our different needs. - My space is your space. Where we all fit and grow.	- Employees are flexible in shifting from 'work at my own desk' to 'work wherever is available'. - People drive their identity largely from the norms and practices of the workplace and environment. - Employees can easily select the right space to support their focus and concentration.

Mindfulness "We are all in it together?"	This value is about the extent to which employees are considerate to each other while working in the workplace.	- Our consideration to each other is key for our success. - Open space is meant to support our interaction and unity. - We value collaboration but not at the expense of privacy and concentration when needed.	- Employees avoid distracting others and use the right voice tone in the right place. - Employees are mindful about the space usage and guidelines. - Employees are mindful about what and where to eat and drink. - Employees always leave a clean and tidy workplace. - Employees avoid unnecessary potential conflicts by respecting others' rights for privacy and autonomy. - Reliance on paper is greatly reduced.
Continuous improvement "We are always improving our space"	This value reflects the degree to which employees are constructive toward the workplace.	- Nothing is perfect, we will be always improving our workplace norms and practices.	- Employees are comfortable with unfamiliar situations in the workspace. - People are open to feedback from others to always improve the norms and practices. - Employees always provide constructive feedback for further improvement.
Small power distance "Who is the boss here?"	This value reflects the degree that the organization is managed using a decentralized and less top-down power and influence.	- Our office space is needs-based allocation not status-based allocation. - High sense of ownership. - Seniors are treated in the same way as the rest of employees.	- Decentralization is popular. - Subordinates expect to be always consulted or involved. - Special status for seniors are not encouraged. - Managers are more tolerant of staff criticism. - Our workplace is cheerful and relaxed.

9.4.5   Deliverable 2.3: Decision-Making Assessment

The objective of this deliverable is to identify how the decisions are being taken inside the organization to ensure the right alignment with the change goals.

Decision making style is one of the main manifestations that shows if leadership "walk the talk" and apply the claimed values or not. Decisions show which values the organization is sticking and abiding to.

Important Note

It is expected that the employees will have less buy-in for the change if they do not accept the way in which decisions are made by their managers.

The decision-making style is normally part of the leadership style. Below are the styles that will be considered in our assessment.

- ▪ **Authoritarian decisions making style:**
  This style can be noticed by using fear-based methods, with major important decisions made by the managers alone. Decisions are made with minimum consultation within a very close circle. Then communicated to the employees.

- ▪ **Paternalistic decisions making style:**
  This style could be common when there are sort of good relationships and trust between the managers and their subordinates. Most important decisions are made in consultation with a close circle. Even though the decisions are not changed, they are explained and justified to the employees before being implemented.

- • **Consultative decisions making style:**
  This style is reflected when the managers consult with their subordinates before they reach their decisions. They listen to their advice, consider it, and then announce their decision.

- • **Participative decisions making style:**
  In this style, the issue is put before the group for discussion. The decision is made based on the majority viewpoint.

Managers move between the different decisions making styles. However, there is one style that will closely correspond to them. The technique that we use is to ask the subordinates to rate their satisfaction of the decisions making style. It is also good practice to ask the managers to conduct a self-assessment. A sample results is shown in Table 9-11.

Table 9-11. *Decision-Making Assessment Template*

	# of participants	Authoritarian	Paternalistic	Consultative	Participative	Dominant style	Satisfaction with style	Preferred style
Self-assessment		20%	20%	30%	30%	Participative		Participative
Subordinates	20	40%	30%	20%	10%	Authoritarian	Not satisfied	Participative
Comment: Manager needs to be less autocratic								

The output of this assessment provides an understanding of the level of satisfaction employees have with their managers' decision making style. This may give some indication of whether or not the managers will be able to lead the change with their current decision making style.

The satisfaction and acceptance of the decision making style among employees is an important cultural element that must be assessed.

Previous surveys indicate that most employees prefer a participative style. It is difficult to change the style in a short period of time. Generally, the best style is the one that keeps the subordinates motivated and committed to the change.

9.4.6   Deliverable 2.4: Leadership Assessment

The objective this deliverable is to identify to what degree the organization's leaders follow the required behaviors and mindsets of the change. The assessment should be communicated to all involved managers so they are aware of what is expected of them.

The higher the impact of the change, the more crucial the change leadership role will be. Therefore, leading by example is a very powerful strategy to indirectly communicate the change's message and establish the new required behaviors.

As Kotter indicated, the most undermining element of a change is when the behaviors of the leaders are inconsistent with their verbal communication.

The leadership assessment can be conducted by using a tool called the 360-degree leadership match. This tool includes three categories in which the evaluation is conducted: (1) the manager's superiors, (2) the manager's peers at the same level, and (3) the manager's subordinates. Each manager will also conduct a self-assessment.

This assessment is a direct change tool as the managers will pay attention to the list of behaviors and mindsets that are included in the evaluation.

It is good practice to conduct this 360-degree evaluation during the sustaining and realizing benefits phase as it helps bring attention to the change. This tool is not supposed to measure the management performance.

The tool should be designed based on the behaviors and mindsets required for the change values. In the survey, the current behaviors of managers are compared with the desired behaviors, which they should endeavor to apply.

This assessment is important as wrong behaviors by a manager may have a very negative impact and may hinder the realization of the change benefits.

Figure 9-21 shows a sample output for a specific manager in which the subordinates see a real conflict between the words and actions while the manager believes that he has a very high match.

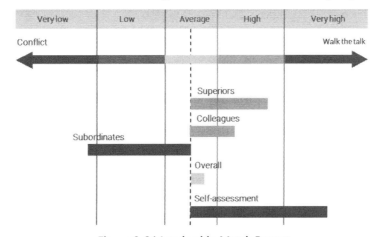

Figure 9-21. Leadership Match Report

9.5   COMPONENT 3: ASSESSING ORGANIZATIONAL ALIGNMENT

9.5.1   Overview

In change management, organizational alignment ensures that the organization has the capabilities, capacity, and resources required by the change the change. It also ensures that all organizational elements support and enable the change implementation.

9.5.2   Objective

The objective of this component is is to assess the readiness of the organizational elements, the required resources, and risks of the change.

The objective of this component is achieved by developing four deliverables. Depending on the change size, we decide which deliverables to develop. The four deliverables are shown in Figure 9-22.

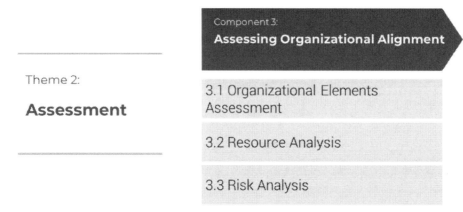

Figure 9-22. Deliverables of Assessing Organizational Alignment Component

9.5.3   Deliverable 3.1: Organizational Elements Assessment

The objective of this deliverable is to determine to what level the organizational elements are ready and aligned with the change goals.

We will use ElKattan's Organizational Alignment Framework along with its assessment tools to assess the organizational readiness. This framework provides a map of the elements that must be aligned with the change initiative. As shown in Figure 9-23, the framework is made of three perspectives; each perspective consists of a number of elements. The perspectives are as follows: (1) Strategic, (2) Capabilities, and (3) Capacity.

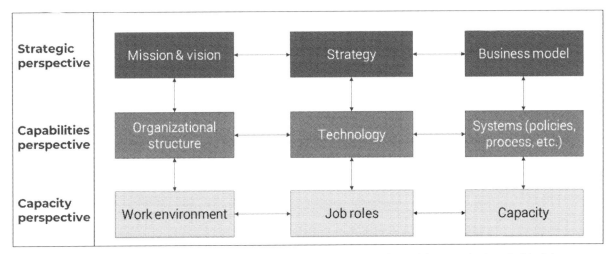

Figure 9-23. ElKattan's Organizational Alignment Framework. Adapted from Burke-Letwin Model

If all elements are not considered, the change will probably fail. Therefore, we need to assess the elements in the three perspectives to be able to have the right change management enablers and sustainers. As shown in Figure 9-24, the combination of the elements of the three perspectives indicates the organizational readiness to change.

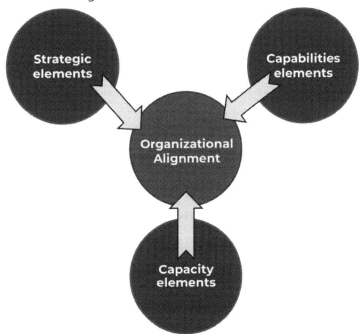

Figure 9-24. Perspectives of the Organizational Readiness

9.5.3.1   Strategic perspective

Strategic elements include: mission and vision, strategy, and business model. Elements are rated from very low to very high to reflect how ready they are to the change.

Table 9-12 below demonstrates sample criteria that can be used for rating.

Table 9-12. *Strategic Alignment Assessment*

Rate = Very low	Rating	Issues	Recommendations
1. Mission and vision			
1. Organizational mission and vision are inspiring and active.			
2. There is no conflict between the mission and the change objectives and goals.			
3. It is clear that the change initiative is one step toward achieving the long-term goals of the organization.			
2. Strategy			
1. There is a clear and direct link between the change outcomes and benefits and the organizational strategic objectives.			
2. The organizational strategic objectives are cascaded to all levels with clear measures and targets.			
3. Business model			
1. The organization is financially ready for the change.			
2. The internal value chain is well-designed to support and implement the change initiative.			
3. The change goals will positively impact the value proposition of the target customer.			

9.5.3.2   Capabilities perspective

Capabilities elements include: organizational structure, technology, and systems (business processes, procedures, regulations, performance management system, etc.). Elements are rated from very low to very high to reflect how ready they are to the change.   .

Table 9-13 below demonstrates sample criteria that can be used for rating.

Table 9-13. *Capabilities Readiness Assessment*

Rate = Very low	Rating	Issues	Recommendations
1. Organizational structure			
1. The organizational structure does not require any modifications to support the change implementation.			
2. We are ready and capable to change the organizational structure in case the change initiative requires.			
2. Technology			
1. The technology we have will support the change requirements and implementation.			
2. We are ready and capable to introduce any new technology the change may require.			
3. Systems (Processes, procedures, regulation, etc.)			
1. Current processes and regulations are well-suited to the change requirements.			
2. We are ready to adapt our systems in case the change requires.			
3. Existing systems can provide robust data to measure the change progress and performance.			

9.5.3.3   Capacity perspective

Capacity elements include: work environment, job roles, and individuals. Elements are rated from very low to very high to reflect how ready they are to the change.

The capacity indicates the availability of staff or gaps in resources or in specific positions that will require attention during the implementation of the change.

Table 9-14 below demonstrates sample criteria that can be used for rating.

Table 9-14. *Capacity Readiness Assessment*

Rate = Very low	Rating	Issues	Recommendations
1. Work environment			
1. Work environment is perfect in support of the change requirements. No changes are required.			
2. Job roles			
1. The job roles of the impacted stakeholders are suitable for the change requirements and implementation.			
3. Staff capacity			
1. We have enough staff capacity to implement the new change.			
2. The staff are mentally and psychologically ready to adapt to the new change.			

Figure 9-25 shows a sample output for such an assessment.

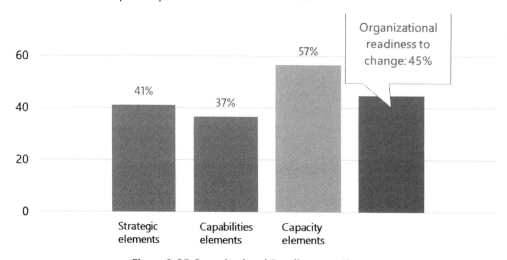

Figure 9-25. Organizational Readiness to Change

Depending on the context, the assessment is conducted either on the organizational level or on the unit level.

9.5.4   Deliverable 3.2: Resource Analysis

9.5.4.1   Objective

The objective of this analysis is to identify the existing and missing resources required by the change and who can provide these resources.

This analysis could be useful to refine our theory of change that was developed in the vision and sponsorship theme in Chapter 8. Managing the available resources could be the key to the game; if we know how to play it, our chance of winning will be high.

Now, let us see how to analyze the resources in light of the intended change. To do this, we need to have answers for the following questions:

I. Questions related to the resources that we have:

   1. What specific resources do we have that can be used to achieve the change goals?

   2. Who can provide these resources in question #1? And what do they need?

   3. What are the recommendations to utilize the existing resources to achieve the change goals?

II. Questions related to the resources that we do not have:

   4. What other specific resources do we need to achieve the change goals?

   5. Who can provide the resources identified in question #4? And what do they need?

   6. What are the recommendations to get the required change resources?

In some cases, the resource analysis could be a good tool to be used to identify the theory of change.

Example 9.2 has sample answers to the above questions that were slightly modified according to the context of the project. You can use a similar template that is used in Example 9.2 to answer the above six questions.

Example 9.2 - Resources Analysis

Table 9-15 below shows an example of a resources analysis that was conducted for a planned change to the teaching methods in a university. Please refer to Examples 8.1 and 8.2 for the change statement and vision map of the same project.

Table 9-15. *Resources Analysis*

Resources that you have	Resources that you do not have
1. What specific resources do we have that can be used to achieve the change goals? - Support of the president. - Access to external experts and trainers. - Course evaluation. - Good relations with the members of the student union, which plays an independent role in the university. - Knowledge about student-centered approach. - Social media, especially the university Facebook page.	4. What other specific resources do we need to achieve the change goals? - The buy-in and engagement of the opposition and resistance stakeholders. - Dedicated team to follow up and monitor. - Budget for the new unit and training. - Many managers do not have authority. - Lack of knowledge about how to redesign the courses. - Agreement on the new approach among all directors.
2. Who can provide these resources? And what do they need? - This is a new initiative. - Instructors who apply a student-centered approach do it as an individual way of teaching. They do not care to have it as a new initiative as the university has no interest in this regard. Therefore, they will not get any support. - They also know that other instructors have been using their methods for a long time. Everybody uses this method, which is basically one way of pushing the information from the lecturer to the students.	5. Who can provide these resources? And what do they need? - The president, VP Admin, and VP Education have the power to decide about having a dedicated team for the initiatives. - VP Admin and VP Education have the power to allocate a new budget. - Dean of Engineering and Dean of Computer Science have the authority in other schools. - The leadership team can work on securing an agreement on the new approach. - The instructors have their own courses. It is very difficult to have control the part-time instructors. And they need the following: - The interest and approval of the president. - Success stories. - Voice of the students. - Good word of mouth.
3. What are the recommendations to utilize the existing resources to achieve eh change goals? - The supporters from the faculties must agree on the same goals and start applying the new approach. - The supporters from among the students can start using social media to help promote the new initiatives. - The student union can start implementing related activities.	6. What are the recommendations to get the required change resources? - Apply change management activities to engage, motivate, and coach the different stakeholders. - Organize communication campaigns offline and online. Engage the student union in this campaign. - Provide extensive training and orientation. - Change the culture of the university.

Skill Practice 9.2 - Develop the Resources Analysis for Your Project

Use the same template that is used in the resource analysis in Example 9.2 to develop a resources analysis for your project.

Make sure that the analysis is linked with the previous analysis that you did for your project.

9.5.5   Deliverable 3.3: Risk Analysis

The objective of this deliverable is to identify the anticipated risks that may hinder the implementation of the change.

In order to analyze the risk issues, each risk should be classified according to its potential impact on change and the probability of it happening. Once you identify the potential impact of each risk of the change if it happens, you need to have a mitigation and contingency strategy and tactics. However, selecting the mitigation and contingency actions is to be done while working on the strategizing and tactics themes.

Below are the steps of performing risks analysis as discussed:

- Identify the risks that may happen.

- Assess the impact of the change if the risk happens.

- Assess the probability of each risk to happen.

- Identify the risk category.

When identifying the risks, try to avoid using generalized statements such as *workload may increase.* As much as possible, specify and quantify the increase you are referring to. Accordingly, the statement could be, for example, *workload may increase 20%-30% depending on the impacted unit.*

Figure 9-26 shows the four quadrants that are created by combining the two dimensions (impact on change and probability). You need to focus on the high risks issues.

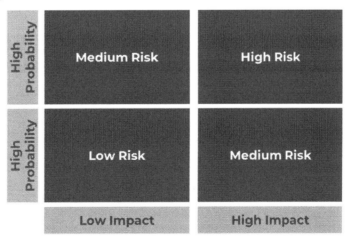

Figure 9-26. Risk Categorization

Table 9-16 presents a sample template of risks analysis.

Table 9-16. *Risks Analysis*

Risk	Impact	Probability	Category	Recommendations
Category A				
Category B				

9.6   COMPONENT 4: ASSESSING COMMUNICATION

9.6.1   Overview

Communication is considered by many researchers to be the most important element in change management. Effective communication helps increase employee readiness, create awareness, and ensure an appropriate sense of urgency. Good communication is the most effective way of encouraging people to commit to taking a risk and taking action.

In addition to the standard ways of communication, in change monument, we also depend on change narratives. So what is the difference between a narrative and a story? First, some people use them interchangeably. However, we differentiate between them as the narrative is the way you tell the story. Therefore, the story can have many different narratives depending on the narrator of the story.

"You can't really change the heart without telling a story." Martha Nussbaum.

Change management should address the heart, talk to the mind, and mobilize the emotions. Stories, like movies, can reach the heart and influence people to take new choices and actions. Narrative (or storytelling) is one of the most effective tools that addresses the heart and helps unfreeze the employees from the current state to make sure they are ready to accept the new change.

Ganz says about stories:

> "... stories are what will help others make choices. Stories are how we learn to access the moral and emotional resources of others so that they can face the uncertain, unknown, and unexpected. Because stories speak the language of emotion and the language of the heart, they help us learn not only how we and others should act, they can also inspire us – and others - with the courage to act. Because values are an important emotional resource, stories help us translate our values into action."

9.6.2 Objective

The objective of this component is to assess the internal communication and identify the stakeholder narratives regarding the change.

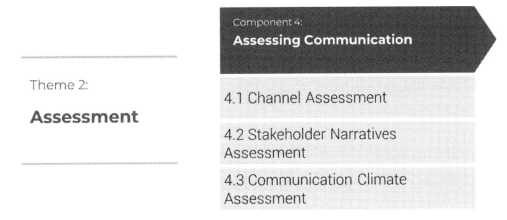

Figure 9-27. Deliverables of the Assessing Communication

9.6.3 Deliverable 4.1: Channel Assessment

The objective of this deliverable is to assess the effectiveness of the organization's communication channels that are used to deliver the messages to the stakeholders. Communication channels are the means through which people in an organization communicate. Accordingly, the management's use the most suitable and effective channels for the change. Below are the different channels that could be used:

- Staff meeting (one-on-one, group meeting, workshops, etc.)
- Social media (Facebook, Twitter, Instagram, etc.)
- Corporate internet (internal portal, company website, etc.)
- Electronic groups (WhatsApp, Telegram, etc.)
- Email
- Gathering and events

As shown in Table 9-17, effectiveness of each channel should be quantitatively rated by the both the senders and recipients. Also, issues related to each channel are to be identified.

Table 9-17. *Channel Assessment*

Channel	Effectiveness (1 to 5) (by senders)	Effectiveness (1 to 5) (by recipients)	Issues
1. Staff meeting			
2. Social media			

Channel	Effectiveness (1 to 5) (by senders)	Effectiveness (1 to 5) (by recipients)	Issues
3. Corporate internet			

9.6.4 Deliverable 4.2: Stakeholder Narratives Assessment

The objective of this deliverable is to identify the change stories that are being narrated by the impacted stakeholders themselves.

In general, there are two main levels of narrative that we will cover in this book. We will refer to them as the "stakeholder narratives" and the "sponsor narratives." The "stakeholder narratives" are the stories about the change told by the impacted stakeholders themselves.

The sharing of the positive personal stories is a good change management practice and they should also be within the change's larger stories told by the sponsors. In addition, the "sponsor narratives" should address the main aspects of the "stakeholder narratives".

People will respond to the change in different ways; and accordingly, they have different types of narrative. Stakeholder narrative can be generally categorized according to the six main resistance categories that were identified in the stakeholder assessment. Therefore, the stakeholder narratives can be classified into the following: (1) Supporters narrative, (2) Adapters narrative, (3) Accommodators narrative, (4) Rejectors narrative, (5) Neutralists, and (6) Apathetic narrative,. Below is the description of the five types of narratives.

1. **Supporters narrative.** This is the story of the stakeholders who totally accept the change to move forward to the future desired state.

2. **Adapters narrative.** This is the story of the stakeholders who partially accept the change to move forward to the future desired. state.

3. **Accommodators narrative.** This is the story of the stakeholders who partially reject the change to keep to current state.

4. **Rejectors narrative.** This is the story of the stakeholders who totally reject the change to keep to current state.

5. **Neutralists narrative.** This is the narrative of the stakeholders who feel indifferent .

6. **Apathetic narrative.** This is the narrative of the stakeholders who have no energy as a result of being frustrated and/or exhausted from previous experiences.

The stakeholder narratives can be obtained by conducting interviews and/or qualitative surveys. Figure 9-28 shows the four main stakeholder narratives.

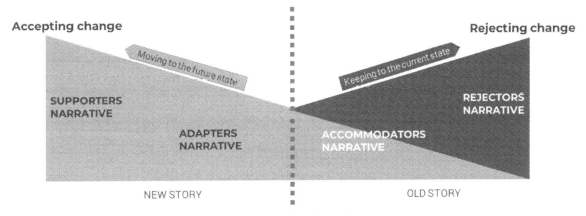

Figure 9-28. Stakeholder Narratives

9.6.5   Deliverable 4.3: 4.3 Communication Climate Assessment

The objective of this deliverable is to identify to effectiveness of the internal communication climate.

This deliverable is important to develop the right 2-way communication strategy. This assessment is related to the organizational culture dimension: Open vs Closed that was discussed in Chapter 6. The more the open the culture is, the more open feedback the organization will have.

9.7   CHAPTER IN A BOX

A summary of the assessment theme is shown in Table 9-18.

Table 9-18. *Summary of the Assessment Theme*

Theme objective	The objective of this theme is to assess stakeholders, culture, organizational alignment, and communication inside the organization, in order to enable developing the appropriate change strategy and tactics.			
Theme components	1. Assessing stakeholder readiness	2. Assessing culture	3. Assessing organizational alignment	4. Assessing communication
Component objective	The objective of this component is to identify how much the stakeholders are prepared and ready for the change along with the issues that may drive them to either support or resist the change.	The objective of this component is to identify the culture elements that may hider or motivate the change implementation and to ensure having the right change values and core values in	The objective of this component is to assess the readiness of the organizational elements, the required resources, and risks of the change.	The objective of this component is to assess the internal communication and identify the stakeholder narratives regarding the change.

		place.		
Deliverables	<ul><li>Stakeholders influence analysis</li><li>Stakeholder register and map</li><li>Stakeholder readiness assessment (ACE assessment)</li><li>Change energy index</li><li>Sponsorship assessment</li></ul>	<ul><li>Culture readiness assessment</li><li>Value assessment</li><li>Decision-making assessment</li><li>Leadership assessment</li></ul>	<ul><li>Organizational alignment assessment</li><li>Resource analysis</li><li>Risk analysis</li></ul>	<ul><li>Channel assessment</li><li>Stakeholder narrative assessment</li><li>Communication climate assessment</li></ul>

CHAPTER 10

STRATEGIZING THEME

Chapter 10 - Strategizing Theme

10.1   OVERVIEW

In change, strategizing is defined -as indicated by Marshall Ganz, as the process of making purposeful choices in the face of uncertainty. Such choices are actually assumptions that we believe will effectuate the progress of change regardless of its challenges and uncertainties. It is how we find ways to make the change happens.

Every change has its own unique dynamics, context, barriers, and best-fit strategy.

We call it "strategizing" to indicate that it is an ongoing process throughout the whole change life cycle. Ganz stated:

> "... strategy is not a single event, but an ongoing process continuing throughout the life of a change initiative. We plan our strategy, we select our actions, we evaluate the results of our actions, we plan some more, we act further, evaluate further, etc. We strategize, as we implement, not prior to it."

We actually started the strategizing process in the vision theme when we formulated our theory of change while developing the change statement. The theory of change is the most important strategy or assumption that we believe -if done- will make the change happen.

How to Continue Reading the Book

This is our third theme of the model, through which we learn how to determine the change strategy. At first, we began by developing a vision and building sponsorship (Chapter 8). Next, an assessment was conducted along our four work streams: stakeholder management, culture management, organizational alignment, and communication management (Chapter 9). In this chapter, we will develop the strategy to be used along the four work streams. Next, in Chapter 11, we will identify the change management tactics. Finally, in Chapter 12, we will appraise the change and develop the change management plan.

In case you are interested to understand a particular work stream, you can continue reading only its components in both this chapter (strategizing theme) and the next chapter (tactics theme). Figure 10-1 shows the four work streams of the model as discussed in Chapter 7.

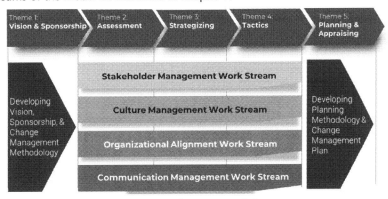

Figure 10-1. The Four Work Streams

10.2 OBJECTIVE

The objective of the strategizing theme is to formulate the assumptions that -if done- will presumably make the change happen. This includes the stakeholder strategy, culture strategy, organizational alignment strategy, and communication strategy. This objective would be achieved by implementing the related components and deliverables along the model's four work streams as presented in Figure 10-2.

Theme 3: Strategizing			
Component 1: Developing stakeholder management strategy	**Component 2:** Developing culture management strategy	**Component 3:** Developing Org. alignment strategy	**Component 4:** Developing comm. management strategy
1.1 Involvement strategy	2.1 Direct vs. indirect change strategy	3.1 Organizational elements objectives	4.1 Two-way communication strategy
1.2 Motivation strategy	2.2 Culture management objectives	3.2 Resource objectives	4.2 Communication theme strategy
1.3 Managing resistance strategy	2.3 Leadership objectives	3.3 Risk management strategy	4.3 Relationship strategy
1.4 Stakeholder management objectives (ACE objectives)			4.4 Change narrative strategy

Figure 10-2. Components and Deliverables of the Strategizing Theme

I will include here the summary of the components and deliverables that are shown in Figure 10-2 so that you have the choice of focusing, skimming, or skipping whatever you want based on what is of most relevance to your case.

COMPONENT 1: DEVELOPING STAKEHOLDER MANAGEMENT STRATEGY

The objective of this component is to have the assumptions, that if done, will keep the stakeholders aware, competent, and engaged to achieve the change outcomes and benefits.

Deliverable 1.1: Involvement Strategy

The objective of this deliverable is to determine to what extent the different stakeholders are involved in the change.

Deliverable 1.2: Motivation Strategy

The objective of this deliverable is to define the motivation types to use for the different stakeholders.

Deliverable 1.3: Managing Resistance Strategy

The objective of this strategy is to define the strategy that will be used to manage the resistance to change.

Deliverable 1.4: Stakeholder Management Objectives (ACE Objectives)

The objective of this deliverable is to formulate the objectives to have the stakeholders aware, competent, and engaged throughout the implementation of the change.

COMPONENT 2: DEVELOPING CULTURE MANAGEMENT STRATEGY

The objective of this component is to formulate the assumptions of what culture aspects to be changed to motivate acceptance and implementation of the change.

Deliverable 2.1: Direct vs. Indirect Change Strategy

The objective of this deliverable is to define to what degree the direct and indirect approaches will be used to reshape the organizational culture.

Deliverable 2.2: Culture Management Objectives

The objective of this deliverable is to determine to what degree the values will be managed to help reshape the organizational culture.

Deliverable 2.3: Leadership Objectives

The objective of this deliverable is to decide what change the leaders should do based on their leadership match and decision-making assessments.

COMPONENT 3: DEVELOPING ORGANIZATIONAL ALIGNMENT STRATEGY

The objective of this component is to formulate the assumptions, that if done, will presumably ensure that the organizational elements and resources help enable and sustain the change.

Deliverable 3.1: Organizational Elements Objectives

The objective of this deliverable is to formulate the objectives that will help prepare the organizational elements to enable and sustain the change initiatives.

Deliverable 3.2: Resource Objectives

The objective of this deliverable is to identify how to get and utilize the required resources for the change.

Deliverable 3.3: Risk Mitigation Strategy

The objective of this deliverable is to identify the risks that should be managed along with their mitigation and/or contingency plans.

COMPONENT 4: DEVELOPING COMMUNICATION MANAGEMENT STRATEGY

The objective of this component is to ensure that the change vision along with its outcomes and benefits are communicated in an effective way to all target stakeholders.

Deliverable 4.1: Two-Way Communication Strategy

The objective of this deliverable is to define to what degree the two-way communication activities will be used to help understand the stakeholder perceptions.

Deliverable 4.2: Communication Theme Strategy

The objective of this deliverable is to define to what degree the communication content reflects emotional and rational messages.

Deliverable 4.3: Relationship Strategy

The objective of this deliverable is to define to what degree building the relationship with the stakeholder will be done one-to-one or one-to-many.

Deliverable 4.4: Change Narrative Strategy

The objective of change narratives strategy is to define what type of change narrative to develop.

10.3 COMPONENT 1: DEVELOPING STAKEHOLDER MANAGEMENT STRATEGY

10.3.1 Overview

The stakeholder management strategy is built around our assumptions that we believe will make the change progress in spite of the challenges and uncertainties that come with the change. It is how we find ways to keep the stakeholders engaged and competent to achieve the required outcomes and benefits.

In order to formulate the right stakeholder management strategy, we should have answers to the following questions that are supposed to be addressed in the vision and the assessment themes:

- What is the problem that triggered the change?
- How are the power and influence distributed inside the organization?
- Who are the potential resistors to the change? And why?
- Do we anticipate a harmful resistance? And why?
- Who is unsatisfied with the current state? And why?
- What are the stakeholders shared needs and interests?
- What is the change governance?
- Who are the potential ambassadors for the change?
- What are the issues that prevent having a high stakeholder readiness?
- What are the dominant emotions toward the change?
- What are the apparent change resistance behaviors?
- What is the change energy index?

Important Note

As movement away from the present state toward a new state occurs, different strategies can be selected based on the context to give affected stakeholders the time to disengage from the pain of the loss.

10.3.2 Objective

The objective of this component is to have the assumptions, that if done, will keep the stakeholders aware, competent, and engaged to achieve the change outcomes and benefits. The objective is achieved by developing the five deliverables shown in Figure 10-3.

Theme 3:

Strategizing

Component 1:
Developing Stakeholder Management Strategy

1.1 Involvement Strategy

1.2 Motivation Strategy

1.3 Managing Resistance Strategy

1.4 Stakeholder Management Objectives (ACE Objectives)

Figure 10-3. Deliverables of Developing the Stakeholder Management Strategy Component

Important Note

"Getting into my territory" is usually one of the greatest sources of resistance to planned change and requires extensive resistance management.

10.3.3 Deliverable 1.1: Involvement Strategy

10.3.3.1 Overview

When it comes to change, *involvement* is one the most frequently used words. Most researchers agree that involvement is one of the most important practices for change management (Pihlak & Alas, 2012). This is simply because involvement is the quickest way to get commitment, increase engagement, and mitigate the risk of the expected resistance.

Involving employees creates both a sense of co-ownership and a corporate sense among all employees that "we are all in it together." Some people who are not involved will psychologically lack the value of commitment and may therefore feel as though the intended change is being imposed on them (Burke, 2010). As we discussed in Chapter 1, many people who resist the imposed idea are psychologically resisting the imposition, not the idea itself.

One major drawback of involvement is the fact that it may be enormously time-consuming (Kotter and Schlesinger, 1979). Also, involvement may be a double-edged sword, as employees may view their involvement as a method of manipulation to get their buy-in without really taking their feedback into consideration. If involvement is perceived as manipulation, it will have very harmful and negative consequences. Therefore, change leadership team must have a clear and transparent process of getting feedback, analyzing, communicating, revisiting, and taking corrective action.

Important Note

Most researchers agree that involvement is one of the most important practices for change management as it leads to engagement and commitment (Pihlak & Alas, 2012).

Even though involvement may help achieve better coordination, commitment, alignment, and buy-in from the stakeholders, it should be implemented carefully during crises or when a quick change must be implemented for urgency purposes (Pihlak and Alas, 2012). We should also note that culture has its own influence. For example, in some cultures, such as India, employees may not expect very much involvement from their supervisors.

Getting feedback that yield in corrective actions should be considered throughout the implementation of the change initiative. Afterward, clear and effective communication that is built on the results of the feedback should follow with whoever was part of the involvement process cycle.

Figure 10-4 shows the involvement process cycle, which has the following five steps: (1) Request to get feedback from concerned stakeholders, (2) Inform the stakeholder when you will revisit the actions and decisions, (3) Analyze the current situation in light of the given feedback, (4) Decide on the corrective actions, and finally (5) communicate back to the stakeholders with whatever decisions that have been taken with the why behind.

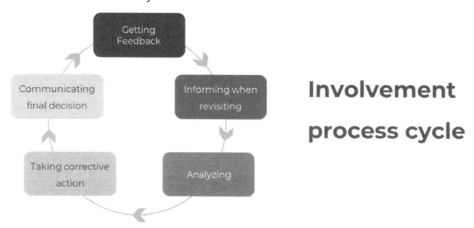

Figure 10-4. Involvement Process Cycle

Now, we know the involvement process, so what do I mean by the involvement strategy?

Involvement strategy is the degree of involvement to be achieved with the stakeholders to make the change happen.

10.3.3.2   Objective

The objective of this deliverable is to determine to what extent the different stakeholders are involved in the change.

10.3.3.3 Dimension of the involvement strategy

Normally, the overall involvement strategy is determined by giving a score from 0 to 100 for the whole organization or for each group. The higher score, the more involvement will be used indicating that the change is not planned and managed in a closed room. The lower the score, the more imposition will be used.

Referring to Figure 10-11, a score of 0 represents an extreme push strategy (total imposition). This strategy can be translated into "*do what you are told to do.*"

The score of 25 means there will pushing for the decisions with less involvement. This strategy can be translated into "*we will keep you informed.*" Usually, in this case, the leader (alone or with his closed circle) identifies the problem, suggests the solution, and starts pushing for actionable items to achieve the target using one-way communication. This may be an effective strategy if the subordinates are very low caliber with low maturity and/or experience. It may also result in a faster change, as readiness and engagement will take less time. However, it is ineffective in terms of ownership and buy-in and will make it very difficult to engage both the heart and head in the change.

Usually the decision makers, especially in a high power distance culture, prefer to have the pull strategy (full involvement) with a small number of people.

A score of 50 means a hybrid option between the push and pull strategies. Engagement will still be the goal and two-way communication will be used to generate sufficient commitment and buy-in.

On the other hand, the score of 75 means there will be more pulling with less pushing for the required actions. This strategy can be translated into "*we will proceed after getting your feedback.*" This will cultivate great engagement, buy-in, and commitment. It will also sustain the change. However, it will be far more time consuming, especially when some involved people do not have the required experience to participate.

While a score of 100 represents an extreme pull strategy (total involvement). This is translated to the message: "*Let us create out future together.*"

Important Note

A reduction in the stakeholders' problems should not be a goal in itself and is not evidence of progress in the change effort, as change may create new problems in the process of reaching its end result.

Figure 10-5 represents the dimension of the involvement strategy.

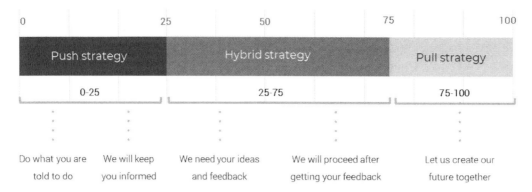

Figure 10-5. Dimension of the Involvement Strategy

In a general sense, the more we involve people, the more commitment and buy-in we get from them, which is good for the change. However, it also depends on the context of the organization, along with its level of maturity. An in-between strategy or hybrid approach will probably suit most situations.

As shown in Figure 10-6, power and interest greatly impact the involvement strategy. These two factors were analyzed in the "stakeholder influence analysis" deliverable in the assessment theme.

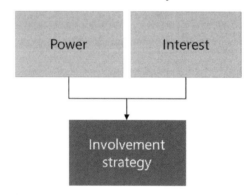

Figure 10-6. Inputs to the Involvement Strategy

The stakeholder influence was classified as: A+, A, B, C, and C-. These five influence groups can generally match the different involvement strategies as follows:

1. **Pull strategy (Score: 75-100)**

   This strategy can be used with the A+ and A groups. These two groups of stakeholders should be involved while taking decisions throughout the implementation of the change.

2. **Hybrid strategy (Score: 25-75)**

   This strategy is mainly used with the B group. This group of stakeholders should be at least consulted while taking decisions throughout the implementation of the change.

3. **Push strategy (Score: 0-25)**

   This strategy can be used with the C and the C- groups. These groups of stakeholders should at least be informed about the progress of the change and the decisions pertaining to it.

Depending on the context, the involvement score and strategy (pull, hybrid, or push) can be selected on either the organizational level, the unit level, or the individual level. Table 10-1 presents a template that can be used to indicate the involvement strategy on the different levels.

Table 10-1. *Stakeholder Involvement Strategy*

#	Name	Involvement score	Involvement strategy	Comments
	Organization	50	Hybrid strategy	
Key Individuals				
1	Key stakeholder 1	50	Hybrid strategy	
2	Key stakeholder 2	75	Pull strategy	
Units				
1	Unit A	50	Hybrid strategy	
2	Unit B	25	Push strategy	

10.3.4 Deliverable 1.2: Motivation Strategy

10.3.4.1 Overview

The motivation strategy is the heart of our stakeholder management strategy. You need to understand the stakeholders personal needs and interests before selecting the motivation types to use. Also, it is important to know what previous actions motivated the stakeholders.

10.3.4.2 Objective

The objective of this deliverable is to define the motivation types to use for the different stakeholders.

Human beings are complex creatures. They are a complicated mix of feelings, desires, and ambitions. They are by nature enthusiastic and engaged when performing any type of work if they are motivated. However, everyone has their own motivational profile. There are many theories that address how to determine an individual's motivational profile, such as the outcome-based theory, the content-based theory, and the process-based theory.

Important Note

Two of the most effective engagement strategies are increasing the sense of urgency and increasing the level of dissatisfaction with the current status quo.

The ElKattan's Model adapts the outcome-based theory to understand how stakeholders can be motivated.

I will give a summary of the outcome-based theory, and how it helps develop the motivation strategy for any change initiative. This theory states that the consequences of an action reinforce a person's future behaviors. It classifies motivation into four types: extrinsic, intrinsic, contribution, and relational. Below are the descriptions of the four types:

Extrinsic motivation

The extrinsic motivation is the stakeholders' willingness to act because of the positive or negative extrinsic motives that they expect to receive.

It is about what reward or punishment people will receive in exchange for their behaviors. Positive extrinsic motives are the formal rewards that the individual may receive, such as an increase in salary, a bonus, a cash incentive, recognition, status, or promotion. Negative extrinsic motives are the punishments that the individual may receive, such as financial sanctions, loss of face, and suspension of promotion.

Intrinsic motivation

The intrinsic motivation is the stakeholders' willingness to act because of the internal satisfaction they will receive.

It is about what satisfaction people will get from carrying out their behaviors. There are also positive and negative intrinsic motives. Examples of positive intrinsic motives are the desire to learn, enjoyment of the task, passion for the task, and personal challenge. Negative intrinsic motives could be finding the task boring and not challenging.

Contribution motivation

The contribution motivation is the stakeholders' willingness to act because of the benefits they expect others to experience as a consequence of their actions.

The keyword is "others". It is about acting for the benefit of others, such as helping people who have problems through community development projects. Another example of a contribution motive is helping achieve the mission of the organization. There are also negative contribution motives, as people may be motivated to act to cause negative consequences for others for whatever reason.

Relational motivation

The relational motivation is the stakeholders' willingness to act because of the expected impact in the relationship with their external environment.

For example, an individual may act to improve the relationship with their boss. Examples of relational motives are gaining the trust of others, fulfilling commitments, and pleasing the boss. In many cases, having good relationships is an important step in satisfying extrinsic motives.

As shown in Figure 10-7, the actions of individuals will be influenced by the four types of motivation. The weight of the four types for any individual represents their motivational profile.

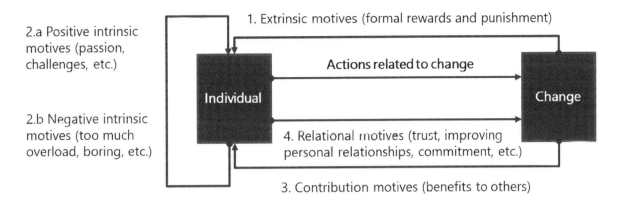

Figure 10-7. Individual's Motives Toward a Change. Adapted from Basics in Work Motivation, IESE, 2004.

The motivation strategy highly depends on the adapted motivation types. The organization (or each department, unit, or individual) could be assigned a relative weight so that the total weight is 100%. The weight of the four types will make the generic motivation strategy.

For example, as shown in Figure 10-8, if Extrinsic: 30%, Intrinsic: 20%, Contribution: 10%, and Relational: 40%, then the motivation strategy for the change initiative should be mainly balanced between extrinsic and relational motives. This motivation strategy reflects how the employees inside the organization are best motivated.

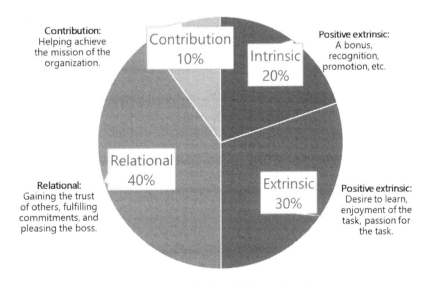

Figure 10-8. Organizational Motivation Strategy

10.3.5   Deliverable 1.3: Managing Resistance Strategy

10.3.5.1   Overview

As indicated in Chapter 2, having the right amount of resistance to change can be healthy; however, if the resistance increases to reach a certain threshold, it can become a real obstacle to change.

Sources of resistance should not be overcome, avoided, or excluded; rather, it should be managed, dealt with, and utilized properly. We do not overcome or exclude the resistance as is mainly an emotional process that stems from experiencing certain feelings, and feelings are to be addressed not excluded.

People will not invariably resist the change. It is quite obvious that people will not resist if they believe that the change is going to serve their own personal interests. On the other hand, people will normally resist if they believe personal disbenefits will result from the change. Therefore, it is important to manage resistance on the individual level together with the organizational level.

Generally, everyone's brain automatically makes a benefit analysis based on the perceived picture of the change. If the brain perceives that the short-term and long-term benefits do not greatly outweigh the effort required, it will not be motivated to participate.

Resistance to change develops as a result of many reasons, and it largely depends on the context. For example, change may be resisted if people have the perception that it is purposed for personal or political reasons. They also resist for more personal reasons, for instance, if they do not like, or trust the manager.

It is recommended to keep an eye on the energy index introduced in Chapter 9. You should not only focus on people who show resistance, but also on neutralists and apathetic groups so as to maintain the project's energy and momentum. Also, having a good network of supporters and ambassadors reduces resistance to a manageable level.

Managers in a large power distance culture may assume that stakeholders will be engaged with the change as soon as the project is announced. They may not notice the silent resistance due to the huge gap between the top management and employees.

10.3.5.2   Objective

The objective of this strategy is to define the strategy that will be used to manage the resistance to change.

Having the right resistance management requires a detailed analysis of the context, culture, stakeholders' personalities, awareness, and capabilities.

10.3.5.3   Managing resistance strategy

There are different strategies that can be selected for managing resistance. One of these strategies is the Pushing/Pulling strategy. This strategy is your choice to measure to what degree resistance is pulled out to be discussed openly with neither fighting nor precluding it. This strategy uses a scoring model on a scale from 0 to 100.

The higher the score, the more the people encouraged to express their concerns freely and openly in a completely safe environment with no fights or head-on battles. In this case, the company may bear more lose-win situations, especially when many people are having emotional resistance due to losing some of their benefits. A Lose-win situation indicates that the company is willing to give more than expected to people who show resistance.

The lower the score is, the larger the magnitude of the pushing back against resistance and its prohibition from being discussed. Pushing too much may intensify resistance, cause frustration, and drain energy.

Figure 10-9 shows the dimension of the managing resistance strategy.

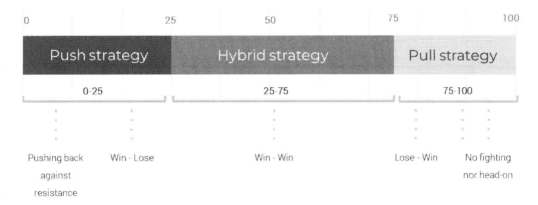

Figure 10-9. Managing Resistance Strategy

The more managing resistance push strategy, the more assertiveness and/or anger that is used especially with the apathetic people. Also, confronting managers could be terminated or moved out from the way.

The more managing resistance pull strategy, the more trade-off and/or reassurance approaches to be used especially with the political resistance people.

10.3.6 Deliverable 1.4: Stakeholder Management Objectives (ACE Objectives)

10.3.6.1 Objective

The objective of this deliverable is to formulate the objectives to have the stakeholders aware, competent, and engaged throughout the implementation of the change.

10.3.6.2 Issue analysis

Before selecting our ACE objectives, we need to identify the importance of the issues that were identified during the ACE assessment. The issues should be classified according to their importance. Figure 10-10 shows a sample of a suggested classification for the issues.

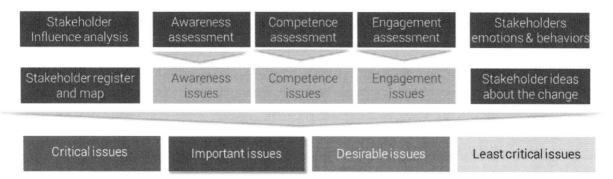

Figure 10-10. Classifications of the Stakeholder Issues

The analysis can be done intuitively using the experience and knowledge about the context.

The identified issues are to be managed by selecting the right stakeholder management objectives. The objectives should be based on one of the following change management practices:

1. Stakeholder management

    o   Involving

    o   Motivating

    o   Managing resistance

    o   Coaching

    o   Developing technical competence

    o   Sponsoring

2. Culture management

    o   Developing behavioral competence

3. Organizational alignment

    o   Managing resources

    o   Mitigating risks

4. Communication management

    o   Communicating

    o   Understanding perception

    o   Building relationships

5. Planning

    o   Agile (iterative) planning

Figure 10-11 shows the change management practices that can be selected to formulae the stakeholder management objectives.

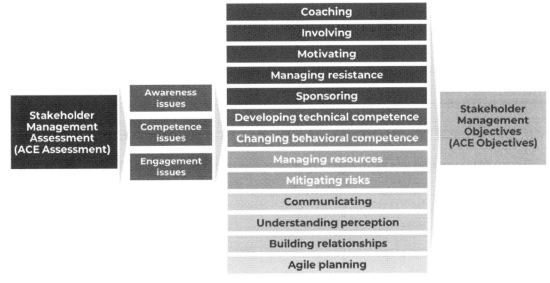

Figure 10-11. ACE Objectives

Table 10-2. *Sample ACE Objectives*

Issue	Stakeholder	Issue category	CM Practice	Recommended objective
Not interested in the change.	Stakeholder A	Critical	Communicating	Communicate the support that is provided, including training, coaching, resources, and sponsorship.
Talking negatively about the change goals.	Stakeholder B	Important	Coaching	Conduct one-on-one coaching to highlight the risks of not changing.
Does not want to support the change.	Stakeholder C	Least critical	Involving	More involvement in the change processes.

10.4   COMPONENT 2: DEVELOPING CULTURE MANAGEMENT STRATEGY

10.4.1 Overview

It is said that culture eats new changes for breakfast! The culture strategy is all about deciding what change is required for the current behaviors and mindsets inside the organization. Such a change is critical, as behaviors and mindsets highly influence the acceptance or rejection of new ideas within a group. Therefore, when culture is aligned with the change goals, it releases a great amount of energy toward achieving the change goals.

People often ask: "What are the aspects of a good organizational culture?" Generally speaking, there is no good or bad organizational culture. When it comes to business, organizational culture could be functional or dysfunctional depending on the industry, context, maturity, and specific issues related to the organization.

Change is mainly about managing people, and culture is one of the most powerful influencers over how people behave and how they relate to each other.

When it comes to change, the organizational culture could motivate or hinder the change. This mainly depends on the fit between the change goals and the behaviors, norms, and mindsets inside the organization. Therefore, we need to define what change we wish to see in our culture – and this is the culture strategy.

This book uses the six culture dimensions (values) and the eight culture styles (values) that were identified and assessed in Chapter 9 to answer the above questions. These values can be used for most of the projects. However, some projects may require other specific values as explained in Example 9.1.

10.4.2 Objective

The objective of this component is to formulate the assumptions of what culture aspects to be changed to motivate acceptance and implementation of the change. It is not recommended to change many culture aspects at the same time.

The objective of this component is achieved by developing the deliverables shown in Figure 10-12.

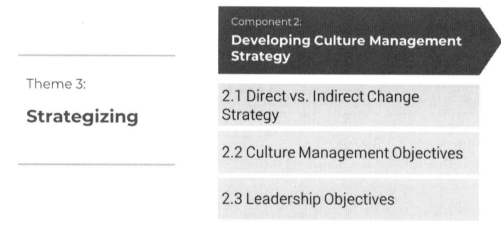

Figure 10-12. Deliverables of Developing the Culture Strategy Component

This component mainly answers the question: What are the desired values along with their mindsets and behaviors that we want to have to motivate the change implementation?

Before start developing the component along with its deliverables, we should have -based on culture assessment- answers for the following questions:

1. What are the mindsets and behaviors of the people in our organization? How well are they aligned with the intended change? If there is a misalignment, what problems can we expect due to this misalignment?

2. What is the culture readiness to change? And how can we enhance this readiness?

3. Do the norms and etiquette help sustain the change? And if not, what new norms and etiquette do we need to have?

10.4.3   Deliverable 2.1: Direct vs. Indirect Change Strategy

The objective of this deliverable is to define to what degree the direct and indirect approaches will be used to reshape the organizational culture.

There are two approaches that can be used to change behaviors: direct change and indirect change. The direct change approach, also called the "tell and see" approach, is what most managers use. In using this approach, managers use their authority to tell their subordinates what new changes in behavior they need to adopt.

Changing behaviors using this approach may not work, as changing behaviors is not that straightforward. If it does work, it may not be sustainable as it is not deeply embedded in the culture. However, in some cases the direct approach may be convenient to use with top management.

However, the indirect change is done by changing the work environment to such a degree that employees would prefer to adjust their behaviors accordingly.

Both approaches are important and required. However, which approach to use more depends on the context and the profile of the target people. For example, in the case of top management, direct change is to be used and will be more effective. If they do not change, they could be replaced. Also, direct change will be more effective in case of crises. On the other hand, indirect change is more effective when the organization has a low authority culture style. The effectiveness of indirect change is normally higher than of a direct approach, but it should always be supported by direct change.

Normally, this strategy is determined by giving a score from 0 to 100 for the whole organization, group, or individuals. A score of 0 represents a total direct approach for reshaping the culture, while a score of 100 represents a total indirect approach. If a score of 75 is given, this generally means that the indirect approach is almost 75% of the activities. Figure 10-13 represents the dimension of the direct vs. indirect culture change. strategy.

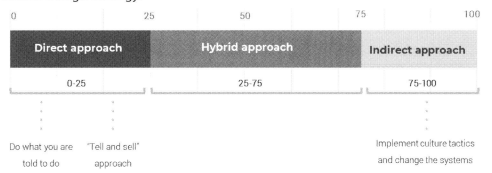

Figure 10-13. Dimension of the Direct vs. Indirect Culture Change

10.4.4   Deliverable 2.2: Culture Management Objectives

The objective of this deliverable is to determine to what degree the values will be managed to help reshape the organizational culture.

As explained in the value assessment deliverable, we have different types of values to consider. The change values, the culture values, and the organizational core values.

We should check the results of the value assessment on two levels: (1) The values level and (2) The behaviors and mindsets level.

Figure 10-14 shows value assessment results on the values levels for three values (Value 1, Value 2, and Value 3) as well as the value assessment results on the behaviors and mindsets level for three behaviors associated with Value 1 (Behavior 1, Behavior 2, and Behavior 3).

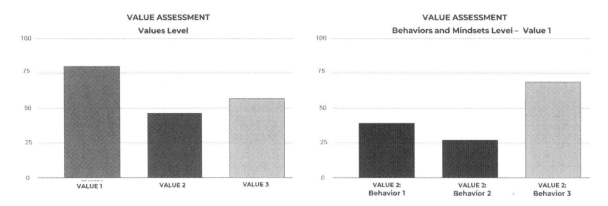

Figure 10-14. Value Assessment Levels

Referring to the example in Figure 10-20, the value objectives could address only Value 2 with two objectives to manage behavior 1 and behavior 2.

It is not recommended to change everything at the same time, as this will create an overload of work that may not be easily managed.

Tables 10-3 and 10-4 show templates that could be used for this deliverable.

Table 10-3. *Value Objectives – Level 1*

Value	Score	Objective

Table 10-4. *Value Objectives – Level 2*

Behavior/Mindset	Score	Objective
Value name:		

10.4.5 Deliverable 2.3: Leadership Objectives

The objective of this deliverable is to decide what change the leaders should do based on their leadership match and decision-making assessments.

The leadership match assessment results will have similar results as presented in Figure 10-20.

As shown in Table 10-5, the objective is to be formulated for each manager based on the manager's 360 degree evaluation.

Table 10-5. *Leadership Objectives*

Behavior/Mindset	Superior assessment	Peer assessment	Subordinate assessment	Self-assessment	Objective
Manager name:					

10.5 COMPONENT 3: DEVELOPING ORGANIZATIONAL ALIGNMENT STRATEGY

10.5.1 Overview

The organizational alignment strategy should lead to having tangible results that can be easily realized. Also, it reflects how serious the top management are regarding supporting the change initiative.

The organizational alignment strategy is to be developed based on the organizational elements assessment, the resource analysis, and the risk analysis that are conducted in the assessment theme.

As shown in Figure 10-15, the organizational alignment strategy is the consolidated objectives of organizational elements objectives, the resource objectives, and the risk management objectives.

Figure 10-15. Organizational Alignment Strategy

Theoretically, each issue should be managed be an associated objective.

10.5.2 Objective

The objective of this component is to formulate the assumptions, that if done, will presumably ensure that the organizational elements and resources help enable and sustain the change.

As we need to both enable and sustain the change, the change management objectives can be generally classified as enablers or sustainers.

The enabler objectives are those objectives related to increase readiness and manage the transition phase, while the sustainer objectives are those objectives related to reinforce the change and make it last.

This deliverables of the component are shown in Figure 10-16.

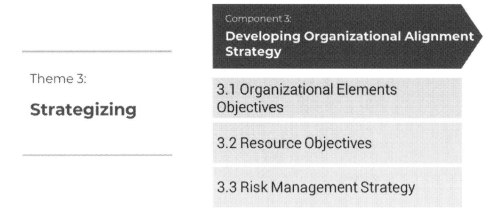

Figure 10-16. Deliverables of Developing the Organizational Alignment Strategy Component

10.5.3 Deliverable 3.1: Organizational Elements Objectives

The objective of this deliverable is to formulate the objectives that will help prepare the organizational elements to enable and sustain the change initiatives.

The organizational elements were assessed in Chapter 9 using ElKattan's Organizational Alignment Framework that was adapted from the Burke-Litwin Model (Brief description about the Burke-Litwin Model is provided in Appendix A).

The framework has three perspectives (strategy, capacities, and capacity) that include nine elements. Every element has bilateral arrows with other elements.

The question is why do we have two-sided arrows between all the elements?

Because there is a relation that happens between all the elements. When we have a change in one element, this change will influence other elements as well.

An organizations is just like the human body when one organ complains the rest of the body suffers sleepless and fever.

The change leadership should develop an organizational alignment strategy in a way to address all possible impacted elements and to make sure that all organizational elements help enable and sustain the change.

To develop the organizational elements objectives, we do the following steps:

1. Analyze the organizational elements issues in each one of the three perspective: (1) Strategy, (2) Capabilities, and (3) Capacity.

2. Categorize each issue as: (1) Critical, (2) Important, (3) Desirable, or (4) Least critical.

3. Formulate the organizational elements objective for the issues.

4. Check the impact of each objective on the remaining elements.

These four steps of developing the organizational elements objectives is shown in Figure 10-17 below:

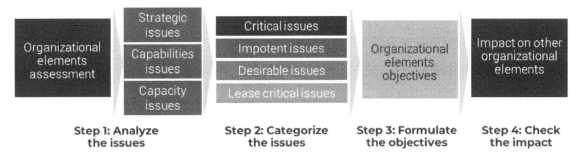

| Step 1: Analyze the issues | Step 2: Categorize the issues | Step 3: Formulate the objectives | Step 4: Check the impact |

Figure 10-17. Steps of Developing the Organizational Elements Objectives

Table 10-6 shows a sample of this deliverable.

Table 10-6. *Organizational Elements Objectives Template*

#	Issue	Issue category	Recommended objective	Impact on other elements
Strategic elements				
Capabilities elements				
Capacity elements				

10.5.4 Deliverable 3.2: Resource Objectives

The objective of this deliverable is to identify how to get and utilize the required resources for the change.

Figure 10-18 has the relationship between the resource analysis and the resource objectives.

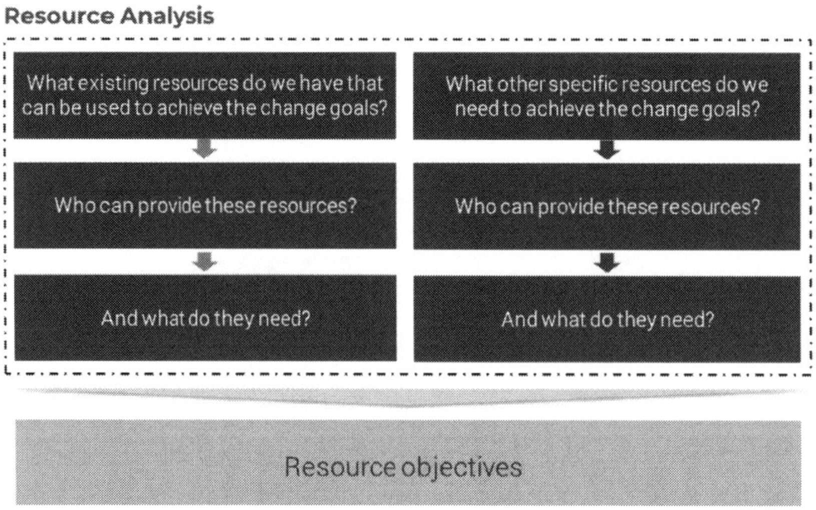

Resource Analysis

Figure 10-18. Relationship Between the Resource Analysis and the Resource Objectives

The objectives will be based on the resource assessment that was explained in Chapter 9. This deliverable should answer the following two questions:

1. What can we do to utilize the existing resources to achieve the change goals?

2. What can we do to get the required change resources?

10.5.5 Deliverable 3.3: Risk Management Strategy

The objective of this deliverable is to identify the risks that should be managed along with their mitigation and/or contingency plans.

Human beings naturally identify risk and carry out risk management. For example, if you are travelling by car, then you identify that having a flat tire is a risk, so you complete two actions. Firstly, you make sure that the tires have enough air to reduce the chances of the risk occurring. This is called a risk mitigation plan. Secondly, you ensure that you have a backup tire. This is called a risk backup or contingency plan.

Risk management is common in both project management and change management. Project management focuses on risks related to time, scope, and budget. However, change management focuses more on risks related to readiness, sustainability, enabling outcomes and realizing benefits.

The risk management strategy for the identifies risks will one of the following: (1) Prepare mitigation and contingency plans, (2) Prepare contingency plan only, (3) Accept the risk, and (4) Avoid the risk completely.

Table 10-7 presents a sample template of the risk management strategy.

Table 10-7. *Risk Management Objectives Template*

Risk	Mitigation and contingency	Contingency	Accept	Avoid
Category A				

Risk	Mitigation and contingency	Contingency	Accept	Avoid
Risk A	√			
Risk B		√		
Category B				
Risk C			√	
Risk D				√

10.6 COMPONENT 4: DEVELOPING COMMUNICATION MANAGEMENT STRATEGY

10.6.1 Overview

Communication is very important in all aspects of leadership and management. However, when it comes to change, communication is considered by many researchers to be the most critical component. Effective communication is one of the best ways to encourage people to commit to take the risk and act.

Researchers indicated that one of the most common mistakes that causes a change not to be successful is the failure to have an effectively communication. Effective communication requires developing the right communication strategy.

> **Important Note**
>
> In a change effort, communicating what will not be changed and what is unknown is just as important as communicating what will be changed and what is known.

Depending on the assessment and strategizing of the other work streams, communication may tackle critical issues related to change, such as complacency, fear, apathy, and uncertainty.

It must also elevate the sense of urgency if it is required int eh stakeholder management strategy and tactics.

Ideally, the change communication should include all individuals to make it absolutely clear to them how and why the change is happening. Some stakeholders will experience the dilemma of losing control and changing the way they have done things for years. They also may no longer be the main point of reference. For those stakeholders, you need to acknowledge their previous efforts and give them some time to adjust to the idea of the new change. Then, show commitment helping them adapt to the new way of doing things. Finally, point to their behaviors that need to be changed.

Do not expect that people who will blindly resist the change due to organizational politics would quickly accept the change. Give them time to get used to the idea of the new change. Negotiate and try

CHAPTER 2: BRIDGING THE GAP

to come up with a win-win strategy. It is good practice to start from a common ground and discuss long-term benefits instead of short-term benefits.

10.6.2 Objective

The objective of this component is to ensure that the change vision along with its outcomes and benefits are communicated in an effective way to all target stakeholders. The deliverables of the component are shown in Figure 10-19.

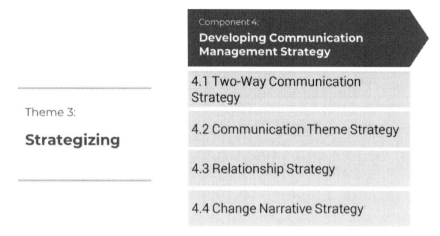

Figure 10-19. Deliverables of Developing the Communication Strategy Component

10.6.3 Deliverable 4.1: Two-Way Communication Strategy

The objective of this deliverable is to define to what degree the two-way communication activities will be used to help understand the stakeholder perceptions.

Normally, the change message is translated on the receiving end, as shown in Figure 10-20, into the following aspects: (1) Perceived loss, (2) Perceived gain, and (3) Business message.

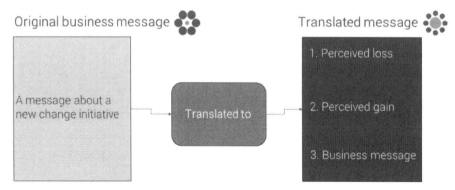

Figure 10-20. Translation of a Business Message

Perceived loss and perceived gain are widely referred to by the question: How will this impact me? The communicated message may be totally distorted in terms of the perceived message.

But, how can you disclose this perceived message?

Page 266 of 410

In order to understand how the message is perceived, you need to have a two-way communication to understand the recipients' perception.

Important Note

The first question asked by most people about organizational change concerns the personal impact, not the business objectives or the general nature of the future state.

As shown in Figure 10-21, we can have a two-way communication dimension. This dimension has a scale from 0 to 100, where 100 represents total two-way communication. A score of 10 means that the communication will be primarily pushing the information without much interaction with the audience.

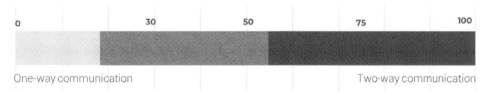

Figure 10-21. Two-Way Communication Dimension

The required degree of the two-way communication should be reflected in the communication plan and activities.

The more the pull strategy, the more two-way communication approaches to use. Two-way communication is very important to use to determine how people perceive the message and their degree of awareness. Communication must be designed to address both the awareness aspect (head) and the engagement aspect (heart) in order to increase the readiness to change.

Figure 10-22 shows the relationship between effective communication and readiness to change.

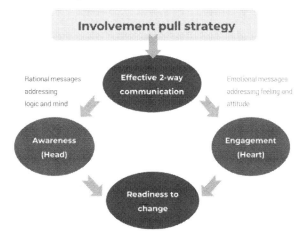

Figure 10-22. Relationship Between Communication and Readiness to Change

10.6.4   Deliverable 4-2: Communication Theme Strategy

The objective of this deliverable is to define to what degree the communication content reflects emotional and rational messages.

Change management can be defined as management of the acceptance of new choices and actions. So, how do people accept new choices and actions?

People see the world through two lenses: rational/logical (head) and emotional (heart). Therefore, the communication them strategy should be selected to take into account the degree to which both the heart and the head need to be addressed. This commognition theme strategy should be reflected in al the commutation messages and activities.

The theme should also determine whether the intended communication would be addressing the rational side (head) or the emotional side (heart).

As shown in Figure 10-23, we have two prospective dimensions for the theme (emotional vs. rational), The decision regarding the communication theme is estimated within a scale from 0 to 100, where 0 represents a totally rational theme, and 100 represents a totally emotional theme. As shown in Figure 10-24, a score of 50 means that the key messages need to be balanced between addressing the head and the heart.

Samples of a theme statement for a certain communication plan can be, for example, "You can make a difference" if there is a lack of confidence, or "Let's hope for the best" If there is a fear from the uncertainty.

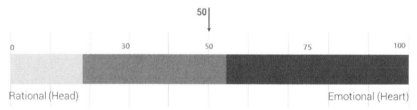

Figure 10-23. Rational/Emotional Dimension

10.6.5 Deliverable 4-3: Relationship Strategy

The objective of this deliverable is to define to what degree building the relationship with the stakeholder will be done one-to-one or one-to-many.

Leading transformational change is based on relationship building. It strengthens the inner bonds, which help merge individual self-interests into a shared purpose.

As shown in Figure 10-24, we use the relationship dimension to identify the strategy (one-to-one vs. one-to-many), The dimension has a scale from 0 to 100, where 0 represents a totally one-to-many communication, and 100 represents a totally one-to-one relationship. As shown in Figure 10-24, a score of 50 means we use a hybrid between of one-to-one and one-to-many.

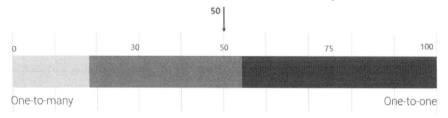

Figure 10-24. Relationship Dimension

By one-to-one strategy, I mean that one person communicates individually with another person; in-person, over phone, or through messaging apps. And be one-to-many, I mean one person communicates with more 2 persons or more; in-person, over phone, or through messaging apps.

Example 10.1 - Call for Ambassadors

Ambassadors, change agents, and change champions can be used interchangeably. Ambassadors are employees who volunteer to support the implementation of the change. Having the ambassadors network in place is a very important tactic, as they will be the link between the leadership team and the rest of the company. It is important to outline the ambassadors' roles and responsibilities pertaining to the change.

It is imperative that the ambassadors are enthusiastic about the benefits the change will bring and committed to enabling and empowering more people to support the change. They need to have a high level of understanding of the initiative and good relationships with all the people being impacted by it. This group of stakeholders needs to be aligned at all times. If they are, they can turn their resources into power to convince the remaining stakeholders of the benefits of the change. In addition, they play a key role in the development of the initial scope of the change.

It is good practice to openly invite people to become ambassadors to encourage active participation and shared responsibilities. As explained, Example 10.1, a "Call for Ambassadors" is to be announced. It should include the following items: (1) Roles and responsibilities, (2) Expected time commitment, (3) Benefits participation, (4) Selection criteria, (5) How to apply, and finally (6) The date of the kick-off meeting.

When ambassadors become involved in defining the change scope and requirements, it is time to develop the Ambassadors Requirements Traceability (ART) document to keep tracing the status of their requirements to maintain credibility and gain their trust.

In one of our projects, below was the outline of the message that was sent to all employees requesting them to volunteer as ambassador for the new program.

1. **Introduction**
   If you are interested in taking part in shaping the future of our organization, please share your interest in being part of the ambassadors group, which will lead the change according to the guidelines below.

2. **Responsibilities**
   - Participate in defining requirements, and recommending options and ideas, etc.
   - Supporting the planning for the execution.
   - Be a communication channel between the project management team and their colleagues (bi-directional communication).

3. **Commitment per week**
   Total period: Approximately 6 months.

4. **Initial plan:**
   1. TELL US HOW YOU WORK? – Two months, 3 to 5 hours per week
   2. CREATING OUR FUTURE WORKPLACE! – Two months, 1 to 2 hours per week
   3. GO-LIVE CAMPAIGN – Two months, 2 to 3 hours per week

5. **Benefits of participation**
   1. Ensure your active participation in shaping our future workplace.

Example 10.1 - Call for Ambassadors

    2.   Provide a proper channel to communicate your voice to the project team.

    3.   Gain experience and stay up to date with the project's progress.

6. **How to apply**
    1. Volunteer if you would love to participate in this initiative.
    2. Nomination or recommendation from managers.
    3. One or two representatives from each department area will be chosen.
    4. If there are multiple volunteers from the same department area, selection will be based on management recommendation and availability.
    5. If there are no volunteer in any area, management nomination is required.

7. **Kick-off meeting**

10.6.6 Deliverable 4.4: Change Narrative Strategy

The objective of change narratives strategy is to define what type of change narrative to develop.

Creating a compelling story is important to address the emotions of others and touch their hearts, which is essential to motivate people to accept the change and face its uncertainties.

Generally speaking, a good story tells: (1) Where we are now, (2) What challenge we have, (3) What will be changed, (5) Where we are heading, (6) Why we should act a certain way, and (7) What we must change to reach our new destination.

We will address the below two types of narrative:

- Story of Self, Us and Now

- The Empathetic Bridge

10.6.6.1   Story of Self, Us and Now Narratives

It is better to use this type in the initiation phase of a change. A change leader tells three linked stories: (1) a story of self, (2) a story of us, and (3) a story of now.

A "story of self" answers the questions: What called you -as a change leader- to lead such a change? This is something people will be interested to know.

A "story of us" answers the question: Why do you think those stakeholders listening to you care about this change?

A "story of now" is a call for action. It answers the questions: (1) Why do you think it is urgent to change now?, (3) What is our strategy?, and (3) What are you asking the "us" to do?

Figure 10-25 shows the three narratives.

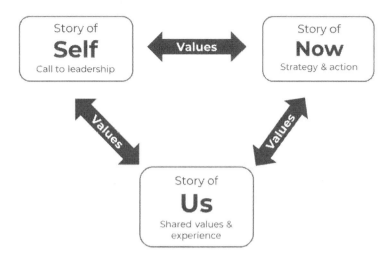

Figure 10-25. Types of Storytelling. Source: Marshall Ganz Leading Change course, Harvard Kennedy School

The three stories should overlap and link together to explain why you are called to lead, why the stakeholders are called to act with you, and why are the stakeholders are called to act now. This means the story should be customized and related to the context. The three types of storytelling can be used alone or as a combination.

Human being are naturally good story tellers. It is part of our daily lives. Of course, some people are more talented. A change story should have a certain structure, which I will explain in the tactics theme.

If people employ both the "head" and the "heart," it will be easier for them to mobilize others to act effectively for the change initiative. The key point is that whoever is communicating must understand other people's values in order to inspire their actions accordingly. The aim of the story is to help lead everyone to a state of solidarity, create a sense of ownership, and ensure commitment.

10.6.6.2   The Empathetic Bridge Narratives

This type of narratives should deal with the existing stories narrated by different stakeholders.

Based on the stakeholder narratives assessment, we should know where the people are from the change and what the different existing narratives are. Accordingly, we use the empathetic bridge to develop a narrative for each one of the four groups (supporters, adapters, accommodators, and rejectors).

Our second narrative is the empathetic bridge, which is developed to address the existing stakeholder change narratives. As I presented earlier, it is a four-step narrative tool used to turn the inhibitor emotions, that are experienced toward the change, into enabler emotions, so that the stakeholders respond positively toward the change.

When a change is communicated, stakeholders will different emotions based on the perceived message. They may inhibitors emotions that will lead them to resist the change like: (1) Complacency, (2) Loss, (3) Apathy, (4) Fear, (5) Self-doubt, (6) Distrust, and (7) Isolation.

And they may feel enablers emotions such as: (1) Urgency, (2) Dissatisfaction, (3) Bein energized, (4)

Hope, (5) Self-efficacy, (6) Trust, and (7) Solidarity. And the objective of the empathetic bridge narratives is to turn the inhibitors emotions toward the change into enablers emotions

The structure and detailed description of narrative types will be provided while presenting the Tactics theme in the next chapter.

10.7   CHAPTER IN A BOX

A summary of the strategizing theme is shown in Table 10-8.

Table 10-8. *Summary of the Strategizing Theme*

Theme objective	The objective of the strategizing is to formulate the assumptions that -if done- will presumably make the change happen.			
Theme components	1. Developing stakeholder management strategy	2. Developing culture management strategy	3. Developing organizational alignment strategy	4. Developing communication management strategy
Component objective	The objective of this component is to address the assessment issues to make sure the stakeholders are aware, competent, and engaged throughput the implementation of the change.	The The objective of this component is to formulate the assumptions of what culture aspects to be changed to motivate acceptance and implementation of the change.	The objective of this component is to formulate the assumptions, that if done, will presumably ensure that the organizational elements and resources help enable and sustain the change.	The objective of this component is to ensure that the change vision along with its outcomes and benefits are communicated in an effective way to all target stakeholders.
Deliverables	▪ Involvement strategy ▪ Motivation strategy ▪ Managing resistance strategy ▪ Stakeholder management objectives (ACE objectives)	▪ Direct vs. indirect change strategy ▪ Culture management objectives ▪ Leadership objectives	▪ Organizational elements objectives ▪ Resource objectives ▪ Risk management strategy	▪ Tw-way communication strategy ▪ Communication theme strategy ▪ Relationship strategy ▪ Change narrative strategy

CHAPTER 11
TACTICS THEME

Chapter 11 - Tactics Theme

11.1   OVERVIEW

As indicated by Ganz, the word "strategy" comes from the Greek word "strategos," which means the military general; the word "tactics" comes from the Greek word "taktikas," which means soldiers. During a war, the strategos (generals) decide the general plan and directions. However, on the ground, it is the taktikas (soldiers) who get the job done. Tactics are the activities that put our strategy into action and, if all goes according to plan, make us win the war. A strategy without tactics is nothing more than a list of wishes. Tactics without strategy are a waste of our resources.

Here is another example: in a football game, setting the team to play as 4-3-3 (four in the back, three in the middle, and three strikers) is a strategy, while the one-two passing movement that is used by two players to go beyond the defenders is a tactic.

Which is more important: strategies or tactics? You definitely need both to win a war. In some circumstances, tactics without a strategy may win a battle. However, it is impossible for a strategy to win a war without tactics. Many people may disagree with me on this point, but this discussion illustrates how tactics in change management can, in some situations, be more important than the strategy.

> **Important Note**
> An increasing sense of urgency and a state of dissatisfaction are critical tactics that should be used to increase the readiness for the change before starting the implementation

A tactic is a specific activity selected to achieve an objective in the change management strategy. Therefore, a tactic is the "how" for the change outcome's "what." Even though a tactic is an activity, sometimes it may require some actions for its implementation; in this case, the actions would be the "how" for the tactic's "what." To clarify, a tactic is the "how" for its outcome and the "what" for its actions. A tactic as an activity may not require actions for its implementation if it is actionable by itself. If this is still confusing, read the Rally case study that will be presented in this chapter for further clarification.

Up to this point, we have developed the change vision and sponsorship, and then we did the assessment of the current state of stakeholder readiness, culture, organizational alignment, and communication. And based on the assessment we went ahead and developed our change management strategy. In this chapter, we will move one step further, to identify the tactical actions of our change management strategy.

> **Important Note**
> Change leaders usually find it more difficult to determine the tactics and ways of implementing the change than

identifying the change vision, strategy, and goals.

11.2   OBJECTIVE

The objective of this theme is to identify the change management tactics that help achieve the change management strategy to ensure having the right readiness and engagement on both the individual and organizational levels. This objective is achieved by the components and their deliverables presented in Figure 11-1.

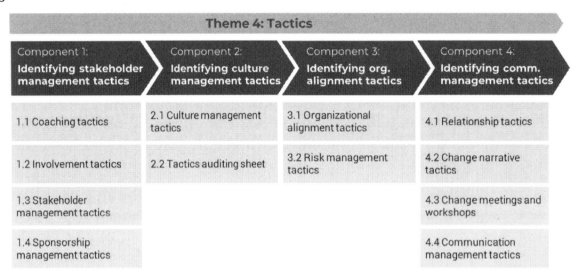

Figure 11-1. Components and Deliverables of the Tactics Theme

I will include here the summary of the components and deliverables that are shown in Figure 11-1 so that you have the choice of focusing, skimming, or skipping whatever you want based on what is of most relevance to your case.

COMPONENT 1: IDENTIFYING STAKEHOLDER MANAGEMENT TACTICS

The objective of this component is to identify the tactical activities that will help achieve the objectives of the stakeholder management strategy.

Deliverable 1.1: Coaching Tactics

The objective is to identify what coaching techniques to use in order to achieve what is required in the stakeholder management objectives.

Deliverable 1.2: Involvement Tactics

The objective of this deliverable is to define the involvement roles of the stakeholders based on the involvement strategy.

Deliverable 1.3: Stakeholder Management Tactics

The objective of this deliverable is to identify the tactics that will help achieve the stakeholder management objectives.

Deliverable 1.4: Sponsorship Management Tactics

The objective of this deliverable is to identify the tactics that will assure achieving the sponsorship objectives and governance.

COMPONENT 2: IDENTIFYING CULTURE MANAGEMENT TACTICS

The objective of this component is to identify the tactical activities that will help achieve the culture management strategy.

Deliverable 2.1: Culture Management Tactics

The objective of this deliverable is to select the culture management tactics that will help achieve the culture management strategy.

Deliverable 2.2: Tactics Auditing Sheet

The objective of this deliverable is to design the process that will be used to make sure that the change in the culture is sustained.

COMPONENT 3: IDENTIFYING ORGANIZATIONAL ALIGNMENT TACTICS

The objective of this component is to identify the tactics that will help achieve the organizational alignment strategy.

Deliverable 3.1: Organizational Alignment Tactics

The objective of this deliverable is to identify the tactics that will help achieve the organizational elements and resource objectives.

Deliverable 3.2: Risk Management Tactics

The objective of this deliverable is to identify the mitigation and contingency tactics of the identified risks.

COMPONENT 4: IDENTIFYING COMMUNICATION MANAGEMENT TACTICS

The objective of this component is to identify the communication tactics based on the communication management strategy, and the communication objectives and tactics that are developed in the stakeholder management, culture management, and organizational alignment work streams.

Deliverable 4.1: Relationship Tactics

The objective of this deliverable is to develop the techniques to be used to build relationship with the stakeholders.

Deliverable 4.2: Change Narrative Tactics

The objective of this deliverable is to develop the right change narratives based on the change narrative strategy.

Deliverable 4.3: Change Meetings and Workshops

The objective of this deliverable is to provide a communication climate that can increase awareness and motivate collaboration, engagement, and open feedback.

Deliverable 4.4: Communication Management Tactics

The objective of this deliverable is to identify the communication tactical activities that will help achieve the communication management strategy and the change management objectives.

Next, I will introduce our fourth case study: Rally. A fictional name and change in the data had to be used as the organization only granted permission to use the case study under a fictional name. This case study was originally written, under my supervision, by one of my MBA students at Nile University. I rewrote it to illustrate the relationship between strategies, tactics, and actions. Another important objective of the Rally case study is to illustrate how organizations can translate their values into consistent behaviors and practices in the culture.

11.3   RALLY CASE STUDY

"... my dream is to transform our company into a very big start-up. And we have to bring our people on board in this transformation."

These words were said by the Rally CEO during an interview in which he was explaining the company's new change initiative to embed their core values in their organizational culture around the world.

11.3.1 Company Background

The Rally story began in the 1950s in a workshop in a small town in Germany. Almost 70 years later, it is now a global automotive supplier operating in 10 countries with over 40,000 employees.

The company's 2017 revenue statement showed approximately US$21B in revenue. Both the CEO and the chairman of the group are involved in the daily operations of the organization.

11.3.2 Mission and Core Values

The mission that guides the company in its operations is *to* guarantee the best quality satisfaction for all customers.

The mission of the company is tied to its core values, whose primary aim is to increase employee competency in order to serve the customers more efficiently. The end goal is for the customers to feel satisfied and have a great experience with the company. The core values are: (1) Ethics and integrity, (2) Continuous improvement, and (3) Operational excellence.

11.3.3 The Vehicle Spare Parts Industry

The vehicle spare parts industry is extremely competitive. The competition has increased significantly over the last few decades. Some of the major trends shaping the industry include value addition for products, customization of products, and research and development initiatives. As the Rally CEO said in an interview:

"... the trends have increased the competition because each business aims at retaining the current

customers it has as well as acquiring new ones."

11.3.4 Continuous Improvement Through Continuous Changes

With regard to the purpose behind implementing so many new change initiatives, the CEO explained:

> *"... all the change initiatives that the company makes aim at achieving better customer satisfaction."*

He added that because customers are an integral element of the industry, they greatly influence the sales and growth of the company. He also stressed that the many change initiatives that the company implements are due to the fact that Rally is an externally driven company. He said:

> *"... the increased competition is making it rather difficult to achieve the target without continuous improvement and having major challenges."*

On this note, Rally has been seeking ways to improve its operations to meet the demands of its customers across the globe.

11.3.5 Demonstration of the Dilemma

The CEO and top management believe that the organization's core values are the main enablers that the company can leverage to better serve its customers. In order to replicate the same customer experience across all its branches, management did its best to hire the same caliber of employees and enforce identical values. Despite this, customer satisfaction varied, with not all customers reporting the same positive experience. Consequently, the company's image differed in different parts of the world.

In an effort to ensure the core values are consistently reflected in the culture, the same organizational structure and processes are applied in all branches. All employees are hired and managed using the same set of rules and policies and treated on equal terms. However, it was not easy to instill the values in all of them. Upon analyzing the root causes of the differences in customer experiences across the branches, it was found that they varied greatly in the following areas:

1. Level of employee involvement in decision-making
2. Following the same production activities
3. Number of implemented new innovative ideas
4. Level of employees' awareness and engagement
5. Following the new processes

All these factors linked back to the core value: continuous improvement. Therefore, the company believed that a transformational change related to this core value must be initiated, otherwise these inconsistencies would irreparably harm the brand image and negatively impact the financial targets.

11.3.6 The New Change Initiative: Translating Values into Culture

The issue at Rally was that employees at some branches treated the core values as nothing more than pleasant slogans to be hung on the walls. Management believed that if they could infuse the values into the culture as practices, behavior, and attitude, it would provide a leap toward better customer satisfaction and planned growth.

Management applied the following methodology: five objectives were selected for the continuous improvement core value. Each objective was to be implemented through a number of tactical actions. The following five objectives were selected:

1. Building a wellbeing environment.

2. Conducting one-on-one personal, competence, and engagement coaching.

3. Getting employees more involved.

4. Moving toward a more results oriented culture.

5. Empowering first line managers and their teams.

Figure 11-2 shows the core values, objectives, and tactical actions.

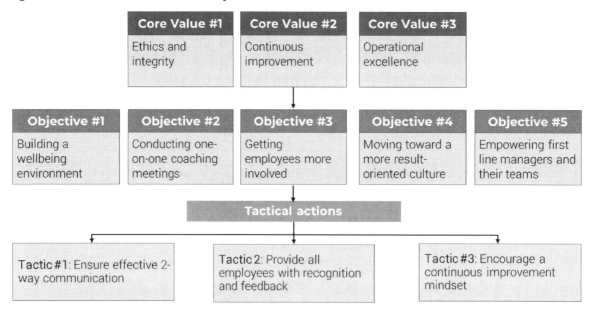

Figure 11-2. Relationship Between the Core Values, Objectives, and Tactical Actions

11.3.7 Tactical Actions for the Implementation

Rally decided to give managers the freedom to select at least three tactics to implement for each objective. Some tactics were provided as best practices for each objective to allow managers the option of selecting from them. Table 11-1 shows the list of suggested best practices tactics for the objective: Getting employees more motivated.

Table 11-1. *Tactics of the Objective: Getting People More Involved*

	Objective: Getting employees more involved
	Suggested best practices tactics
1	Ensure effective 2-way communication
2	Provide all employees with recognition and feedback
3	Encourage a continuous improvement mindset

11.3.8 Auditing the Implementation of the Five Objectives

In order to ensure the implementation of the five objectives, Rally placed the following guidelines to be followed in each branch:

1. An owner is to be assigned to each objective.

2. The owners and the managers select the tactics that will be implemented.

3. The managers define the requirements for each tactic and get them approved through the objective owner.

4. A plan is submitted for the tactics of each objective.

5. Each objective owner has a yearly target.

6. At the end of the year, each manager shows evidence of the implementation of the tactics for each objective.

7. An official auditor visits the site, checks the self-assessment ratings, and gives their assessment of the implementation.

An objective auditing dashboard is designed to keep track of the performance of each objective for each manager. Table 11-2 shows a sample objective auditing dashboard.

Table 11-2. *Sample Objective Auditing Dashboard*

	Tactic	Manager's self-assessment	Manager's comments and evidence	Auditor's assessment	Auditor's comments
	Objective: Getting employees more involved **Objective target: 80%**				
1	Ensure effective 2-way communication	80%	Compliance rating is 80% (no further action needed)	40%	Most of the communication was only informing
2	Provide all employees with recognition and feedback	70%	Workload prevented giving feedback to all employees	70%	Agree with the manager's comments

	Tactic	Manager's self-assessment	Manager's comments and evidence	Auditor's assessment	Auditor's comments
3	Encourage a continuous improvement mindset	90%	Compliance rating is 90% (no further action needed)	70%	Not enough evidence is provided
	Overall Objective Compliance	80%		60%	Target is not achieved

11.3.9 Reflection

The methodology that Rally applied to translate the core value into the culture is similar to the methodology explained in Figure 11-2.

As demonstrated in the case study, the core values should be infused into the organizational culture. This can be done by selecting the right tactics for each core value and the right actions for each tactic. This technique of selecting tactics and actions is the main method we use in this book to make the change happens inside organizations.

11.4 COMPONENT 1: IDENTIFYING STAKEHOLDER MANAGEMENT TACTICS

11.4.1 Overview

Stakeholder management tactics are the main players in the change management game. There are many best practices tactics and techniques that can be used. I will present the coaching techniques and samples of many tactics. In real change initiates, tactics are the activities that help achieve the stakeholder management strategy.

It is important to do the right analysis and be very specific when selecting the change management tactics. If the most efficient tactics are chosen, they are supposed to increase employees readiness and ensure the right level of awareness and engagement.

11.4.2 Objective

The objective of this component is to identify the specific activities that will help achieve the objectives of the stakeholder management strategy.

The objective of this component is achieved by developing the deliverables are shown in Figure 11-3.

Theme 4:

Tactics

Component 1:
Identifying Stakeholder Management Tactics

1.1 Coaching Tactics

1.2 Involvement Tactics

1.3 Stakeholder Management Tactics

1.4 Sponsorship Management Tactics

Figure 11-3. Deliverables of Identifying the Stakeholder Management Tactics Component

11.4.3   Deliverable 1.1: Coaching Tactics

The objective is to identify what coaching techniques to use in order to achieve what is required in the stakeholder management objectives.

Generally, coaching provides directions and guidance by asking the right questions. In change management, coaching could be an effective tool to manage the issues that prevent having a high readiness to change.

Managers should sometimes act as coaches not as supervisors. In their role as coaches, it is important for managers to recognize what coaching technique to use to address the identified issues based on the stakeholder readiness assessment.

As shown in Figure 11-4, for the awareness issues and objectives, we may use the awareness coaching technique; for the competence issues and objectives, we use the competence coaching technique; and finally for the issues and objectives related to the engagement element, we use the engagement coaching, which it is also known as the motivational coaching.

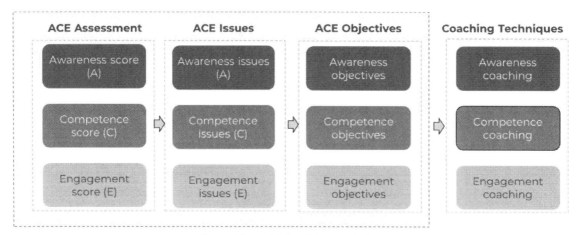

Figure 11-4. ACE Coaching Techniques

A coach is like a doctor who has a patient with chest pain as shown in Figure 11-5. The doctor first asks the patient about the symptoms in order to understand the problem. They then ask deeper questions to make a diagnosis. They may then ask for a detailed scan to enable them to recommend the right treatment. Finally, they give the patient a debrief about their condition and what shold be done about it.

Figure 11-5. A Patient with Chest Pain

Similarly, in change management, the coach does the same by asking questions to understand more the identified issue, then ask questions to pinpoint or confirm the root causes. Next, the coach defines the goals to be achieved, and finally both should agree on the next steps to be done. Figure 11-6 shows the coaching cycle in change management.

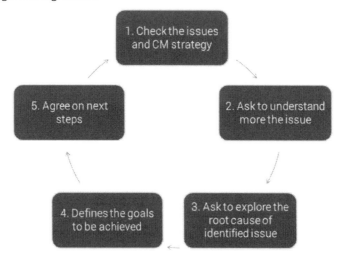

Figure 11-6. ACE Coaching Cycle

The coaching questions should stimulate deep thinking and self-reflection in the resistant person.

Important Note

In a change effort, approaching people on a one-on-one basis may be more effective than in groups.

The critical question is: Have we really identified the right root cause? To make sure the right root cause is identified along with the right tactic, people should not only depend on the score of the ACE assessment as the remaining three elements (rationale, emotions, and behaviors) must be identified and monitored. This may require a sense of empathy to sense what other people might be thinking or feeling. For example, when someone says that he is sad, the coach should get deeper and asks why is he sad till he gets to the bottom of it.

11.4.3.1 Awareness coaching

Awareness coaching emphasizes what has been communicated about the change in a more direct, one-on-one way. This will ensure that everyone understands what is driving the change, how it will be implemented, and what its benefits will be. Orientation should first be provided for the managers who will be coaching the other employees.

For awareness coaching, in addition to the questions listed in Appendix E, the coach could start by asking questions such as:

* Do you think this change initiative is a waste of time?
* If the current status quo is fine, why do you think we need this change?
* Are you aware of what is going on?

11.4.3.2 Competence (Developmental) coaching

Competence coaching is used to analyze the competence issues. For competence coaching, the coach could start by asking questions such as:

* How confident are you about implementing the first steps of the change?
* Do you require further knowledge to proceed?
* Do you believe it is important to apply the newly acquired skills?

11.4.3.3 Engagement (Motivational) coaching

Analysis of the emotional issues that were identified during the assessment phase can be done by sort of an engagement coaching. Emotional engagement will be very low if individuals are not motivated enough, which could occur for a variety of reasons.

This level of emotional engagement can be determined by the amount of effort the individual made with regard to the change. It is also largely evident in the attitudes of individuals toward showcasing their skills and helping other develop themselves.

For engagement coaching, in addition to the questions listed in Appendix E, the coach could start by asking questions such as:

- How do you think this change will impact you?

- To what degree are you interested in the change?

- Do you believe the management is committed to the change?

> **Important Note**
>
> The coach must point out to the unacceptable behaviors that may hinder the change implementation. These behaviors are categorized as: (1) Avoiding, (2) Submissive, (3) Denial, and (4) Rejecting.

11.4.4   Deliverable 1.2: Involvement Tactics

The objective of this deliverable is to define the involvement roles of the stakeholders based on the involvement strategy.

Based on the stakeholders involvement strategy, an involvement role is defined for every stakeholder for the different deliverables. The involvement roles are described in Table 11-3.

Table 11-3. *Involvement Roles*

Involvement role	Description
Approve	Responsible for approving the final output.
Accountable	Responsible for the final scope and quality of the output.
Responsible	Responsible for the execution to deliver the output.
Participate	Participate in the execution to deliver the output.
Feedback	Must be consulted to get feedback.
Inform before and after	No feedback may or may not be required.
Inform after	Informed after the deliverable is finished. No feedback is required.

Each deliverable should also be assigned to both an accountable and a responsible person. The accountable person is the one who approves the final decision, while the responsible person is the implementer. If one person has the role of being both the accountable and responsible, they are called the deliverable owner.

11.4.5   Deliverable 1.3: Stakeholder Management Tactics

The objective of this deliverable is to identify the tactics that will help achieve the stakeholder management objectives.

Before we identify the tactic, we need to put all the bits and pieces together to see the full picture. This is done by: (1) Identify the triggering issue, (2) Identify the impacted stakeholders by this issue, (3) List the change management practice(s) that will be used to manage the issue, (4) List the formulated stakeholder management objective, and finally (5) Identify the tactics that will help achieve the objectives. Figure 11-7 shows the relationship between all the elements.

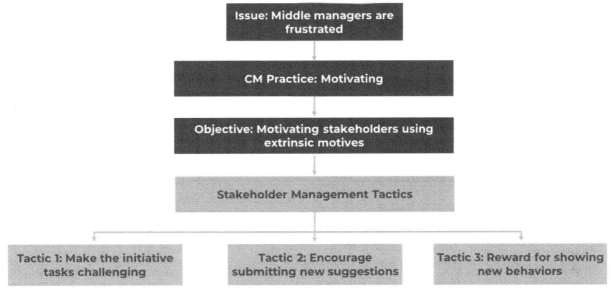

Figure 11-7. Relationship Between Assessment Issues, Objectives, and Tactics

Important Note

It is essential to keep monitoring the disbenefits resulting from the change as they will generate unhealthy resistance.

It is important for the people who work on the stakeholder management tactics to know the relationship between the assessment issues, the change management practices, the stakeholder management objectives, and the tactics to know why these specific tactics are being implemented.

As shown in Figure 11-7, the leadership team may identify a number of tactics for each objective. Check Tables 10-4, 10-5, and 10-6 as they show some generic objectives and tactics for the ACE elements. When developing your change management objectives and tactics, you need to take into consideration the specific identified issues, impacted stakeholders, context, etc.

Table 11-4. *Generic Objective and Tactics for Awareness Issues*

Practice	Objectives	Tactics
Awareness issues		

Practice	Objectives	Tactics
- Communicating - Understanding perception	Objective 1: Ensuring the reason of the change is clear.	Tactic 1: Conduct small meetings to explain what problems are addresses by the change and why and conduct a survey to understand the perception.
		Tactic2: Send messages on the internal portal of the risk of not changing.
- Communicating - Involving	Objective 2: Regularly updating the change status	Tactic 1: Arrange regular group meetings to present the change status, progress, and get the feedback.
- Coaching	Objective 3: enhancing the level of awareness on the individual level.	Tactic 1: Conduct one-to-one awareness coaching. Give all relevant information (analysis, financial, statistics, etc.). Explain the criteria for making the decisions.
- Involving - Communicating - Building relationship	Objective 4: Involving stakeholders in the implementation and communication process.	Tactic 1: Form an ambassadors structure and develop their role and responsibilities
		Tactic 2: Conduct one-on-one sessions with each ambassador to discuss their feedback.

Table 11-5. *Generic Objective and Tactics for Competence Issues*

Practice	Objectives	Tactics
Competence issues		
- Developing technical competence	Objective 1: Developing change related competence.	Tactic1: Create a community of practice (COP) that reflects the new competence and capabilities of the change.
		Tactic 2: Support senior managers to develop their full technical potential related to the change.
		Tactic 3: Provide training
		Tactic 4: Provide assurance that the required resources will be made available.
		Tactic 5: Remove obstacles and conflict with day-to-day operations.
		Tactic 6: Provide support, training, and coaching.
- Agile planning - Coaching	Objective 2: Making the first steps of the change implementation as simple as possible.	Tactic 1: use Agile planning with simple requirement in the first iteration.
		Tactic 2: provide one-to-one coaching during the first phase of the change implementation.

Practice	Objectives	Tactics
- Motivating	Objective 3: Increasing tolerance while implementation.	Tactic 1: Accept mistakes when using the new systems.

Table 11-6. *Generic Objective and Tactics for Engagement Issues*

Practice	Objectives	Tactics
Engagement issues		
- Managing Resistance	Objective 1: Reducing complacency.	Tactic 1: Conveying a sense of urgency with complacent attitudes.
- Communicating	Objective 2: Gaining more trust.	Tactic 1: Assure more transparency in all commutation.
		Tactic 2: Managers to assure better approachability.
		Tactic 3: Track and keep all promises.
	Objective 3: Seeking solidarity.	Tactic 1: Arrange workshops between all department till reaching one agreement about the technical solution.
	Objective 4: Getting the negatively impacted stakeholders away.	Tactic 1: Keep the people who will be negatively impacted by the change as busy as possible.
	Objective 5: Increasing ownership.	Tactic 1: Avoid the feeling that the change was imposed, and let people be part of it.
- Coaching	Objective 6: Highlighting the risk of not changing.	Tactic 1: Conduct one-to-one awareness coaching. Start the discussion from a common ground and highlight the risks of not changing
- Involving	Objective 7: Providing continuous feedback channel.	Tactic 1: Provide the right channels and opportunities for issues to be raised and addressed.
- Motivating - Sponsoring	Objective 8: Motivating stakeholders using <u>extrinsic</u> motives.	Tactic 1: Integrate the change results and benefits into the performance management system.
		Tactic 2: Ensure that the change goals are reflected in the plans, targets, and budgets of all business units.
		Tactic 3: Link promotion to initiative results.
	Objective 9: Motivating	Tactic 1: Always encourage and/or reward stakeholders for showing new behaviors related to change.

Practice	Objectives	Tactics
	stakeholders using <u>intrinsic</u> motives.	Tactic 2: Encourage people to come up with suggestions that help achieve the change.
		Tactic 3: Make the initiative tasks always challenging.
		Tactic 4: Make sure doing the initiative tasks add new experience to stakeholders.
		Tactic 5: For stakeholder who will totally change the way they used to work for a long time, replace something of value with something else of value. Recognize and appreciate the previous work done.
	Objective 10: Motivating stakeholders using <u>contribution</u> motives.	Tactic 1: Ensure that across all business units, staff are committed and keen to contribute to the successful realization of the change benefits.
		Tactic 2: Ensure max ownership by most key stakeholders.
		Tactic 3: Make sure that the results of the initiatives will bring benefits to other people.
	Objective 11: Motivating stakeholders using <u>relational</u> motives.	Tactic 1: Link between the new results and improving the relations with the customer.
		Tactic 2: Link between the new results and improving the relations with the boss.

11.4.6   Deliverable 1.4: Sponsorship Management Tactics

The objective of this deliverable is to identify the tactics that will assure achieving the sponsorship objectives and governance.

In our model, we have four standard objectives that we recommend having for all sponsors. These four objectives are as follows:

1.   Commit to being active and visible.

2.   Use effective two-way communication.

3.   Assure accessibility and power.

4.   Manage the people side.

Table 11-7 has sample of some sponsorship tactics that could be identified for the objectives.

Table 11-7. *Generic Sponsorship Objectives and Tactics*

Objective	Tactic
Objective 1: Commit to being active and visible	Tactic 1: Regularly attended project status meetings.
	Tactic 2: Ensure that each member of the sponsorship team is interested in

Objective	Tactic
	achieving the objectives of the new initiative, in both the short term and the long term.
	Tactic 3: Have regular face-to-face meetings with frontline supervisors.
	Tactic 4: Regularly attended committee meetings.
	Tactic 5: Be active, visible, and present at all special events (kick-off, training, etc.).
Objective 2: Use effective two-way communication	Tactic 1: Listen to and address the concerns of subordinates and peers.
	Tactic 2: Communicate effectively in different ways throughout the implementation.
	Tactic 3: Be consistent between the communicated message and actions (walk the talk).
Objective 3: Assure accessibility and power	Tactic 1: Be always accessible to provide support.
	Tactic 2: Have a high degree of control over the people being impacted by the change.
	Tactic 3: Have a high degree of control over the systems being impacted by the change.
	Tactic 4: Be powerful enough to make strategic decisions and remove obstacles.
	Tactic 5: Remain always accessible to provide support.
Objective 4: Manage the people side	Tactic 1: Motivate and engage the team with the new change.
	Tactic 2: Link the team performance appraisal with the change objectives.

Important Note

Integrating change objectives and benefits into the performance management system (PMS) is one of the most effective change management tactics. The change goals should also be reflected in the plans, targets, and budgets of the business units.

11.5 COMPONENT 2: IDENTIFYING CULTURE MANAGEMENT TACTICS

11.5.1 Overview

The culture management tactics are the most effective in making the change a sustained one. The tactics should be based on the culture management strategy and assessment.

The culture management tactics will mainly address the behaviors and mindsets of the target values 'that are going to reshape the organizational culture. As previously explained, values are not in themselves either good or bad; they are rather the sense of broad feelings and emotional tendency toward particular attributes.

Values should not be confused with virtues. A virtue is a quality valued as being always good. The opposite of virtues are vices, which are understood, always, as bad. The opposite of a cultural value is not a vice but rather another value in the same cultural dimension.

Values are the guiding principles of the employees' actions and behaviors. They are manifested in decisions, mindsets, behaviors, and systems. You can also identify values within stories that are being narrated in the organizations.

11.5.2 Objective

The objective of this component is to identify the tactical activities that will help achieve the culture management strategy. The objective of this component is achieved by developing the deliverables shown in Figure 11-8.

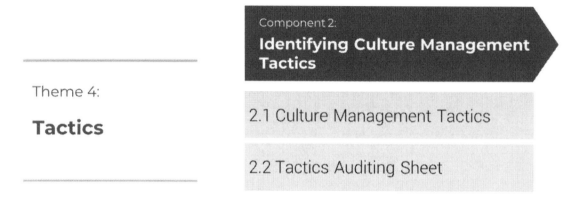

Figure 11-8. Deliverables of Identifying the Cultural Tactics Component

11.5.3 Deliverable 2.1: Culture Management Tactics

The objective of this deliverable is to select the culture management tactics that will help achieve the culture management strategy.

In order to reshape the culture, the culture tactical activities should be identified according to whether the direct vs. indirect change strategy, that was developed when the culture management strategy was drawn up, is a direct one or an indirect one.

In whichever way, the tactics need to be identified to address the issues along the culture levers . I have already presented the culture levers that we adapt in our model, in Chapters 4 and 6, which are: (1) Values, (2) Mindsets, (3) Practices, and (4) Behaviors.

The more change that is required in the culture, the greater the number of approaches, both direct and indirect, will need to be used.

Before starting the process, the values should: be written down and given a clear definition; be associated with a related set of mindsets and behaviors.

Culture change requires a lot of work. Therefore, it is recommended that only one or two values be changed at any one time. The number of objectives needed for each change, together with the tactics deployed to achieve them', indicate the scope of the improvement. Also, the more tactics you select, the more expensive the process will be.

For the indirect change, you identify the tactics for the following culture management indirect approaches:

* Symbols

* Heroes and stories

* Norms

* Leadership

* Organizational elements (HR, structure, processes, regulations, etc.)

* Rewards and sanctions

For the direct change, you identify the tactics for the following culture management direct approaches.

* Relationship

* Change narrative

* Communication channels

* Ceremonies

Figure 11-9 shows the process of both the direct and indirect culture change.

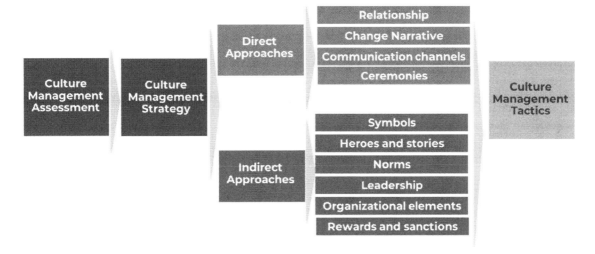

Figure 11-9. Culture Change

Important Note

Successful change efforts typically require changing the organizational reward system to support the change.

Example 11.1 - Changing the Culture

The management of a multinational company wanted to have a high results culture style to increase the willingness to change for a new program being introduced. To achieve a results-oriented culture style, the organization needed to have both high goal-oriented and externally driven cultures.

Based on a culture assessment, the goal-oriented culture had a rating of "very low" (this means the culture is means-oriented). In order to have a high goal-oriented culture, it was decided -during the strategizing theme- that the following four culture management objectives would be implemented:

Objective 1: We should not stick too much to the rules while implementing our projects.

Objective 2: We should link promotion to innovation and new initiatives.

Objective 3: We should have more inspiring leadership.

Objective 4: We should make more effort to gain people's trust.

Table 11-8 shows a sample of tactics that could be selected for objective 1 for using both direct an indirect approaches.

Table 11-8. *Tactics Implementation on the Culture Levers*

Objective 1: We should not stick too much to the rules while implementing our projects
I. INDIRECT APPROACH
Relationship, Narrative, Ceremonies, and Communication channels
Tactic 1: A special meeting is to be organized in which leaders are to be transparent and honest. Facilitate bi-directional open communication channels where employees can discuss their views.
Tactic 2: Arrange regular meetings with frontline employees who perfectly understand the process to get rid of bottlenecks.
Tactic 3: Enable employees to become involved by arranging one-on-one meetings with workgroup leaders who are responsible for implementing the change.
Tactic 4: Increase people's level of dissatisfaction with the current state of not being very results-oriented.
II. INDIRECT APPROACH
Heroes and Stories
Tactic 1: We should acknowledge those who add real value, rather than those who perfectly follow the rules.
Tactic 2: Call out for new heroes related to being results-oriented in monthly meetings.
Symbols
Tactic 1: Put up visible signs and banners around the workplace related to the problems associated with being too process-oriented.
Tactic 2: Use the right slogan throughout the organization. For example: "Did you solve a problem today?"
Leadership

Example 11.1 - Changing the Culture

Tactic 1: Managers need to delegate more and stay away from their team to enable them to get used to unfamiliar situations instead of continuously asking for help.

Tactic 2: Give frontline employees more authority to troubleshoot issues and make decisions before asking for support.

Tactic 3: Provide flexible deadlines that do not affect the achievement of the required results.

Tactic 4: An understanding of how and when the rules can be bent should be conveyed across the team, while providing a shadowing and coaching program between juniors and seniors.

Tactic 5: Encourage the leaders to be role models "walk the talk".

Organizational elements (HR, Structure, Processes, regulations, etc.)

Tactic 1: Align performance indicators with the goal rather than with the tools and processes.

Tactic 2: Refine the process of the techniques to remove all steps that do not help achieve the final results.

Tactic 3: Refine the systems to be more automated.

Tactic 4: When defining new processes, make sure the stakeholders get involved to motivate them to become more goal-oriented.

Rewards and Sanctions

Tactic 1: Announce a reward to encourage employees to challenge the process and rules in order to achieve better results.

Tactic 2: Reward those who go above and beyond their daily job to achieve the targets.

Tactic 3: Managers will be sanctioned if they claim to walk the talk but do otherwise.

11.5.4 Deliverable 2.2: Tactics Auditing Sheet

The objective of this deliverable is to design the process that will be used to make sure that the change in the culture is sustained.

As explained in Rally case study, changing the culture has the following steps: (1) selecting the values to managed, (2) identifying the objectives to be achieved, (3) selecting tactics for each objective, and finally (4) auditing the implementation of the tactics.

The advantage of letting the managers come up with their own tactic is that it increases their engagement and ownership. The unit specific tactics will be totally selected by units' manager based on their own context. Please check the Rally case study for more details about these tactics.

The process should include the following steps:

1. Target of each culture objective is to set to each manager.

2. Managers identify the tactics that they will implement to achieve the culture objectives.

3. At the end of a pacified period, managers self-assessment by specifying the percentage of achieving

the objective by each tactic.

4. Manager submit the evidence to justify their self-assessment.

5. Member of the culture sustainability committee audit the results of each manager.

Figure 11-10 shows an overview of how to change the culture in order to have a more caring culture in the organization. A number of tactics are to be selected for each objective along the different culture levers.

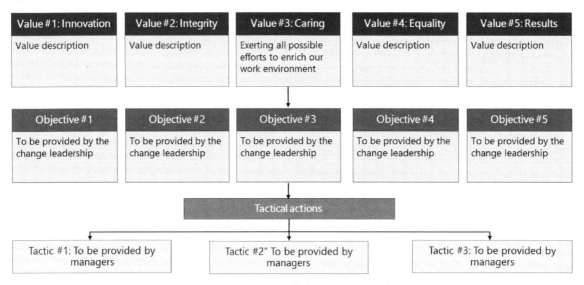

Figure 11-10. Process of Changing the Culture

As shown in Table 11-9, the tactics auditing sheet is a good tool to use to implement this process.

The objective of the auditing is to make sure that the managers are effectively implementing the selected tactics to achieve the desired culture management strategy.

Important Note

It is essential to keep monitoring the disbenefits resulting from the change as they will generate unhealthy resistance.

Table 11-9. *Tactics Auditing Sheet Template*

Tactics Auditing Sheet				
Objective:				
Description:				
Accountable:				
Objective target: 80%				
Tactics				
Tactics	Self-assessment	Comments and	Change auditor's	Comments and evidence

		evidence	assessment	
Tactic 1				
Tactic 2				
Overall compliance				

Important Note

Successful change efforts typically require changing the organizational reward system to support the change.

Example 11.2 - Polytechnique University Objectives and Tactics

Below are the change management objectives that were selected for the Polytechnique change management strategy.

* Rebuilding a strong and powerful sponsorship team.
* Building trust and commitment with all instructors.
* Increasing the sense of urgency regarding not changing the current learning methods.
* Removing all challenges identified in future desired state gap analysis.
* Maximizing emotional engagement with the change initiative.
* Increasing involvement at all levels, especially for part-time instructors.
* Reshaping the culture to be more student-centered.

Table 11-10 below shows the objective profile sheet of the first objective in the above list.

Table 11-10. *Tactics Auditing Sheet Sample*

Tactics Auditing Sheet				
Objective: Building a strong and powerful sponsorship team.				
Description: The change initiative is mainly led by the two of the top management. Therefore, rebuilding a powerful and balanced sponsorship committee is a must.				
Accountable: CEO				
Objective target: 80%				
Tactics				
Tactic	Self-assessment	Comments and evidence	Change auditor's assessment	Comment and evidence
1. Conduct governance assessment	90%		60%	
2. Form the change governance structure	80%		50%	
3. Develop governance	70%		70%	

framework				
Overall compliance	80%		65%	Target is not achieved

11.6 COMPONENT 3: IDENTIFYING ORGANIZATIONAL ALIGNMENT TACTICS

11.6.1 Overview

The organizational alignment tactics help the change management team focus on achieving the change goals and get the internal conflicts out of the way.

As indicated by Ganz, from a change management perspective, tactics are the activities that turn the available resources into the power needed to achieve the desired change.

Achieving the organizational objectives identified in the strategizing theme is one of the most critical results of the change management. Complete alignment between the tactics of all work streams (stakeholders management, culture management, and communication management) is very important.

11.6.2 Objective

The objective of this component is to identify the tactics that will help achieve the organizational alignment strategy.

The objective is achieved by developing the deliverables shown in Figure 11-11.

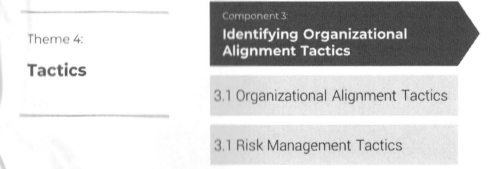

Theme 4:

Tactics

Component 3:
Identifying Organizational Alignment Tactics

3.1 Organizational Alignment Tactics

3.1 Risk Management Tactics

Figure 11-11. Deliverables of Identifying the Organizational Alignment Tactics Component

11.6.3 Deliverable 3.1: Organizational Alignment Tactics

The objective of this deliverable is to identify the tactics that will help achieve the organizational elements and resource objectives.

Table shows a template of the organizational alignment tactics.

Table 11-11. *Organizational Alignment Tactics Template*

Objective	Impact on other elements	Tactic
Strategic perspective		
Objective 1		
Capabilities perspective		
Objective 2		
Capacity perspective		
Objective 3		
Objective 4		
Resources		
Objective 5		

11.6.4 Deliverable 3.2: Risk Management Tactics

The objective of this deliverable is to identify the mitigation and contingency tactics of the identified risks.

Table 11-12 shows a template of the risk management tactics.

Table 11-12. *Risk Management Objectives Template*

Risks	Mitigation tactics	Contingency tactics	Avoidance tactics
Category A			
Category B			

11.7   COMPONENT 4: IDENTIFYING COMMUNICATION MANAGEMENT TACTICS

11.7.1 Overview

There are a variety of communication tactics and techniques that can be used in change management. In this section, I will present techniques that are aligned with the communication management assessment and strategizing that were introduced in Chapters 9 and 10.

Some examples of these communication techniques are the change narratives or the storytelling, the relationship techniques, and the change team meetings.

11.7.2 Objective

The objective of this component is to identify the communication tactics based on the communication management strategy, and the communication objectives and tactics that are developed in the stakeholder management, culture management, and organizational alignment work streams. The objective of this component can be achieved by developing the deliverables shown in Figure 11-12.

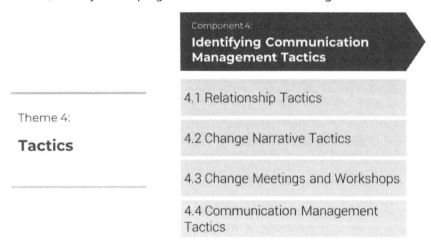

Figure 11-12. Deliverables of Identifying the Communication Management Tactics Component

11.7.3 Deliverable 4.1: Relationship Tactics

The objective of this deliverable is to develop the techniques that are to be used in building the relationship with the stakeholder.

Have you ever had a personal or a professional relationship with others?

Think about any valuable relationship you have had before with your colleagues, teachers, manager, or others. What I am trying to point out is that we all naturally build relationships. In this deliverable, we will step back and reflect on how this process works. And also, on how this is to be done intentionally.

Building relationships is a more or less unstructured part of our daily lives. However, in change management, it is a process of a definite and particular kind.

I will recommend some techniques to be used to build intentional relationships and for communicating the change vision to secure people's commitment or their performance of certain tasks related to the change initiative. The relationship techniques available to us are as follows:

- One-to-one relational meeting

- 4Cs

- Change meet-up

11.7.3.1   One-to-one relational meeting technique

The one-to-one relational meeting is a five-step conversation that you can use to build formal relationships with individuals.

This technique is used only when one-to-one conversations are being conducted. The technique has the five steps: (1) Check-in, (2) Goal, (3) Exploration, (4) Exchange, and finally (5) Commitment. Below is a description of the five steps:

1. **Check-in**. From the outset, gain the attention of the other person so that they are ready to engage in that meeting.

2. **Goal.** Set a clear goal for the meeting. Why are you interested in meeting this person, and also, of what interest is the meeting to the other person, do you think?

3. **Exploration.** Explore your shared needs, values, interests, and resources by sharing and asking questions to understand each other's story and motivation. Keep the conversation here focused on your interests and the contribution each of you can make.

4. **Exchange**. Talk about the change initiative and listen to the other person's thoughts. Discover what you can exchange for the sake of the change. This can be insights, support, recognition, actions, etc.

5. **Commitment**. Take the other person's commitment on what is next for both of you. This may vary from changing a behavior to talking to other stakeholders about the change initiative, acting as a change ambassador.

The last step is to secure the other person's commitment, which is key to the success of any change initiative. Figure 11-13 shows the five steps.

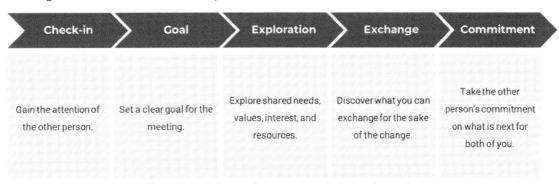

Figure 11-13. Steps of One-to-One Relational Meeting

The one-to-one relational meeting technique, like all other tools, needs to be practiced; remember, as discussed in Chapter 2, you did not learn how to ride a bike on the first attempt.

11.7.3.2   4 C's technique

The second relational tactic is the 4Cs, which is a four-step process used to mobilize effective commitment on a clear and specific action.

This technique can be used as one-to-one or one-to-many. It can be used as a quick conversation or even through emails. The 4Cs stand for: Connect, Context, Commitment, and Capitalize. Below is a description of the four steps:

1. **Connect**. In this step, be clear about what are you asking them to do. Talk about why you care about the change initiative, and why you think they might care about it as well.

2. **Context**. In this step, you start talking about why the change is important, why it is urgent. What are the consequences if it not implemented?

3. **Commitment**. The goal of this step is to get a clear commitment from the other person. If this tactic is used within a conversation, ask them directly whether you can count on them or not? If it is used in an email, create a simple form to submit, or ask them to reply to the email. The bottom line is to get a definitive commitment from them (Yes or No).

4. **Capitalize**. In this step, you capitalize on their being committed to the action, by giving them an opportunity to take ownership of a course of action, talking to another person, say, or preparing something with you that is based on the nature of the action agreed upon between you.

11.7.3.3   Change meet-up

The change meet-up is gatherings of about 60 minutes' duration, involving around 10 stakeholders to build relationships between the host and the attendees and between each other. The change meet-up is focused completely on motivating people through values and moving them to action. The debating of issues should be totally avoided.

Below is a typical agenda for the meeting:

1. **Intro.** The meeting starts with an introduction of the goal of the meeting. A quick check-in or icebreaker activity can be done, if needed.

2. **Host's self, us, and now narrative.** Then share your story of self, us, and now as a host. If there are co-hosts, they could share their story of self as well, if the time allows.

3. **Attendees' story of self.** In this step, have the attendees break into pairs to share their story of self.

4. **Group discussion around change.** Then facilitate a group discussion around why this change is important. And why do they care about it? And what are the sources of inspiration toward this change?

5. **Action ask.** After this discussion, tell them what you are asking them to do. Make sure it is clear, specific, and meaningful.

6. **Evaluation.** At the end of the meet-up; get their evaluations; what worked well in the meet-up? What could be improved? What are their take-aways?

11.7.4 Deliverable 4.2: Change Narrative Tactics

The objective of this deliverable is to develop the right change narratives based on the change narrative strategy.

In the change narrative strategy deliverable, I explained the difference between using the self, us, and now narrative and the empathetic bridge narrative, and we decide while developing the communication management strategy which type of narratives to use. In this deliverable, I will go through the structure of the narratives and how to develop them.

Storytelling, like building relationships, is part of our daily lives. However, in change management, the storytelling should have specific content and a specific structure.

A story is not properly a story if it does not include three key elements: character, plot, and moral. The plot is the main event of the story that engages the audience and makes them pay attention. The plot should have three components.

Let me tell you a short story to explain:

"Today, I got up early, had my breakfast, and went to my office to write a new chapter of this book."

Is this an engaging story? Or a boring one? Does it have a plot?

Let me tell you another version of the story:

"Today, I got up early to head to the studio, had my breakfast as usual, but it tasted differently. Then I started feeling a pain in my stomach, my heart beat was so fast,. I started asking myself': was the food poisoned?"

Is the story getting more interesting now? What is the difference?

I added a challenge; something unusual happened, and this is the first component of the plot: a challenge.

The second component is choice: What was my choice when I had this challenge? How did I act?

And the third component is the outcome of my choice? And the outcome -in a good story- should take the audience to the moral of your story.

A good story presents a challenge we face, the choice we make, and the outcome we experience.

11.7.4.1   Story of Self, Us, and Now narrative

As we know, the first narrative is the three linked stories: Story of Self, Story of Us, and Story of Now. Let us go through each one of them.

A Story of Self

he Story of Self answers the questions: What called you to leadership? Why do you care? What moment from your life can you tell us about, that shows why you are here today?

The character in the story is yourself. To develop the story, select a moment from your life when you faced a challenge and you acted to meet it; and that action resulted in an outcome that leads the audience to the moral of the story, which answers the question: Why are you here today?

It is very important that your Story of Self manages to communicate your values in the course of describing the challenge you faced, as values drive our choices.

Figure 11-14 shows the elements of the story of self.

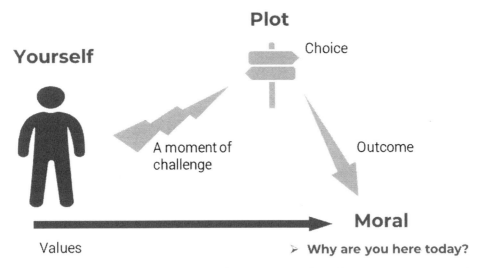

Figure 11-14. Elements of a Story of Self. Adapted from Ganz's Leading Change Course at Harvard Kennedy School

Each element in the story matters; a story without a challenge is boring, like the first story I told you; a story without a choice is a story of a victim; a story without an outcome contains no moral, and a story without values and motives does not mobilize the emotions of others.

A Story of Us

A Story of Us communicates why our organization has been called to its mission. To a great extent, the structure of the Story of Us is similar to the Story of Self, but of course it reflects on the organization rather than the self.

The Story of Us answers these main questions: Why do you think those stakeholders care about the change? What are our shared values and shared experiences?

Here, the character is the Us; or you, together with the people who are listening to you. To develop the story, select a shared challenge that the Us faced together, and you acted upon collectively; and that action resulted an outcome that leads to the moral of the story. The moral of the story should answer the question: Why do you feel proud to be part of this Us? Why do you think the Us care about this change? And why is there a hope related to the change initiative?

It is very important that your Story of Us manages to communicate the shared values and experiences while details about the shared challenge are presented'. For the shared experience, it does have to be a specific situation in one single location. It can be a shared challenge which the Us experienced separately. Like the COVID-19 pandemic, which was also a shared experience for the whole world. The core here is "shared experience."

Figure 11-15 shows the elements of the Story of Us.

Figure 11-15. Elements of a Story of Us. Adapted from Ganz's Leading Change Course at Harvard Kennedy School

A Story of Now

A Story of Now is our third linked story. This story is mainly about what should happen now. It answers the questions: Why is the change urgent on both the individual and organizational levels? What is our strategy in implementing the change? and What are you asking the Us to do now?

The story has three elements and ends with a call to collective action.

The first one is the "nightmare," which should address both the individual and organizational levels, and it is conveyed by means of painting a picture of what is happening due to the existence of the problem that the change will address. What are the short and long-term consequences if we do not change now? And what are the short and long-term benefits that will accrue if we address the problem and change?

Remember, the content related to the previous questions was obtained when the change business case was being developed, using the problem map analysis.

The second element is the "choice." It should communicate our choices and answers the question: What is our strategy?

The third element is the "dream." It leads to the collective action that you are asking the Us to take. It should be specific, feasible, and measurable.

The inspiring Story of Now should have a "hope" embedded in it. This hope should address the fear of uncertainly that comes with the change. Figure 11-16 shows the elements of the Story of Now.

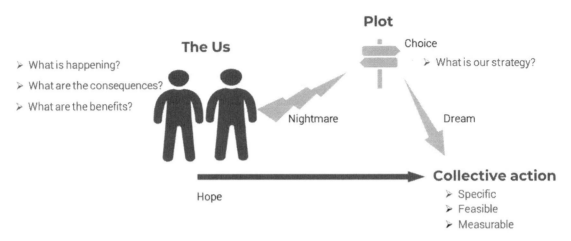

Figure 11-16. Elements of Story of now. Adapted from Ganz's Leading Change Course at Harvard Kennedy School

When you start practicing this narrative, tell the three stories in the same order. However, when you become more familiar with the narrative, you can tell the three stories in any order. You can start with a paragraph from the Story of Now then one from the Story of Self, then one from the Story of Us, then another from the Story of Now again, as a way of linking the stories together.

We link the three stories through the thread of values. Therefore, the values in the three stories need to be aligned.

One person who very effectively utilizes storytelling as per the above structure, is Barak Obama. Please search for his speech from the Democratic National Convention in 2004, and try to identify where he moves between the three stories.

Figure 11-17. Barak Obama and Storytelling

11.7.4.2   Empathetic bridge narrative

Our second narrative is the empathetic bridge, which is developed to address the existing stakeholder change narratives. As I presented earlier, it is a four-step narrative tool used to turn the inhibitor emotions, that are experienced toward the change, into enabler emotions, so that the stakeholders respond positively toward the change.

Step 1: Acknowledge the perceived challenge

The first step is acknowledging the challenge which the change is perceived to represent; this should be categorized under the main change inhibitor emotions.

The challenge should be categorized under the main change inhibitor emotions (complacency, loss, apathetic, fearful, self-doubt, distrust, and isolation). Therefore, this step requires that you had already identified what type of inhibitor emotions the stakeholders experience. It could be the loss of certain benefits, fear of the unknown, etc. Do not ignore people's feelings! And do not just tell them "Don't feel bad."

Step 2: Express empathy

The second step is to express empathy in order to establish an empathetic connection with the Us by sharing a similar experience of your own. Do not just say "I feel what you feel," because most probably you do not.

Step 3: Narrative hope

The third step is the narration of hope, in which you mention what the sources of hope are that the Us can use to overcome the challenges. By the way, the Story of Us can be used in this step.

Step 4: Enable choice

In the last step you identify how the Us can begin to make a choice about what to do. And before developing this step, you need to know what type of enabler emotions you want to head for (urgency, dissatisfaction, being energized, hope, self-efficacy, trust, and solidarity).

Skill Practice 11.1 - Story of Self

Write your story of self. At the end, include two to three sentences of your story of us and your story of now. The story should be no longer than two minutes when read aloud, or a maximum of two double-spaced pages.

11.7.5 Deliverable 4.3: Change Meetings and Workshops

The objective of this deliverable is to provide a communication climate that can increase awareness and motivate collaboration, engagement, and open feedback.

In this deliverable, I will provide general tips which the change team can use when communicating with each other and with stakeholders. Therefore, this deliverable is also addressing the internal communication of the change team, since, if the sponsors and the change team do not meet and communicate with each other in the most suitable way, the change will, most probably, fail.

This deliverable is about the change meetings and workshops; so, do these differ from the other meetings that we know about already?

No, meetings are meetings, but the structure and tips that I will go through are essential for achieving the objective of increasing the awareness, and motivating collaboration, engagement, and open feedback.

In this deliverable, I will go through three elements that are required in change management:

- The meetings' themes

- The launching workshop

- The speedy meeting

11.7.5.1   Meetings' themes

Before we get into the details of the meeting themes, I would strongly suggest that you first of all reflect on your own experience. Think about one of the worst meetings you attended, that left negative reactions in you. Who was there? Where was it? When was it? How were the dynamics between the attendees? And what was bad about this experience?

And let us do it the other way around. Think about one of the best meetings you attended, that left positive reactions in you. Who was there? Where was it? When was it? How were the dynamics between the attendees? And what was good about this experience?

What are the results you generated from this reflection? What do you notice? What interpretations can you make?

If you did not feel like engaging in this activity, at least have one meeting in mind to reflect on when I go through the meeting themes.

Next, I will go through the five themes that I want you to consider while conducting change management meetings and workshops. By the way, applying the tips that I will go through in these five themes can turn what would have been one of the worst meetings you ever had into the best meeting you ever had!

Theme 1: Design and into

The first theme is the design and into, and I will give my tips by asking some questions that you can relate to the meeting you have in mind and that you can reflect on.

- Was the goal for the meeting clear for the whole team? Was the meeting really needed?

- Was the agenda clear and were any materials that were needed for the meeting sent to the attendees, ahead of time?

- Were all the attendees invited based in the goal of the meeting?

- Did the host of the meeting assign different roles for the attendees? Maybe keeping time, taking notes, taking action, facilitating part of the meeting, presenting a case, or some other meaningful responsibility.

- Did the host welcome everyone when they arrived?

- Did the host make sure that the goal for the meeting was clear for everyone at the beginning of the meeting?

- Did the host ask a quick check-in question?

By the way, in change management, the target stakeholder for the meetings and workshops should be identified in the change management tactics.

And for the last one, about the check-in question, let me give you a few samples of the kind of check-in questions that I use most of the time at the beginning of the change management meetings:

- Why are you interested in joining this meeting?

- Why are you interested in joining the change ambassadors group?

- What are your needs and values that the change may fulfill?

- What is your emotion toward the change, in one word?

Theme 2: Time dynamics

The second theme is the time dynamics, and I will also give my tips by asking some questions:

- Did the meeting start and end on time?

- Did everyone come on time? Did someone follow up with the attendees, before the meeting, urging them to come on time?

- Did you stick to the original agenda items? And were you able to go through them efficiently?

When I facilitate a meeting, I usually say that our meetings are time boxed ... start on time and end on time. However, it is not easy to force such a practice in cultures that take a more relaxed approach.

Theme 3: Team dynamics

The third theme is the team dynamics:

- Was there always a safe space for all the attendees to express opinions or new ideas?

- Were all the attendees engaged and focused? And why?

- Was there a lot of complaining in the meeting? And how were the complaints handled?

- Were there some attendees dominating the meeting, as experts?

Having a safe environment is very important in order for the stakeholders to be able to be engaged in the meeting. The host of the meeting should have what I call the "engagometer" to make sure that the attendees are always engaged.

You, as a change leader, need to differentiate between the healthy and the non-healthy complaints, and to handle them differently. As Maslow indicated, you should be happy to hear the healthy complaints or the meta-grumbles that are driven by the motivation and desire to achieve the change goals.

Theme 4: Discussion dynamics

Our fourth theme is the discussion dynamics:

- Did the facilitator use activities to engage the attendees?

- How did people express the disagreements they had?

- Was the facilitator able to make the discussion move forward?

- Was there thoughtful decision-making occurring?

When you facilitate a meeting, use different activities to increase engagement and collaboration. For example, you can let the attendees think in pairs and then share with the others; or ask them to brainstorm in different groups; or ask them to write their ideas on sticky notes and paste them on a flipchart and have an open discussion about them. You do whatever activities you feel comfortable with; the bottom line is to make your meetings and workshops active.

You should always explore different opinions and options before taking a decision.

Sometimes, when I lead meetings, I adopt different positions. For example, if we are brainstorming to develop the theory of change, I ask someone to take an opposing opinion and someone else to defend what is being considered, to encourage the conversation and initiate a healthy debate.

Theme 5: Closing and post-meeting follow-up

And the last theme is the closing and post-meeting follow-up:

- Was there a shared summary for what was resolved and decided on?

- Was it clear, at the end of the meeting, what the action items were? And who was going to do what?

- Did you end the meeting on time? Or were the attendees kept beyond the time that was scheduled in the meeting invitation?

- Did the host make it possible for the attendees leave with a positive experience?

- Did you ask the attendees to conduct a quick evaluation?

- Did someone send a summary of the meeting notes, and follow up on the actions items as per the deadlines assigned?

When you lead a meeting, you can have your attendees leave with a good experience by appreciating their participation with specific examples, or by sharing something positive at the end.

For the meeting evaluation, I usually ask three simple questions:

- What went well?

- What could be improved?

- What are their main insights from the meeting?

11.7.5.2   Launching workshop

The second element is the launching workshop, and it is a suggested structure for your change launching meetings or workshops. It can be used by the sponsorship committee and the change team for their launching meetings. It can also be used for the launching workshops with the ambassadors and key stakeholders.

My suggested structure for the launching workshop has seven items. Next, I will lead you through each one of them.

Item 1: Intro

After welcoming everyone and clarifying who is attending the meeting, make the meeting objectives clear, and ask a quick check-in question to start engaging everyone. I have already presented some examples of check-in questions.

Item 2: Shared purpose

The second item is the team shared purpose. Do not confuse the change purpose and the team purpose. They are both connected, of course, but they are different.

Start this step by presenting the change purpose, and next you get the attendees involved. For example, if this is a workshop with the change ambassadors, you could ask them the following questions:

* Why do you think the change is important?

* Why is it urgent?

* What might the consequences be if no change is made?

Afterward, try to facilitate an activity to define the team shared purpose. That should answer the following two questions:

* What is this team going to achieve?

* How is the team going to achieve this?

Here, you only define the directions of the "how". Do not go into details.

And if the team or the committee purpose is already defined, try to make it clear and have a discussion about what the general understanding of it is, and how the team can achieve it.

Item 3: Team norms

After defining the "what" and the "how" of the shared purpose, define your team norms.

The norms are the ground rules of how the group will work together. How do you manage your time? How do you keep yourselves accountable? How do you handle the discussions and the disagreements? How do you take the decisions?

Item 4: Tactical activities

Now, with your team purpose and norms defined, we reach the core of the workshop, which are the tactical activities.

There are different ways to design this step based on the stakeholders attending the workshop and the context.

You may start by doing a quick assessment of the current state and discussing what should be done to increase the readiness and mitigate the risks.

For example, if you plan to conduct an ACE assessment, you start by explaining the ACE model and its elements and then ask the attendees to assess the awareness, change competence, and engagement to find the issues that you can analyze during the workshop.

Next, facilitate the workshop to arrive at the answers to questions about what you are going to do And about how you are going to achieve your goals. This should be guided by the change visions and by whatever change management strategy you have decided upon.

As explained in the meeting themes element, make this part of the workshop an active one, let the attendees think in pairs then share with others, or brainstorm in groups, or whatever else may be decided.

You need to have decided on clearly defined tactical activities by the end of this step.

Item 5: Team roles

Once the activities are clear, define with the whole team the roles that will be needed to implement these activities, but do not just define roles, break each role down into specific responsibilities. Afterward, let the team assign people to each of the roles.

Item 6: Action plan

After assigning the roles and responsibilities, think about your action plan. For each tactical activity, you need to decide at least the following:

- What are the actions that need to be implemented?

- What are the due dates?

- Who is responsible for each of the actions?

Item 7: Closing

At the end of the meet-up; get evaluations from the attendees. I recommend using the three questions that I mentioned when discussing the meeting themes:

- What worked well?

- What could be improved?

- What are the attendees' main insights or takeaways?

The suggested structure of the workshop is a generic framework that should be customized based on your context and the stakeholders attending the meeting.

11.7.5.3   Speedy meeting

The third element is the speedy meetings; this one, by the way, is my favorite.

The speedy meeting is a very short meeting, of between 10-15 minutes, that has a very focused agenda and requires highly effective facilitation skills to strategize, monitor, debrief, motivate, or celebrate.

You can use it to make amendments to your strategy, monitor your team progress, debrief concerning a specific event or period of time, motivate your team before or during an event, and to celebrate a quick win.

One of the most common speedy meetings that I apply, and really like, is the daily stand-up meeting. It is used to monitor and debrief the team work. The team members gather for 10-15 minutes every day to share their progress, as they answer these questions:

- What have you worked on since our last meeting?

- What do you plan to achieve today?

- What are the challenges that you have?

Now, let me go through some important tips for the speedy meetings.

- First, have the meeting for only 10 minutes or 15 minutes maximum; start it on time and end it on time. This is very important for creating a culture in which meeting times are respected.

- Keep your eye on your agenda and do not get diverted into talking about side issues; this is a common occurrence in meetings of this type. If something important is raised and will take time, park it on the white board, and discuss it with the person concerned later on, or ask people to have another meeting to discuss it.

- Fix the meeting time and place. And if it is online, use the same link for every meeting.

- Ask people to stand-up, this will remind them that it is a speedy meeting and will make them eager to finish quickly and get back to their tasks.

11.7.6   Deliverable 4.4: Communication Management Tactics

The objective of this deliverable is to identify the communication tactical activities that help achieve the communication management strategy and the change management objectives.

The communication management tactics will help achieve the other communication management objectives coming from the other works streams: stakeholder management, culture management, and organizational alignment.

Now, we are supposed to have our change vision clear from the vision and sponsorship theme in Chapter 8, and we have our communication management objectives and tactics for the stakeholder management workstream, the culture management workstream, and the organizational alignment workstream from the strategizing and tactics themes in Chapters 10 and 11.

Then we should review all these objectives and tactics through the lens of the communication management strategy: (1) the two-way communication strategy, (2) the communication theme strategy, (3) the relationship strategy, and (4) the change narrative strategy. Also, we need to take the involvement strategy and managing resistance strategy into consideration.

Finally, we conclude the communication management tactical activities while taking into consideration the communication tactics that I went through before this present deliverable: (1) Relationship tactics, (2) the change meetings and workshops, and (3) the change narrative tactics, to end up by consolidating everything so as to be able to identify our communication management tactical activities.

Figure 11-18 shows all the elements that influence the communication management tactical activities.

Figure 11-18. Relationship Between Communication Management Tactics and Work Streams

Each tactical activity should include the following elements:

- **What to communicate:** Define here what aspects you would like to communicate? Would you like to communicate the change vision? The change statement? The change business case? The change objectives and goals? Or other aspects that answer the why, what, who and when questions related to the change?

- **Target stakeholders:** Specify the target stakeholders to be addressed by these tactical activities.

- **How to communicate:** How are you going to communicate? What channels are you going to use? Social media platforms? Physical meetings? Online meetings? Brochures? 1-to-1 relational meeting? Or other communication channels?

- **Communication measures:** It is how we will know that our communication has succeeded. Communication measures help us plan and track our communication.

Figure 11-19 shows the main elements of the communication tactical activities.

Figure 11-19. Communication Management Tactics

11.7.6.1 Communication measures

The communication measures will be used for the planning and tracking of the communication tactical activities. Without the communication measures, communication may point in random directions. The measures could be measured quantitatively, qualitatively, and by time.

Table 11-13 has samples of the measures that can be used for the communication tactical activities.

Table 11-13. *Sample Communication Measures*

General measures	Two-way communication measures	Response and feedback measures
<ul><li>Level of awareness</li><li>Number of communication channels</li><li>Number of newsletters every month</li><li>Number of events</li><li>Number of workshops per month</li><li>Percentage of stakeholders to reach</li></ul>	<ul><li>Stakeholder perception (% of supporters/ % of rejectors)</li><li>Stakeholder change satisfaction</li><li>Number of surveys per month</li></ul>	<ul><li>Response time to change questions</li><li>Number of change complaints</li></ul> Number of new ideas related to the change

11.7.6.2 Communication messages structure

Change communication messages are like the marketing activities for new products or services. Marketing requires identifying the needs and interests of the target segment in order to send the proper message.

Based on the communication theme strategy, the messages should address the "head" by designing awareness messages to increase the awareness and convince the stakeholders of the importance of the change initiative. They should also address the "heart" by designing emotional messages to increase the engagement and willingness to change and support.

Table 11-14 shows a sample of the commutation messages structure.

Table 11-14. *Communication Messages Structure Sample*

Communications theme
Hybrid between emotional and rational.
Theme name
Develop – Empower – Support
Objectives of the messages
1. Increase awareness.
2. Removing the bad experience from the previous programs.
3. Addressing the heart to increase the emotional engagement and willingness to change.
Messages to include the following aspects:
1. Change vision and benefits.
2. Lessons from previous projects.
3. Risks of not changing.
4. Individual benefits.
Change messages
<message 1>
<message 2>
<message 3>

So, by the end of the whole process, we should be looking at a table in which there is:

- The involvement and managing resistance strategy, as part of the stakeholder management strategy; is it push, pull or hybrid?
- The two-way communication strategy..
- The communication theme strategy: it is either emotional or rational. As well as the Relationship strategy, is it one-to-one, or one-to-many, or hybrid?
- The change narrative strategy: will you use the empathetic bridge or the Self, Us, and Now?
- The communication management objectives? Consolidate all the objectives here, remember that these are coming from the different work streams.
- The communication management tactical activities. They are descried by answering the four questions which we described earlier.

Table 11-15 shows the outputs of the communication management work stream.

Table 11-15. *Communication Work Stream Outputs*

Involvement strategy: _____				
Two-way communication strategy: _____				
Relationship strategy: _____				
Change narrative strategy: _____				
Commination management objectives				
Objective 1				
Objective 2:				
Commination management tactics				
Communication Tactical activity	Communication aspects (What to communicate)	Target stakeholders	How to communicate	Measures
Activity 1				
Activity 2				

Important Note

Communication about the status of the progress should be occurring all the time, as people will not necessarily think positively if an inadequate amount of information about the progress is communicated,

11.8   CHAPTER IN A BOX

A summary of the tactics theme is shown in Table 11-16.

Table 11-16. *Summary of the Tactics Theme*

Theme objective	The objective of this theme is to identify the change management tactics that help achieve the change management strategy to ensure having the right readiness and engagement on both the individual and organizational levels.			
Theme components	1. Identifying stakeholder management tactics	2. Identifying culture management tactics	3. Identifying organizational alignment tactics	4. Identifying communication management tactics
Component objective	The objective of this component is to identify the specific activities that will help achieve the objectives of the stakeholder	The objective of this component is to identify the tactical activities that will help achieve the culture management	The objective of this component is to identify the tactics that will help achieve the organizational	The objective of this component is to identify the communication tactics based on the communication management strategy,

	management strategy.	strategy.	alignment strategy.	and the communication objectives and tactics that are developed in the stakeholder management, culture management, and organizational alignment work streams.
Deliverables	• Coaching tactics • Involvement tactics • Stakeholder management tactics • Sponsorship management tactics	• Culture management tactics • Tactics auditing sheet	• Organizational alignment tactics • Risk management tactics	• Relationship tactics • Change narrative tactics • Change meetings and workshops • Communication management tactics

CHAPTER 12
PLANNING AND APPRAISING THEME

Chapter 12 – Planning and Appraising Theme

12.1   OVERVIEW

This planning and appraising theme, if done effectively, puts the project on the right track. This is one of the most difficult aspects of the change journey. It merges the work of the four work streams to enable the assessment of the value of the change and to develop the change management plan.

By now, we have already developed the change vision and sponsorship, then we did the assessment for the current state for the stakeholder readiness, culture, organizational alignment, and communication. And, based on the assessment and the change vision, we developed our change management strategy. Then, based on our change management strategy; we identified the tactical activities required to achieve the change goals.

In this part, we will be completing out story by introducing our last theme of the model: the planning and appraising theme.

12.2   OBJECTIVE

The objective of this theme is to assess the value of the change, finalize the Go/No-Go decision, and develop a consolidated change management plan of all the work streams.

This objective of the theme is achieved by the components and deliverables presented in Figure 12-1.

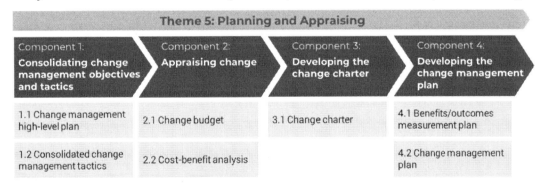

Figure 12-1. Components and Deliverables of the Planning and Appraising Theme

I will include here the summary of the components and deliverables that are shown in Figure 12-1.

COMPONENT 1: CONSOLIDATING CHANGE MANAGEMENT OBJECTIVES AND TACTICS

The objective of this component is to decide on the planning methodology, develop the high-level change management plan and consolidate all change management objectives.

Deliverable 1.1: Change Management High-Level Plan

The objective of this deliverable is to define the number and order of the change management campaigns needed to achieve the change outcomes.

Deliverable 1.2: Consolidated Change Management Tactics

The objective of this deliverable is to assess the change management objectives and tactics for all work streams and assign the tactics for each campaign.

COMPONENT 2: APPRAISING CHANGE

The objective of this component is to estimate the change budget and assess whether or not the change initiative is worth implementing.

Deliverable 2.1: Change Budget

The objective of the change budget is to combine all the expected expenses of the change initiative.

Deliverable 2.2: Cost-Benefit Analysis

The objective of this deliverable is to assess whether or not the benefits of the change initiative exceed its budget..

COMPONENT 3: DEVELOPING THE CHANGE CHARTER

The objective of this component is to give the Go/No-go to start the change initiative.

Deliverable 3.1: Change Charter

The objective of the change charter is to give the Go/No-go to start the change initiative.

COMPONENT 4: DEVELOPING THE CHANGE MANAGEMENT PLAN

The objective of this component is to develop the detailed plan for the change management campaigns and iterations.

Deliverable 4.1: Change Outcome/Benefit Measurement Plan

The objective of this deliverable is to identify how and when the quantification of the outcomes and benefits will be measured to identify the status of the change realization.

Deliverable 4.2: Change Management Plan

The objective of this deliverable is to develop the detailed plan of the change management campaigns and iterations.

12.3 COMPONENT 1: CONSOLIDATING CHANGE MANAGEMENT OBJECTIVES AND TACTICS

12.3.1 Overview

Our change management plan methodology is based on having an iterative and incremental method of planning. This methodology is similar to Agile planning, which is a flexible approach that is needed when a project faces ambiguity and an expectation of undergoing numerous changes.

To decide on the planning methodology, let us look at the four planning approaches that are based on the degree of uncertainty and the frequency of delivery.

- **A predictive approach**: This approach is used in planning when things are known and have been previously proven and there is no need for frequent delivery.

- **An iterative approach:** This approach is used in planning when a lot of changes are expected but there is no need for frequent delivery.

- **An incremental approach:** This approach is used in planning when not many changes are expected but a high frequency of deliveries is required.

- **An Agile approach:** This is the best fit for change management, which includes both the incremental and the iterative approaches.

Why is the Agile approach the best fit for change planning?

Change always comes with new ideas and may face a high level of resistance. And this creates a high level of uncertainty that requires an iterative approach.

And at the same time; in change we work on achieving quick-wins to let people feel the benefits of change, which requires an incremental approach.

As change is accompanied by uncertainty and resistance, it is better for it to be implemented in an iterative and incremental way (Agile approach) to help the achieving of the change outcomes at an early stage.

As you see while developing our change management high-level plan, I will use the Agile approach as our planning methodology.

In addition to the Agile approach being both incremental and iterative, it is also a value driven planning approach and not activity driven, which is consistent with change management principles. Therefore, our planning methodology will also be value-based planning. By the way, the standard way of planning is activity-based planning.

Agile approach is very practical to be used If the change is based on an innovative idea, it is worth mentioning that this new innovative idea may have fuzzy goals. In this case, the level of ambiguity is extremely high; people do not know what they do not know. Innovative changes have goals that depend to a great extent on intuition and only provide a vague sense of direction. The goals are not static and will change over time. Everyone should be aware that, in such a situation, the organization will be entering into a learning process. It is important that the plan is flexible and that the team stops after every phase or iteration to evaluate, strategize, and reframe the vision.

Refer to Appendix B for more description about the Agile planning approach.

12.3.2 Objective

The objective of this component is to decide on the planning methodology, develop the high-level change management plan and consolidate all change management objectives.

The objective of this component is achieved by developing the Change Planning Methodology deliverable shown in Figure 12-2.

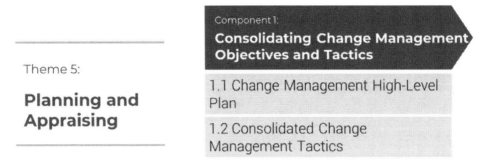

Figure 12-2. Deliverables of Developing the Change Management High-Level Plan

12.3.3 Deliverable 1.1: Change Management High-Level Plan

12.3.3.1 Objective

The objective of this deliverable is to define the number and order of the change management campaigns needed to achieve the change outcomes.

12.3.3.2 Change management campaign

Before going into how we will develop this deliverable, let us understand, first, what we mean by the change management campaigns.

Do you remember where the words "strategy" and "tactics" came from, as I discussed in Chapter 10?

The word "campaign" comes from a similar source as the words "strategy" and "tactics", from the military. It originally comes from a Latin word that means "field."

Campaign in the military was generalized to mean "continued or sustained aggressive operations for the accomplishment of some purpose."

Campaigns have a clear start and end; they are focused and have specific targets.

To win a war you might need to operate multiple campaigns. Each one should end with the achieving of a strategic target. The last campaign should end with the achieving of the final strategic target, which is supposed to be the big one.

Each campaign includes a number of battles; each one of them should end with a sub-target, while the final battle in the campaign should end by achieving the campaign strategic target.

Also, as we all know, the notion of a campaign is also used in politics, so let us talk some politics.

It is defined, in politics, as "a series of operations or efforts designed to influence the public to support a particular political candidate."

The key words "series of operations" in this definition convey the same concept as the battles in military campaigns.

Nowadays, the campaign approach is also used in the Media, social work, and other domains. In the same sense, we are adapting the campaign approach in change management.

In change management, we define a campaign as "a designed stream of iterations focused on achieving specific change outcomes."

Our change goals or outcomes are to be achieved by multiple campaigns; let us assume we will have three campaigns.

Each campaign works on a specific change outcome, and includes a number of iterations, each of which should end with a sub-outcome; while the final iteration in the campaign should end by achieving the campaign outcome.

Again, change management campaigns are like the war campaigns; they should have a clear start and end. They are focused and have specific outcomes.

Change management can have different methodologies for its planning. I will adapt a methodology that is called the campaign-based planning methodology that is adapted from the Agile planning approach.

What is a campaign, in change management?

A campaign is usually conducted and organized around social activities designed to increase awareness and mobilize people toward achieving specific goals. In the same sense, in a transformation program, we need to continuously raise awareness and mobilize people to keep the required energy to assure achieving the change goals.

12.3.3.3 Change management high-level plan

We start our high-level planning by determining how many campaigns we will have and the outcomes that are supposed to be achieved by the end of the campaign. For the sake of simplicity, I assumed that each campaign will achieve only one change outcome.

As shown in Figure 12-3, we assume that our high-level plan has three campaigns, and each campaign ends with the achieving of a change outcome. Let us also assume that campaign #2 has three iterations.

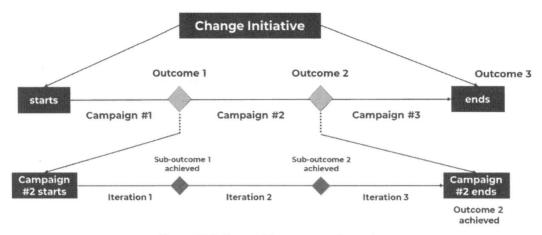

Figure 12-3. Change Management Campaigns

As discussed in Chapter 8, you need to break down each outcome into its sub-outcomes, which I referred to as the nested outcome concept, while developing the change statement. Therefore, we work on achieving the sub-outcomes during the campaign that will help achieve the target outcome of the campaign. The reason for having the sub-outcomes is to assure that incremental delivery of the value of the campaign is achieved as part of the Agile approach that we are using.

Each campaign consists of a number of iterations that end with sub-outcomes or quick wins, that help increase engagement and buy-in.

It is good practice to have a chart for every campaign, based on the required capacity in terms of people, skills, energy, and so on. Figure 2-4 shows a sample of a campaign chart.

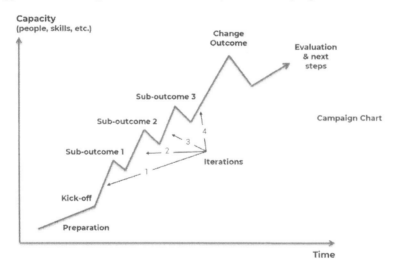

Figure 12-4. Change Management Campaign Chart. Adapted from Marshall Ganz Leading Change Course.

As you can see in this campaign chart, our ultimate goal of the campaign is the change outcome, and we are pursuing this outcome through achieving the sub-outcomes.

We achieve each sub-outcomes through an iteration in which we implement our tactical activities. These tactical activities are strategically achieving the sub-outcomes, and accordingly the ultimate outcome at the end. As you can see, in both Figure 12-3 and Figure 12-4, iteration 1 will end up by achieving sub-outcome 1, but do not forget that we still need to deliver some of the project's other outputs as well to achieve the outcome.

Have you noticed that the capacity or the energy goes down after the end or the peak of each iteration, in Figure 12-4?

At the beginning of the campaign we have a preparation phase, in which we do the team formation and the detailed planning of iteration 1, and prepare for the campaign kick-off meeting. The period of this preparation phase is based on your campaign duration, as well as on the change size.

After the preparation phase we come to the campaign kick-off tactic, which is one of the most important tactics you will implement. It is the official announcement that the campaign has started. It needs to be significant. The tips of the meeting themes and the structure of the launching workshop that I discussed in the communication management tactics, in Chapter 11, should be reflected in the kick-off meeting.

Next, let me go through my recommendations for what should happen in each iteration.

As shown in Figure 12-5, throughout the iterations we hold regular speedy meetings every day, or every second day, depending on your context. I hope you still recall this speedy meeting or the stand-up meeting, that I went through in Chapter 11. These daily meetings are required to make sure that everyone is aligned, and no obstacles are holding the team performance back.

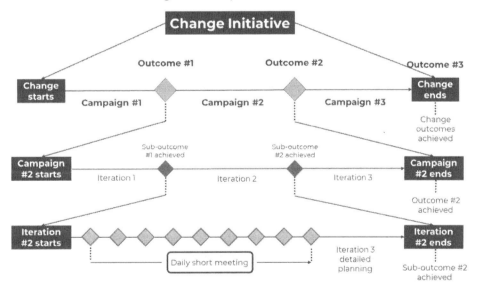

Figure 12-5. Change Management Iteration Planning

By the end of each iteration, we review what happened in the current iteration and hold a planning meeting for the next iteration.

At the end of each iteration, you do an evaluation meeting, which we call a "retrospective meeting." In this retrospective meeting we go over these main questions:

* What worked well during this iteration?

* What would you like to change to achieve our outcome?

- How can we implement that change? Recommended actions?

Our change management campaign approach is iterative, incremental, and value driven, which are the three principles of the Agile approach that I introduced in the overview. It is incremental in that it achieves the outcome through small increments or sub-outcomes. And we work on these sub-outcomes through iterations, and we evaluate, by the end of each iteration, and adapt our work. Also, in campaigns, each iteration and tactic has a strategic value in itself; we are driven by value, not by activities.

Having different iterations in each campaign suits the implementation of a change. The detailed plan for each iteration is finalized by the end of the previous one, to enable the change leadership to take corrective actions as needed along the way. Accordingly, this will help revisit the change management strategy and incorporate employees' feedback.

At the end of the last iteration of the campaign, the leadership team should arrange a retrospective meeting, as I previously discussed. However, prior to this meeting, you may need to send a list of question to the attendees to get them ready and prepared for the meeting. Below is a sample of these questions:

- Are stakeholders engaged with the new change?
- Are the change outcomes still achievable?
- Are we going to realize the change benefits?
- Is the change vision still valid and relevant?
- What should be done to realign and motivate?
- Do we still have the right individual and organizational readiness?
- How effective has our learning and development been?
- Does the culture hinder the change in any way?

Table 12-1 shows -based on the previous discussion- the details of a change management high-level plan.

Table 12-1. *Change Management High-Level Plan*

Comping Planning			
	Duration	No. of iterations	Milestone
Number of change management campaigns: 3			
Campaign #1	6 weeks	3	Sub-outcome #1 achieved
Campaign #2	12 weeks	3	Sub-outcome #2 achieved
Campaign #3	6 weeks	3	Change outcome achieved
Iteration Planning – Campaign #2			

	Duration	Planning activity	Milestone
Number of iterations: 3			
Iteration #1	4 weeks	Detailed plan of iteration #2	Business value A
Iteration #2	4 weeks	Detailed plan of iteration #3	Business value B
Iteration #3	4 weeks	Detailed plan of iteration #1	Sub-outcome #2 achieved

It is good practice to organize a celebration at the end of the important iterations, as a way of injecting energy and increasing engagement. Sponsors should attend all the evaluation meetings and celebrations to show that they are actively participating. If necessary, it will also give them an opportunity to deal with any obstacles that arise.

It is also good practice to link each campaign with its related change statement. As discussed in Chapter 8, a change statement has an immediate outcome (or campaign outcome) that should be achieved within a specific time frame. The change statement also includes the tactics that will be implemented to help achieve this target outcome.

The campaign must have a specific theme. A good theme will reflect the current situation and the expected outcome. It should also help mobilize the stakeholders. A good theme should emotionally link the stakeholders with the purpose of the change. It should be selected based on the target outcomes, and the pattern of the existing stakeholder narratives.

Different themes can be selected for different campaigns that we may have. Examples of the themes could be: "We are here to support you", "Support, Development, and Empowerment", "Employees achieving", and "Think globally, act locally."

> **Important Note**
>
> The change management high-level plan should be communicated upon the completion of the change charter. However, the detailed plan of each iteration will not be complete, as the planning process will continue throughout the implementation of the change.

12.3.4 Deliverable 1.2: Consolidated Change Management Tactics

The objective of this deliverable is to assess the change management objectives and tactics for all work streams and assign the tactics for each campaign.

By finalizing the high-level plan, you already have the change outcomes and the campaign you will implement to achieve each outcome. And you have also identified the iterations that we will go through to achieve the sub-outcomes in each campaign.

One question is still not answered: In which iterations will the change management tactics be implemented? And this is what results from the completing of this deliverable.

By the end of the tactics theme, we had our change management objectives and tactics along the different work streams.

Each objective had its own tactics that needed to be implanted. Tactic are selected to help achieve the change management objective. They should be aligned with the organizational core values. Also, leading a change requires that the tactics be as creative as possible.

I will use two criteria to assess and prioritize our change management objectives; the first is influence, and the second one is resources.

By influence, we mean how the objective is contributing to the achievement of the change outcomes. And we evaluate influence on the scale of 'very low,' 'low,' 'high' and 'very high.'

And by resources, I mean the resources and effort required to implement the identified tactics and so achieve this change management objective. We do its evaluation on a scale of 'very low,' 'low,' 'high' and 'very high.'

For objectives that have a high or very high influence on achieving the change outcomes and their tactics, these will require low or very high resources; these objectives will have the highest priority.

For objectives that have a low or very low influence on achieving the change outcomes and their tactics, these will require high or very high resources; these objectives will have the lowest priority.

The remaining objectives will have medium priority. Figure 12-6 shows a sample result of the analysis.

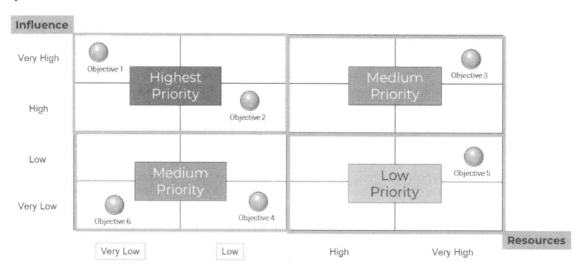

Figure 12-6. Change Management Objective Analysis

I recommend doing this assessment in a workshop style with the change management team, and you do it for each change outcome at a time. Therefore, you end up having the assessment of the objectives, along with their tactics, with respect to each outcome.

Next, you do a further assessment in order to be able to assign the tactics to the different iterations of the campaign.

If you find that some outcomes are not fully supported by your change management objectives, you may need to revisit your change management strategy again. This is normal, and the process should be ongoingly iterative.

And by the end of this workshop you should have the tactics you can implement within each campaign. At this stage, you just need to name the tactics, and later you will develop the details of each tactic, in the iteration planning meeting.

Upon finalizing the analysis, you can also update the theory of change and the tactics that we have in our change statement. To remind you, theory of change is the primary objective or assumption that we believe if done, the change will happen.

12.4   COMPONENT 2: APPRAISING CHANGE

12.4.1 Objective

The objective of this component is to estimate the change budget and assess whether or not the change initiative is worth implementing.

This is the most important component for the top management. This is when we talk money and show value; this is what they have been waiting for.

The objective is achieved by developing two deliverables, as shown in Figure 12-7.

Figure 12-7. Deliverables of Appraising Change Component

12.4.2 Deliverable 2.1: Change Budget

The objective of the change budget is to combine all the expected expenses of the change initiative.

There are different cost structures that can be used to estimate the change budget. Every change initiative is unique; therefore, the cost structure needs to be customized according to the context and type of the change. All possible financial figures must be considered to figure out the total expected investment.

Below is my suggested cost structure to be used for the change budget:

1. Technical projects cost

2. Change management campaigns cost

    2.1 Change management tactics

    2.2 Communication management tactical activities

3. General activities cost

4. Outcome/benefit management cost

5. Assets cost

The cost of the communication management tactical activities can be part of the change management tactics but I prefer to keep them separate.

Table 12-2 presents a sample template of how the budget for these four elements can be estimated.

Table 12-2. *Estimated Budget*

	Description	Estimated date	Estimated cost
1. Technical Project			
Project 1			
Project 2			
3. General change management cost			
Stakeholder management cost			
Culture management cost			
2. Change management campaigns			
Campaign 1			
Campaign 2			
Campaign 3			
3. General activities			
4. Outcome/Benefit management			
5. Assists			
Tangible assets cost			
Intangible assets cost			
Total			

12.4.3 Deliverable 2.2: Cost-Benefit Analysis

The objective of this deliverable is to assess whether or not the benefits of the change initiative exceed its budget.

The change value analysis determines whether or not the change will provide value to the organization. Even though the financial aspect is critical, both a financial and non-financial appraisal should be conducted.

There are certain financial appraisal techniques that can be used to assess the value provided by a change. The popular ones include return on investment (ROI), payback approach, net present value (NV), and internal rate of return (IRR).

While a comprehensive explanation of these techniques is outside the scope of this book, it is easy for interested readers to search online to find a lot of information and comparisons about them. In this section, I will briefly explain the cost-benefits analysis and the decision tree approach, both of which could be used for the appraisal. The appraisal should, in most cases, provide the rationale for investment in a new change initiative.

The cost-benefits analysis will be used as an example of how to conduct the value analysis of a change. This approach checks whether or not the benefits exceed the costs in order to justify the execution of the program. The following steps will be followed for the analysis:

1. Develop the decision tree by identifying the main business risks (paths), along with their probabilities.

2. Calculate the expected cost, revenue, and profit for each path.

3. Calculate the expected revenue ($\sum$ revenue X probability).

4. Calculate the expected cost ($\sum$ cost X probability).

5. Identify the change benefits and disbenefits.

6. Evaluate the change benefits and disbenefits.

7. Conduct a value analysis by comparing benefits vs. costs.

12.4.3.1   Execution decision

If the change initiative provides value for the organization, it should be implemented. The change provides value if its benefits (financial and non-financial) exceed the required costs or resources. Upon finalizing the benefit/cost analysis, we will come up with one of four cases, as shown in Table 12-3.

Important Note

For a large transformation program, the internal rate of return (IRR) must be considered. IRR is the return percentage necessary to break even on an investment. Assuming that the IRR is 30% (calculation of the IRR is beyond our scope here), this means that the change initiative is financially viable as long as the discount rate that will be used to convert the future monetary value to the present value is less than 30%.

Table 12-3. *Change Execution Decision*

Case	Value status	Strategic decision
Value of the change greatly exceeds the change budget	High value	Go ahead

Case	Value status	Strategic decision
Value of the change is slightly higher or lower than the change budget	Medium value	Re-design until benefits are improved for the given budget or the budget is reduced for the given benefits.
Value of the change is much lower than the change budget	No value	Cancel

Important Note

The change provides value when its financial benefits and non-financial benefits exceed the costs or resources required for implementation.

Example 12-1 is a hypothetical cost-benefits analysis that will explain the process.

Example 12.1 - Cost-Benefits Analysis

Let us assume that a company has a yearly revenue of $4.5 million and yearly costs of $2.5 million. The company decides to implement a new change initiative which will presumably increase its revenue to $7 million.

However, the management team anticipates two major business risks, both of which have a 25% probability of occurring. If the first business risk eventuates, the revenue is expected to drop to $4 million instead of increase to $7 million. If the second business risk eventuates, the revenue is expected to drop even further to $3 million.

All paths of the change will have the same cost, which is $3 million. Figure 12-8 translates what we just mentioned into a decision tree, which represents steps 1 and 2.

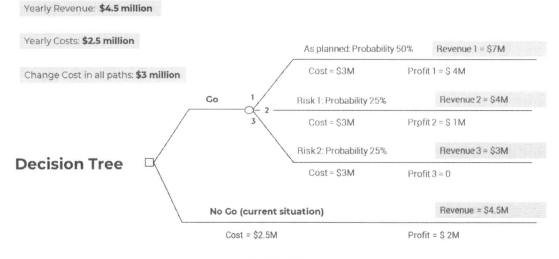

Figure 12-8. Decision Tree

Step 3: Calculate the expected revenue

The expected revenue from the decision tree is calculated as follows:

Expected revenue = (Revenue 1 x Probability 1) + (Revenue 2 x Probability 2) + (Revenue 3 x Probability 3)

Example 12.1 - Cost-Benefits Analysis

Expected revenue = ($7M x 50%) + ($4M x 25%) + ($3M x 25%)

$$= \$3.5M + \$1.0M + \$0.75M = \$5.25M$$

Step 4: Calculate the expected profit

The expected profit from the decision tree is calculated as follows:

Expected profit = Expected revenue − Cost (all paths have the same cost)

Expected profit = $5.25M - $3.0M = $2.25M

Or it can be calculated as:

Expected profit = (Profit 1 x Probability 1) + (Profit 2 x Probability 2) + (Profit 3 x Probability 3)

Expected profit = ($4M x 50%) + ($1M x 25%) + (0 x 25%)

$$= \$2M + \$0.25M + 0 = \$2.25M$$

Next, we compare the financial figures of the two decisions (Go or No-go), as presented in Table 12-4. We then identify the benefits and disbenefits and value them in order to conduct the appraisal analysis to decide the value that the change will provide.

Table 12-4. *Cost-Benefits Analysis*

	Expected costs	Expected revenue	Expected profit	Expected profit margin
No-go	$2.5M	$4.5M	$2.0M	44%
Go (based on the average of the three paths 1, 2, & 3)	$3.0M	$5.25M	$2.25M	43%
	Benefits	Value	Disbenefits	Value
Path #1: As planned	- Benefit #1		- Disbenefit #1	
	- Benefit #2			
	- Benefit #3			
	- Benefit #4			
	- Benefit #5			
Total				
Comments:				

12.5   COMPONENT 3: DEVELOPING THE CHANGE CHARTER

12.5.1   Objective

The objective of this component is to give the Go/No-go to start the change initiative. The objective is achieved by developing the change charter deliverable as shown in Figure 12-9.

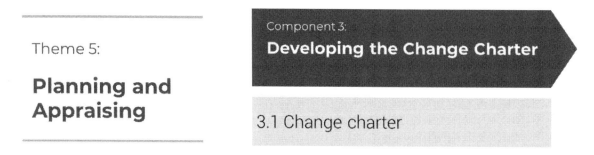

Figure 12-9. Deliverable of the Developing Change Charter Component

12.5.2   Deliverable 3.1: Change Charter

The objective of the change charter is to summarize the change initiative status in one document to let the managers identify whether or not the change is feasible, and accordingly give the Go/No-go decision.

Upon presenting the charter, we should end of one with of the following decisions:

- To go ahead with the change implementation if the value of the change greatly exceeds the budget.

- To redesign or postpone if the value of the change is slightly higher or lower than the budget.

- To cancel if the value of the change initiative is much lower than the required budget.

Approving the charter formally initiates the change initiative and provides the change team with the authority to develop the detailed change management plan to start implementing and leading. As shown in Figure 12-10, the change charter is presented during the planning and appraising theme.

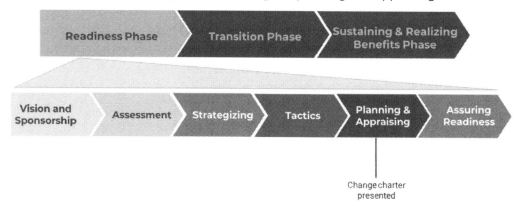

Figure 12-10. Change Charter

This charter has a summary of all analysis to enable the right decisions to be made about executing the change initiative.

I will go through a sample change charter, of course, the content of the charter may change based on the context and the change size.

Below is a suggested content of the change charter:

1. **Executive Summary.**

The executive summary should include the highlight of the charter and to be done when you complete the whole presentation.

2. **Change Vision.**

2.1 Start by defining your understanding of the problem that triggered the change. Show the change problem and then display your analysis of the root causes of the problem as well as the risk of not changing on the short and long time. You do this by showing the the problem map analysis that you did during develop the change business case.

2.2 Once the problem is clear, present the change business case or the change map. Start with the change problem that you already went through and then move though the different elements of the business case in whatever order you want to end up with list with the change outcomes and benefits. While discussing what to change, you may talk from the concept level only about the proposed solution and a brief analysis of the alternatives. And conclude by showing the current state vs. the future desired state from a high-level perspective.

2.3 Display the change objectives and goals using the change logic map, and read from the strategic perspective or from the implementation perspective, Also, try to show the cause and effect relationship between the elements if already identified. You can generally talk about the tactics needed to achieve the output and outcomes but you do not have to go thought the details of the tactics at this point.

2.4 And finally, conclude the change vision section by displaying the change success criteria and here you show the measures and targets for the elements that you displayed in the change logic map.

3   Change Impact

Show the results of the impact assessment along the organizational, culture, and stakeholder perspectives and talk about the findings and results. Also try to mention the most and least impacted units.

4   Change Management Methodology

4.1 Start by giving an introduction into the ElKattan's 5-Theme model and then list the components and deliverables that were delivered.

4.2 And also mention the quantitative methods that you used to collect the data As well as the qualitative methods

4.3 Finally present the inception plan. Notice at this point, the inception plan has not ended yet as it ends by developing the change management plan.

5 Assessment of the Current State

5.1 You can start by showing the results of the stakeholder readiness assessment along the three elements' awareness, competence and engagement and go through the issues that have been identified

5.2 Show the results of the organizational elements assessment along the three perspectives: strategy, capabilities, and capacity and go through the issues that have been identified

5.3 And next talk about the culture assessment and findings and the culture strategy that have been formulated

5.4 Next, show the change energy index and talk about its concept and what you will do to improv it.

5.5 Mention the assessment the stakeholder change narratives and what narrative strategy you will have

5.6 And conclude by the identified risks along with your risk management strategy.

6 Change Management High Level Plan

In this section, present the high-level plan and mention the number of campaign the change will have, and the expected period of each one. Then, explain the sub-outcomes and outcomes that will be achieved at the end of the campaigns. And finally, present the change management tactics that will be implemented in each campaign.

7 Change Management Objectives and Tactics

In this item, present each objective and explain why it was selected and then show the tactical activities that had been identified for it.

8 Change Budget

Display the consolidated budget of the change as per our cost structure. You do not have to go through the details of the budget of each item unless you are asked to do so.

9 Cost-Benefit Analysis

In this item, present the financial and non-financial figures to be able to show your assessment of the change value.

10 Next Steps

You end your presentation by what decision you expect from this meeting and what should happen next.

Once the charter is approved, the change team should go ahead and prepare the change management plan, which we will have next.

12.6   COMPONENT 4: DEVELOPING THE CHANGE MANAGEMENT PLAN

12.6.1 Overview

Many aspects of a typical change initiative are accompanied by a lot of uncertainties and risks. Additionally, as the change progresses, employees move from one state to another, which may cause unexpected resistance resulting in the need to modify the scope of the change initiative. These contributing factors may necessitate a change to the original plan; therefore, it is preferable to plan a change program in an iterative manner (with the plan including sequences of iterations), as it cannot be fully planned from the beginning. Below are some recommended principles to keep in mind when planning for a change:

- The plan does not need to be complete at the beginning of the process.

- The planning process will continue throughout the implementation.

- The planning process should accept feedback along the way.

- Deliver quick wins or show value as early as possible to help mitigate resistance.

- Revisit the change vision and scope continuously.

- The plan should be value-based rather than activity-based.

- The plan should include milestones for achieving outcomes and realizing benefits.

Important Note

Change planning should be designed in such a way that the execution starts as simply as possible, otherwise it will not take long to fail; the change plan should be flexible and agile.

All the above principles can be incorporated if Agile planning is used. Agile is an iterative method of planning that is more suitable than traditional planning for change initiatives.

As explained while discussing the change management high-level plan, the change goals are delivered in small phases called iterations. As our methodology is to have a value-based method of planning, the goal for each iteration is to end with a business value delivered that will help achieve the change outcomes.

As explained earlier in this chapter, the change management plan will have a number of change campaigns where each campaign contains a number of iterations.

Important Note

If a transformational change is not implemented following Agile planning, failure can be expected. The main benefit of Agile is its ability to respond to new changes arising throughout the project.

As a good practice, a planning meeting should be conducted at the end of each iteration in order to evaluate what happened and to plan for the next period.

12.6.2 Objective

The objective of this component is to develop the detailed plan for the change management campaigns and iterations.

The deliverables of the component are shown in Figure 12-11.

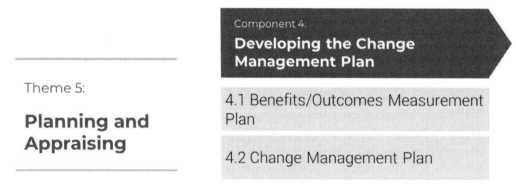

Figure 12-11. Deliverables of Developing the Change Management Plan Component

Tracking and measuring the outcomes and benefits should start as early as possible in the process.

Each plan should include the final consolidated tactics. Each tactic will have its own activities, start date, duration, owner, and budget. Once a plan has been finalized, it should be integrated with the master project plan to ensure good coordination between the change management activities and other activities related to the technical solution or project management.

12.6.3 Deliverable 4.1: Change Outcome/Benefit Measurement Plan

The objective of this plan is to identify how and when the quantification of the outcomes and benefits will be measured to identify the status of the change realization.

Before developing the measurement plan, it is essential to know when the related elements will be achieved. The relationship between the elements are supposed to be identified while developing the change logic map as shown in Chapter 8. In addition to the change logic map, the change business case and the outcome/benefit profile sheet deliverables should have already been finalized.

As shown in Table 12-5, let us begin by having a sample of a benefit profile sheet as presented in Chapter 8. The profile is for the benefit: Increased productivity.

Table 12-5. *Benefits Profile Sheet - Increased Productivity*

Change benefit: Increased productivity	
Description:	This benefit reflects how quickly the organization delivers its services.
Owner:	Sponsor A

Measurement	
Measure:	% Productivity Rate of Employees
Description:	This measure helps evaluate the productivity of an organization over time.
Baseline:	65%
Target:	85%
Scale of improvement:	30%
Measurement process	
Time to full realization:	One year
Measurement start date:	January
Measurement frequency:	Every three months
How to measure:	Dividing the total revenue of the company by the total number of employees.
Measurement responsibility:	HR manager
Measurement cost:	2 days
Impacted stakeholders	
All employees	
Assumptions	
Total revenue is available at the end of every quarter.	
Risks	
Not identified	

According to both the time to full realization and measurement frequency in the profile sheet, we will have four measurements in four different periods. Each period is for three months or one quarter of year.

Each period should have its own target, which is called the period target, where the last period should have the ultimate target which is defined in the profile sheet.

We measure and calculate the actual achievement as well as the cumulative achievement for each period. Tables 12-6 shows the measurements of the four periods.

Table 12-6. *Benefit Measurement Plan*

Change Benefit: Increased productivity			
Benefit owner: Sponsor A	**Measure**: % Productivity Rate of Employees	**Baseline**: 65%	**Target**: 85%

	Quarter 1	Quarter 2	Quarter 3	Quarter 4
Measurement date	1st week of April	1st week of July	1st week of Oct.	1st week of Jan.
Period target value	70%	75%	80%	85%
Target increased value from baseline (Period target – Baseline)	5%	10%	15%	20%
Actual measured value	70%	70%	75%	85%
Actual increased value from baseline (Actual – Baseline)	5%	5%	10%	20%
Achievement index (Actual increased value / Target increased value)	100%	50%	67%	100%
Cumulative achievement	100%	75%	71%	85%

Once the measurement and a comparison between the planned target and the actual measurement has been finalized in each period as shown in the above table, it is time to have the benefit realization status. The objective of the benefits realization status has is to help determine whether the benefits remain achievable or not; and to recommend corrective actions to ensure the change benefits can be realized. Tables 12-7 has a suggested template that can be used for the benefits realization status.

Table 12-7. *Benefit Realization Status Template*

Change Benefit: Increased productivity			
Measure:		Baseline:	Ultimate target:
Last actual value			
Last measurement date			
Cumulative achievement			
Status of related outputs outcomes, benefits			
Achievable (Yes/No)			
Lessons learned			
Corrective actions			

If the company is using its own performance management system tool such as the Balanced Scorecard (BSC) framework, benefits management should be part of this system (refer to Appendix B for more information about the BSC framework).

Important Note

It is very difficult to perfectly predict the future while implementing a change that is full of uncertainties.

Consequently, predicting the right plan is close to impossible. For this reason, any plan should be designed in an iterative way.

12.6.4 Deliverable 4.2: Change Management Plan

The objective of the change management plan is to develop the detailed plan of the change management campaigns and iterations.

As shown in Figure 12-12, the change management plan is developed at the end of the planning sub-phase in the readiness phase. The change management plan is to be executed in the remaining period of the readiness phase, and continues in the transition phase, and finally in the sustaining and realizing benefits phase.

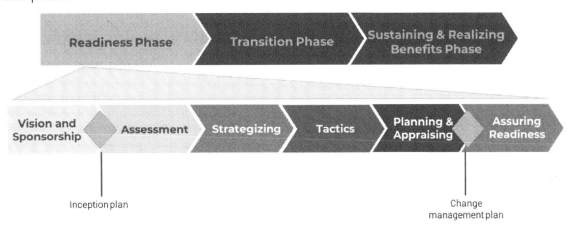

Figure 12-12. Timeline of the Change Management Plan

As shown in Figure 12-13, Let us assume that our high-level plan has five change management campaigns along the three phases of the change cycle. For each campaign, the change management plan should include the detailed plan for the iterations of every campaign. Example 12-2 will have a suggested template.

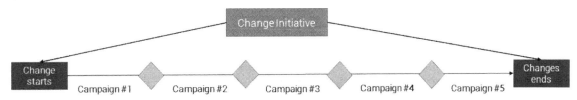

Figure 12-13. Change Management High-Level Plan

Planning in change management is not a deliverable; it is a process that should be happening all the time as we keep assessing based on the progress and feedback, strategizing, and finally replanning.

Example 12.2 - Enterprise Resource Planning (ERP) Project

Enterprise resource planning (ERP) is a software application that provides integrated management of the main business processes. The majority of large companies have an ERP system.

Oracle and SAP are two corporations that are well known worldwide for their ERP systems. Installing an ERP system usually involves many challenges, as many changes in behaviors and the way people work are required. Nowadays, most companies need to add the change management component while deploying a new ERP system to ensure a successful implementation.

The project management cycle of an ERP system is comprised of the following five phases: Preparing, Exploring, Realizing, Deploying, and Going live. We match these phases with the change management, as shown in Figure 12-14.

When we work on such a project, we match the ERP five phases with the three change management phases as shown in Figure 12-14.

The readiness phase will have three change management pans that are to be integrated with the ERP project management plan. These three plans are as follows:

1. Vision and sponsorship plan. In this plan we develop the deliverables of the Vision and sponsorship theme.

2. The inception plan. This plan translates the change management methodology.

3. The change management plan. This plan translates the change management tactics into detailed activities.

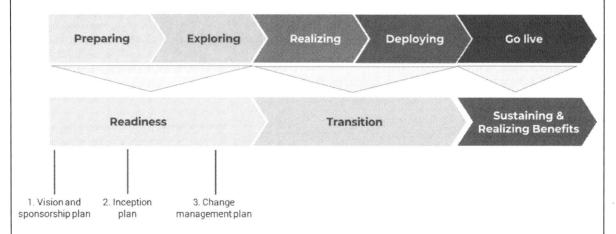

Figure 12-14. CM Life Cycle vs. PM Life Cycle

Table 12-8 provides a template change management plan that can be used for such a project.

Table 12-8. *Sample Change Management Plan*

:	Start date	Duration	Responsible	Involved stakeholders
Campaign #1				
Iteration 1				
Activity 1				
Activity 2				
Iteration 2				
Activity 1				

Activity 2				

Campaign #2				
Iteration 1				
Activity 1				
Activity 2				
Iteration 2				
Activity 1				
Activity 2				

Campaign #3				
Iteration 1				
Activity 1				
Activity 2				
Iteration 2				
Activity 1				
Activity 2				

Campaign #4				
Iteration 1				
Activity 1				
Activity 2				
Iteration 2				
Activity 1				

Campaign #5				
Iteration 1				
Activity 1				
Activity 2				

12.7   CHAPTER IN A BOX

A summary of the planning and appraising theme is shown in Table 12-9.

Table 12-9. *Summary of the Planning and Appraising Theme*

Theme objective	The objective of this theme is to assess the value of the change, finalize the Go/No-Go decision, and develop a consolidated change management plan of all the work streams.			
Theme components	1. Developing the change management high-level plan	2. Appraising change	3. Developing the change charter	4. Developing the change management plan
Component objective	The objective of this component is is to decide on the planning methodology, develop the high-level change management plan and consolidate all change management objectives.	The objective of this component is to estimate the change budget and assess whether or not the change initiative is worth implementing.	The objective of this component is to give the Go/No-go to start the change initiative.	The objective of this component is to develop the detailed plan for the change management campaigns and iterations.
Deliverables	▪ Change management high-level plan ▪ Change management objectives analysis	▪ Change budget ▪ Cost-benefit analysis	▪ Change charter	▪ Change outcome/benefit measurement plan ▪ Change management plan

APPENDICES

Appendix A – A Quick Orientation of Change Management Models

Although numerous change management models have evolved over time, no universal approach is suitable for all circumstances because the context, culture, and scope of the change are different for every situation.

While every model has its own variations, they all share some common features. For this reason, it is essential for senior management to have an understanding of the different approaches to leading a change initiative in addition to the ElKattan's Model.

This chapter will summarize eight change management models.

A.1 LEWIN'S 3-PHASE MODEL

Successful change should follow a specific pattern. Kurt Lewin was one of the earlier scholars to tackle the concept of following a specific pattern during the implementation of change. In the late 1940s, Lewin introduced the first ever change management model, known as the 3-Phase Model.

Lewin's 3-Phase Model stated that, any change must follow a pattern set out in three phases (unfreeze, movement & refreeze). The first phase is to unfreeze the targeted behaviors to be changed. The second is to start changing, and the third is to secure the change and new behaviors.

Even though the 3-Phase Model was developed long ago, both Lewin's name and his model are still dominant in most change management references. The subject model of this book, ElKattan's Model, is also partially based on the same pattern.

Figure A-1 shows the classical change pattern according to Lewin.

Figure A-1. Lewin's Classical Change Pattern

13.1.1 Unfreeze Phase

When a new change is initiated, the status quo must be carefully examined in order to determine how to unfreeze people from what they have been doing for an extended period. Oftentimes, people build what is called "personal pride" in their area of expertise, thus, the *how* of the unfreeze needs to be tailored according to each situation.

Attempting an organizational "unfreeze" can be accomplished through actions such as:

- Presenting gap analysis

- Highlighting weaknesses

- Conducting orientation sessions

- Communicating strategic drivers and new challenges

The primary purpose of these actions is to magnify the level of dissatisfaction with the current status.

13.1.2 Moving Phase

Moving forward and initiating change should not begin unless the driving force outweighs the expected resisting force.

The critical question is: how can this be measured? In other words, how can we be sure that the driving force outweighs the anticipated resisting force?

In this phase, change leaders initiate actions and make changes. Lewin emphasized that these actions are executed in conjunction with the involvement of others in the process.

13.1.3 Refreeze Phase

This phase focuses on stabilizing the desired state by setting up ways to ensure that the new level of behavior is relatively secure. According to Lewin, the *how* of the "refreeze" can be achieved with a level of permanency through:

- Implementation of new policies.

- Changing incentive schemes to reward desired outcomes.

- Establishing new systems.

A.2 KOTTER'S 8-STEP MODEL

A.2.1 Overview

The 8-Step Model is well-recognized and widely referenced in a great deal of literature. Kotter famously explained his model in the 1995 *Harvard Business Review* article entitled "Leading Change: Why Transformation Efforts Fail."

Based on an analysis of over one hundred change initiatives within organizations implementing large-scale change, Kotter found that 70% either failed completely, came in over budget or behind schedule, or were implemented in an atmosphere of extreme frustration.

Thirteen years later, in his book *Creating a Sense of Urgency,* Kotter observed that the success rate of change initiatives remained unchanged, primarily because change has outpaced the skill development of management.

A.2.2 Description of the model

Kotter claimed that a successful change must go through eight steps. Each of these eight steps must complement each other and be initiated in the correct order. Each step was developed from a corresponding mistake. Based on the conclusions made in Kotter's research, the eight steps of this model are as follows:

1. Establishing a sense of urgency

This step corresponds to the mistake of allowing *too much complacency* or the failure to establish a high sense of urgency.

Kotter stressed that without a high sense of *true* urgency, it is difficult to drive people out of their comfort zones. This results in a situation in which the change leader must use coercion to impose the change. As previously mentioned in the Global Trans case study, coercion does not generally create a sense of commitment or ownership, and few people would be interested in participating in such a change.

2. Forming the leadership team

This step corresponds to the mistake of *failing to create a sufficiently powerful leadership team*.

According to Kotter, a transformational change should not be led by just one executive or by a weak change-leadership team. It is usually the case that a single executive or a weak team will struggle with resistance, deep structure, politics, or short-term self-interest. Therefore, it is essential to assemble a team with sufficient power, experience, and credibility to lead the change if it is to be successful.

3. Creating a vision

This step corresponds to the mistake of *underestimating the power of a vision*.

According to Kotter, having a clear vision to steer the change in the right direction is crucial. Clarity of vision for the desired outcome will greatly facilitate the making of decisions during the change implementation process. Once the vision of the change is clear, strategies with dedicated budgets can be formulated and implemented to achieve that vision.

4. Communicating the change vision

This step corresponds to the mistake of *under-communicating the vision*.

The vision and strategies should be communicated repeatedly in a very simple and clear way. According to Kotter, it is very important that employees get on board with the vision, otherwise they will make no effort to ensure the success of the change.

Kotter indicated that if the vision of the change is not adequately communicated, employees will not make any sacrifices to achieve it, as they will not see the potential benefits of that change.

5. Empowering employees to take broad-based action

This step corresponds to the mistake of *permitting obstacles to block the new vision.*

Kotter advised that it is essential to empower employees to get rid of obstacles to the vision. Empowerment will enable the change team to change any systems that undermine the attainment of the change objectives.

6. Generating short-term wins

This step corresponds to the mistake of *failing to create short-term wins.*

Kotter indicated that generating short-term wins is essential to building momentum, getting employees on board, and providing concrete evidence that the change is feasible and on track. The short-term wins should be:

- Visible
- Unambiguous
- Related to the change vision

According to Kotter, without short-term wins it is much more likely that employees will actively join the change resistance front.

7. Consolidating gains and producing more change

This step corresponds to the mistake of *declaring victory too soon.*

Kotter advised using the credibility gained by short-term wins to provide leverage for bigger projects and structural changes that are unrelated to the vision. As Kotter indicated, a change will only be sustainable when it binds to the culture, because any change is naturally subject to degradation as soon as the pressures associated with it are removed.

8. Anchoring new approaches in the culture

This step corresponds to the mistake of *neglecting to anchor changes firmly in the organizational culture.*

As Kotter indicated, changes in any organization can unravel, even after years of effort, if they have not been firmly anchored in the organizational culture.

The more deeply the change team understand the existing culture, the more easily they can figure out how to develop the vision, communicate with employees, increase the sense of urgency, develop strategies to ensure sustainability of the change, and so forth.

A.2.3 The Model Practices

Kotter emphasized that, with the exception of the first step (*Establishing a sense of urgency*), all steps should operate simultaneously once they have been initiated. However, the steps must be initiated in the same order as indicated in the model. If the steps are not initiated in the correct order, there will not be the momentum needed to overcome the enormously powerful influence of inertia.

Each step in the model has some practices that must be implemented. Table A-1 shows a summary of the mistakes and the steps associated with them, as well as the practices that should be implemented with each step.

Table A-1. *Kotter's Eight-Step Model*

Change Mistakes	Model Steps	Practice
Allowing too much complacency	Establishing a sense of urgency	1. Examining the market and competitive realities. 2. Identifying and discussing crises, potential crises, and major opportunities.
Failing to create a sufficiently powerful leadership team	Forming the leadership team	1. Putting together a team with sufficient power to lead the change. 2. Getting the team to work together.
Underestimating the power of a vision	Creating a vision	1. Creating a vision to help direct the change effort. 2. Developing strategies to achieve the vision.
Under- communicating the vision	Communicating the change vision	1. Repeatedly communicating the new vision and strategies to employees. 2. Ensuring the leadership team is a role model.
Permitting obstacles to block the new vision	Empowering employees to take broad-based action	1. Getting rid of obstacles. 2. Changing the systems or structures that undermine the change vision. 3. Encouraging risk-taking and the expression of new ideas.
Failing to create short-term wins	Generating short-term wins	1. Planning for improvements in performance. 2. Creating short-term wins. 3. Recognizing and rewarding people who make wins possible.
Declaring victory too soon	Consolidating gains and producing more change	1. Changing all systems and structures that do not support the change vision. 2. Hiring and developing people who can implement the change vision. 3. Introducing new projects, themes, and change agents.
Neglecting to anchor changes firmly in the organizational culture	Anchoring new approaches in the culture	1. Creating performance-oriented behavior and better leadership. 2. Articulating the connections between new behaviors and success. 3. Developing the means to ensure leadership development and sustainability.

Note. Source: Kotter (1996)

A.2.5 Usage and points of critique

Because Kotter's model is generic, it can be used for different kinds of change implementation. It also demonstrates the benefits of being willing to adapt a change management model to a specific situation. In addition, it can be used to anticipate potential mistakes in the implementation of the change, allowing the change leader to avoid making those mistakes.

This model is good when it comes to a change with a high level of complacency and lack of commitment, especially in radical change initiatives.

Even though I agree with the importance of including Kotter's first step (Establishing a sense of urgency) when implementing any change initiative, I also recognize that a change can be successful without a high sense of urgency if it has a clear and inspiring vision with well-planned actions. It is also worth keeping in mind that an excessive sense of urgency may cause anxiety and frustration amongst employees.

Although Kotter recommended that the change would be implemented as a project, his model had no clear component to act as a guide for this. In addition, the order of the eight steps in his model, which he insisted must be followed, may not be appropriate for all change initiatives.

A.3 ADKAR MODEL

A.3.1 Overview

The ADKAR Model was developed by Jeff Hiatt in 2003. Hiatt emphasized that a change could not be effectively managed at an organizational level unless the change leaders knew how to manage this change with every single individual. Therefore, this model is more relevant to the management of people, as it is a framework for understanding change at an individual level (Bashir & Afzal, 2008).

This has been one of the change management models most commonly used by organizations for many years. The reason is that this model is very simple, yet powerful and can be easily explained and applied.

A.3.2 Description of the Model

This model outlines five building blocks that are required for any change to be successfully implemented.

Hiatt placed the five building blocks in the order in which an individual should experience the change. Desire cannot come before awareness because awareness is what triggers the desire and engagement. Knowledge cannot come before desire because people will not be keen to learn until they are motivated to do so. Ability cannot come before knowledge because people cannot do something before they know about it. Finally, reinforcement cannot come before ability because people can only reinforce something that has already been achieved.

Figure A-2 shows the five ADKAR building blocks, along with their descriptions.

1 Awareness

Person's understanding of the nature of a change.

2 Desire

The willingness to support and get engaged in a change.

3 Knowledge

The information, training, and education necessary to know how to change.

4 Ability

The execution of a change and turning knowledge to action.

5 Reinforcement

Internal and external actions that sustain a change.

Figure A-2. ADKAR Model

A.3.3 The Model Practices

This model also has five practices that should be implemented to achieve its five building blocks. These are: (1) Communication, (2) Sponsor roadmap, (3) Coaching, (4) Training, and (5) Resistance management.

Table A-2 shows the five ADKAR building blocks, practices, and related resistance factors.

Table A-2. *ADKAR Model Building Blocks, Practices, and Resistance Factors*

Building Blocks	Practices	Resistance Factors
Awareness	- Communication	Comfort with status quo
	- Sponsor roadmap	Credibility of change leader
	- Coaching	Debate or denial that change is needed
Desire	- Sponsor roadmap	Being in a comfort zone
	- Coaching	Fear of the unknown
	- Resistance management	Change conflicts with the individual's self-interest or values
Knowledge	- Coaching	Gap between current and required knowledge
	- Training	Insufficient time or resources
Ability	- Coaching	Lack of support and limitations of individual ability
	- Training	Psychological blocks
Reinforcement	- Communication	Reward not meaningful or associated with achievement
	- Sponsor roadmap	Negative peer pressure to revert to old ways
	- Coaching	Incentives that directly oppose change

Note. Source: Hiatt (2006)

A.3.5 Usage and points of critique

The model provides a very easy and practical framework for managing the people side of a change initiative. However, the life cycle of this model only begins after a change has been identified. It does not cover the envisioning phase of the change. Therefore, the model has points of weakness in terms of creating the vision, developing the change objectives, assessing readiness for the change, and evaluating the culture of the organization. The model also lacks the concept of having a life cycle for the change, which has been added by Prosci as we will see in the next model.

A.4 PROSCI ADKAR MODEL

A.4.1 Overview

Prosci is a company that specializes in change management training and products. The name comes from the two words: **Pro**fessional and **Sci**ence. Prosci developed a change management model based on the ADKAR model.

The Prosci ADKAR Model complements the ADKAR Model and is therefore a very comprehensive and useful model for handling change.

A.4.2 Description of the Model

The Prosci ADKAR model has three phases as shown in Figure A-3.

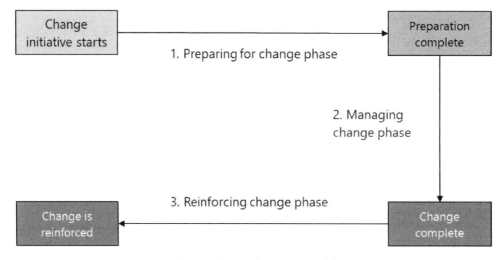

Figure A-3. Prosci ADKAR Model

Below is a description of the three phases of the model:

1. Preparing for change phase

The first phase of the model has three processes:

1. Define the change strategy.

2. Prepare the change team.

3. Prepare the sponsors.

2. Managing change phase

The second phase encompasses the development and implementation of the change plan. It has two processes:

1. Develop change plans.

2. Implement change plans.

3. Sustaining change phase

The third and final phase consists of four main processes:

1. Collect and analyze feedback.

2. Diagnose gaps.

3. Implement corrective measures.

4. Celebrate changes.

Table A-3 shows the phases and processes of the Prosci ADKAR model.

Table A-3. *Prosci ADKAR Model*

	Phase Name	Processes	ADKAR
Phase 1	Preparing for change	1. Define strategy 2. Prepare change team 3. Prepare sponsors	
Phase 2	Managing change	1. Develop change plans 2. Implement plans	Integrate the ADKAR model's five building blocks and five practices into the project plan
Phase 3	Sustaining change	1. Collect and analyze feedback 2. Diagnose gaps 3. Implement corrective measures 4. Celebrate changes	

A.4.4 Usage and points of critique

The company provides a very practical and user-friendly way to integrate the change into the project management plan. It even provides a paint-by-numbers toolkit that can be used to implement the change over the three phases.

Unfortunately, this model is missing the culture assessment component, which is crucial for determining how an organization's culture may influence the implementation of the change. This may result in confusion about the phases, processes, building blocks, and practices.

A.5 BURKE-LITWIN'S MODEL

A.5.1 Overview

The Burke-Litwin model helps the change leader to understand the different elements within an organization and how they influence each other both during and after the implementation of a change.

This model highlights how the theoretical principles of the open-system theory apply to organizations. Describing an organization as an open system suggests that it is like any living being in that it is largely influenced by external environmental factors.

So what are the external environmental factors that influence an organization?

External factors can be either macro or micro. Macro factors potentially impact all industries and include things such as political, economic, social, and technological conditions. Micro factors potentially impact the industry specific to the organization and include things such as competition, barriers to entry, substitution of the products, supplier power, and customer power.

It is the external factors that drive a company's strategy because products and services are developed to serve the external environment. That is why the first step in the creation of a strategic plan for any organization is an analysis of the external environment.

Burke (2010) described why organizations can be an open system in this way:

> "... begins with the cyclical process of input-throughput-output; that is, transforming input into a usable product or service. The transformation of the output into the external environment (a customer, for example) creates the potential for feedback, which in turn generates another form of input so that the organization can correct its throughput to improve its future output, thus helping to ensure long-term survival. Therefore, systems are composed of cycles of events."

A.5.2 Model Description

This model provides a map of the elements comprising almost every organization. The elements are arranged in a top-down order according to their influence on each other. See Figure A-4 for the model's organizational elements.

The model states that the change in the elements at the top of the model (external environment, organization culture, leadership, mission, and strategy) will be the drivers for a transformational change. The rest of the elements (in the middle and at the bottom of the model) are the drivers for a transactional change on either the operational or the individual level. As discussed in Chapter 2, transactional changes can be either incremental or transitional.

For a change to be successful, the strategy, culture, and leadership must be aligned from the beginning of the implementation process. While the alignment of these elements is critical in a transformational change, they are less critical in a transitional or incremental change.

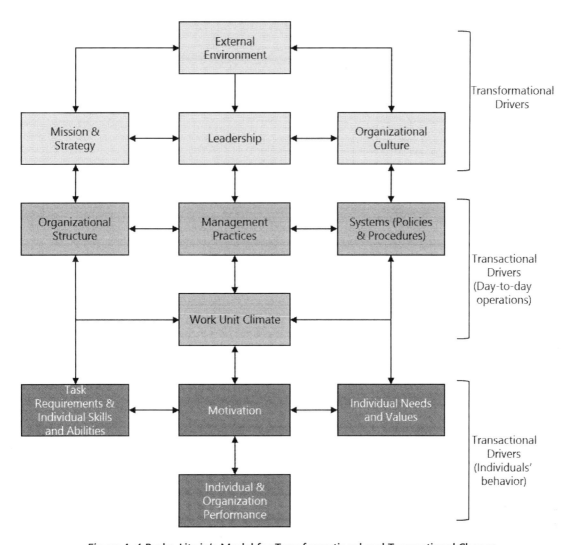

Figure A-4. Burke-Litwin's Model for Transformational and Transactional Change

The elements at the bottom of the model are key to making any kind of change stick. A change will only be sustainable if it is eventually managed at the individual level. Therefore, the following must be considered before implementing any change:

- Motivation

- Individual needs and values

- Task requirements

- Individual skills and abilities

This model also differentiated between the culture and climate within an organization. Climate defines how the workplace looks like and is manifested in things such as the work atmosphere and environment. Throughout the book, this was assumed to be part of the symbols of the organizational culture. Therefore,

I view the organizational climate as a subpart of the organizational culture; it can easily be changed. Many elements contribute to the nature of the organizational climate, such as management practice, leadership approach, norms (shared expectations & rules), and systems of operations (processes, regulations, etc.).

A.5.4 Usage and Points of Critique

The model is useful to:

- Explain the bilateral changes that happen between all the elements when a change is implemented.

- Prevent focusing on only one element of the organization during change implementation.

- Find the connection between the elements.

- Recognize the elements that might enable or hinder a change.

Nevertheless, this model is more of a guiding tool than a systematic change management model, especially with regard to transformational changes.

A.6 BURKE'S MODEL

A.6.1 Overview

Burke's model combines the concepts and practices of several other models, particularly Kotter's Eight-Step Model. Burke strongly believed that an organization is an open system, and emphasized the importance of gathering information about the external environment before starting the change implementation process. This information may include changing customer needs, changing technology in the industry, changing government regulations, learning what competitors are up to, and the status of the general economy.

A.6.2 Description of the Model

Burke's Model has a change life cycle consisting of four phases. The four phases contain 16 practices.

Unlike other multi-phase change management models, Burke emphasized that the phases of his model are not discrete; they overlap and are interconnected, with more than one phase running at the same time.

Figure A-5 shows the four phases of Burke's model.

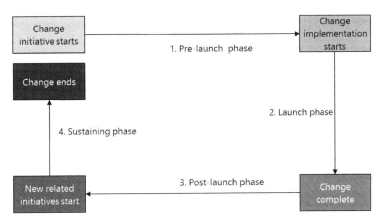

Figure A-5. Burke Model Life Cycle

A.6.2.1 Phase 1: Pre-launch phase

The main objective of this phase is to develop the vision. It is the vision that provides the roadmap that directs an organization's change effort and enables it to be fruitful. Burke indicated that without this roadmap, an organization would not be able to successfully implement the desired change.

This is also the phase in which the leadership team is formed and the need for change is established. It consists of the following practices:

- Leader self-examination
- Gathering information from the external environment
- Establishing a need for change
- Providing clarity of vision and direction

A.6.2.2 Phase 2: Launch phase

The first step in this phase is to communicate the vision. Burke stressed that people need to be reminded about the change – and why it is necessary – in a variety of ways (meetings, in person, face-to-face, via the internet, video meetings, and written documents and so forth).

Burke indicated that resistance can occur at three levels, and the resistance behavior that takes place should be managed at each level. These levels are:

- Individual level
- Group level
- Larger system level

At the individual level, a change leader must differentiate between three different types of resistance:

- Blind
- Ideological

- Political

Different strategies are required for each type of resistance.

This phase consists of the following practices:

- Communicating the need for change

- Initiating key activities

- Dealing with resistance

A.6.2.3 Phase 3: Post-launch phase

This phase is difficult for change leaders because it is the phase in which things are most likely to spiral out of control. Therefore, it is important for the change leader to step in and establish a new order, and be persistent in respect of what is going to make the desired change successful. Furthermore, the change leader should strive to get people out of their comfort zone.

This post-launch or implementation phase consists of five practices:

1. Multiple leverage

2. Taking the heat

3. Consistency

4. Perseverance

5. Repeating the message

A.6.2.4 Phase 4: Sustaining phase

This last phase of the model is primarily about using the credibility gained from implementing the change to push forward faster and introduce new related change initiatives. It consists of the following four practices:

1. Dealing with unanticipated consequences

2. Maintaining the momentum

3. Choosing successors

4. Launching new initiatives

A.6.3 The model Practices

Table A-4 summarizes the different practices of this model.

Table A-4. *Burke's Model Practices*

Phase #	Phase Name	Practice
Phase 1	Pre-launch Phase	1. Leader's self-examination. 2. Gathering information about the external environment. 3. Establishing the need for change. 4. Providing the vision and direction.
Phase 2	Launch Phase	1. Communicating the need for change. 2. Initiating key activities. 3. Dealing with resistance.
Phase 3	Post-launch Phase	1. Multiple forms of leverage. 2. Taking the heat. 3. Maintaining consistency. 4. Showing perseverance. 5. Repeating the message.
Phase 4	Sustaining Phase	1. Dealing with unanticipated consequences. 2. Maintaining momentum. 3. Choosing successors. 4. Launching new initiatives.

Note. Source: Burke (2010)

A.6.5 Usage and Points of Critique

Because this model is general, it is suitable for preparing and managing any kind of change, especially large-scale projects.

Even though the model has a procedure for developing the vision, its weakness lies in the fact that it is unable to measure the success of the change and how the change is linked to strategy.

In addition, the model is also missing the culture assessment and a method of integrating the change plan with the project management plan.

A.7 The 'BIG SIX' MODEL

A.7.1 Overview

Phil Merrell developed the processes for his 'Big Six' model based on the findings of a study done on over 600 organizations. The study was conducted by Towers Watson, which used to be one of the world's largest employee benefits consulting companies. These six processes are: (1) Leading, (2) Communicating, (3)

Learning, (4) Measuring, (5), Involving, and (6) Sustaining.

Merrell maintained that these six processes are the ones that most successful change initiatives go through, regardless of the type of change that a company experiences.

A.7.2 Description of the model

This model has a change life cycle consisting of the following three phases:

A.7.2.1 Phase 1: Understand and segment

In this phase, Merrell indicated that it is not only the business environment that needs to be understood, but also the underlying needs of the business and how its key stakeholders define success.

A.7.2.2 Phase 2: Design and build

This is the phase in which the plans must be set, including tools, tactics, and timing. Change owners must verify that the awareness and behaviors that support the change are in place.

A.7.2.3 Phase 3: Implement and improve

In this last phase, the change management plan is executed and its effectiveness is measured. If all goes according to plan, the success of the change initiative will be celebrated at the end of this phase. Improvements will be found and implemented along the way.

Figure A-6 shows these three phases of the model along with the 'Big Six' processes.

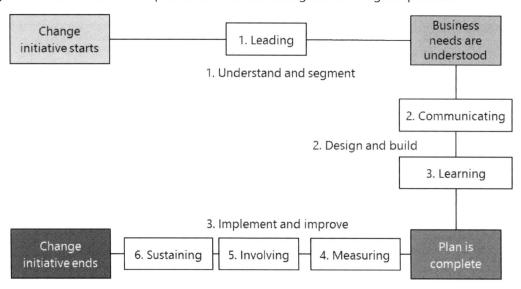

Figure A-6. The 'Big Six' Model Life Cycle

Below is the description of the 'Big Six' processes:

A.7.2.4 Process 1: Leading

For Merrell, most of the organizations that effectively managed a change implementation had a clear-cut vision of the objectives and purposes of the changes. They also had the support of their top management; this is a vital element, because leaders inspire confidence in changes, create clarity among employees, and foster a sense of community.

This process also implies of the following practices:

* Finding executive support for the change.

* Developing a clear vision for the change.

* Creating a strategy for communication and implementation of the change.

* Creating a strong motivation for employees to get on board with the change.

A.7.2.5 Process 2: Communicating

Merrell maintained that organizations that are good at change management are those who clearly communicate their rationale for the changes. Good communication about a change fosters understanding, aligns organizations from top to bottom, guides the change, and motivates employees to be involved in its successful implementation.

This process also has several implied practices:

* Communicating the business rationale for the change.

* Communicating how the change will affect individuals.

* Encouraging employees to provide input.

* Communicating what employees need to do differently to be successful.

* Avoiding the spread of misinformation about the changes being made.

A.7.2.6 Process 3: Learning

Merrell stressed that employees need to have the knowledge and skills needed to adapt to a change. There is a learning process that will help push a change initiative forward in the right direction. This includes:

1. Creating accountability for employees to learn any new skills needed for the change.

2. Creating accountability for employees to exhibit the new behaviors needed for the change.

3. Encouraging employees to give feedback about the new behaviors and skills that are needed to implement and sustain the change.

A.7.2.7 Process 4: Measuring

According to Merrell, organizations that are effective at change management use a balanced set of metrics to define success and support continuous improvement. Setting clear and measurable objectives up front helps an organization use its resources efficiently, make corrections as needed along the way, and assess whether change initiatives are achieving what they set out to do.

As with the previous three processes, this one also has its implied practices, which are:

11 Defining clear and measurable objectives for the changes.

12 Measuring progress against the established objectives of the change.

A.7.2.8 Process 5: Involving

Based on Merrell's conclusions, the organizations that involve their employees in the design and implementation of a change are more likely to be effective at change management and less likely to face resistance to the change from those employees. The practices included in this process are:

13 Recruiting the support of a sufficient number of employees.

14 Creating a sense of co-ownership of the change among the employees.

15 Dealing with any resistance to the change initiatives from the employees.

A.7.2.9 Process 6: Sustaining

Merrell asserted that one of the biggest mistakes a change leader can make is to assume the finish line is located at the end of the project. It is vital that an organization puts in place all the elements needed to ensure the intended change is firmly embedded in its culture. To do this, it needs to consider all the processes, policies, technology, and structures necessary to support and sustain the post-change environment. The practices implied in this process are:

16 Continuing to exhibit the new behaviors and skills after the change has been implemented.

17 Making continual improvements in subsequent years.

18 Avoiding reversion to the previous status.

A.7.3 The Model Practices

Table A-5 provides a summary of the 'Big Six' processes and their practices.

Table A-5. *The 'Big Six' Change Management Model*

Process	Practice
1. Leading	1.1 Finding executive support for the change. 1.2 Developing a clear vision for the change. 1.3 Creating a strategy for communication and implementation. 1.4 Creating strong motivation for employees.
2, Communicating	2.1 Communicating the business rationale for the change. 2.2 Communicating what the change means to individuals.

Process	Practice
	2.3 Encouraging employees to provide input.
	2.4 Communicating what the employees need to do differently to be successful.
	2.5 Avoiding any misinformation about the changes being made.
3. Learning	3.1 Creating accountability among employees to learn any new skills needed for the change to be successfully accomplished.
	3.2 Creating accountability among employees to exhibit any new behaviors required for the change to be successfully accomplished.
	3.3 Encouraging employees to provide feedback on the new behaviors and skills.
4. Measuring	4.1 Defining clear and measurable goals.
	4.2 Measuring the progress against the goals.
5. Involving	5.1 Developing sufficient support from the employees.
	5.2 Creating a sense of co-ownership among the employees.
	5.3 Dealing with resistance.
6. Sustaining	6.1 Continuing to exhibit the new behaviors.
	6.2 Finding additional improvements.
	6.3 Avoiding reversion to the previous status.

Note. Source: Merrell (2010)

A.7.5 Usage and points of critique

The 'Big Six' model is simple but very powerful. It can be used for any project regardless of the size of the change as it provides the most commonly used practices. It is also very useful for managers who are not familiar with change management models and concepts.

Because of the simplicity of the model, the change leader can easily implement its phases and select from the practices while planning for the change.

However, it does have limitations because it is missing the components related to understanding organizational culture and assessing the organization's readiness for the change. It is also missing components such as coaching and training that can be added to the learning process.

A.8 The MANAGING CHANGE MODEL

A.8.1 Overview

The Managing Change Model was developed by Columbia University. It provides a holistic view of change management that highlights the phases and practices that are essential to the successful implementation of a change.

A.8.2 Description of the model

This model emphasizes the importance of maintaining the momentum of the change. This includes directing positive energy toward the change goals, monitoring progress, and providing feedback to employees when any change milestone is reached, no matter how small it may seem. The model has the following four phases:

1. Understanding the nature of the change and the individual responses to it.

2. Planning for the change.

3. Managing the people side and the organizational side of the change.

4. Evaluating the change.

Figure A-7 shows the four phases of this model.

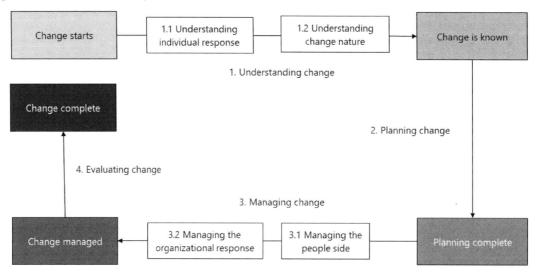

Figure A-7. The Managing Change Model Life Cycle

A.8.4 Usage and Points of Critique

This simple model focuses on the main issues of any change. It also emphasizes the importance of employee involvement during the planning process, along with the importance of voicing any dissatisfaction with the current state and articulating a vision for the future state.

It addresses the issue of communication; what, how much, and how to communicate during the change implementation process. It also addresses the difficulty of determining the vision for the future state of the organization, as well as the importance of allowing time for employees to disengage from the present state.

However, this model is lacking two important things: firstly, the element of culture assessment; and secondly, a method for integrating the change plan with the project management plan.

A.9 SUMMARY

This chapter took us on a journey through seven change management models. The selected models are generic and can be used for many different types of changes. The highlights of the chapter are as follows:

- There is no single recipe that is appropriate for all changes. The more skilled and experienced a manager is, the better they can choose the best tools for their specific circumstances.

- The selected model should be customized according to the size of the initiative, the culture of the organization, and the context of the change.

- Almost all models have similar change life cycles. Mapping between the models and ElKattan's Model was presented.

- The common elements in most of these models is the absence of the "culture" component, and the fact that they fail to address how to integrate change management with project management.

Table A-6 shows the outline of the models discussed in this chapter.

Table A-6. *Summary of the Change Management Models*

	Model	Components
1	Lewin's 3-Phase Model	(1) Unfreeze (2) Moving (3) Refreeze
2	Eight-Step Model	(1) Establishing a sense of urgency (2) Forming the leadership team (3) Developing the vision (4) Communicating the vision (5) Empowering employees (6) Generating short-term wins (7) Consolidating gains and producing more change (8) Institutionalizing new approaches in the culture.
3	AKDAR Model	(1) Awareness (2) Desire (3) Knowledge (4) Ability (5) Reinforcement
4	Prosci ADKAR Model	(1) Preparing for change (2) Managing change (3) Sustaining change.
5	Burke-Letwin Model	(1) Transformational elements (2) Transactional elements (3) Individual elements
6	Burke's Model	(1) Prelaunch phase (2) Launch phase (3) Post-launch phase (4) Sustaining phase
7	The 'Big Six' Model	(1) Leading (2) Communicating (3) Learning (4) Measuring (5) Involving

	Model	Components
		(6) Sustaining
8	The Managing Change Model	(1) Understanding (2) Planning (3) Managing (4) Reviewing

Appendix B – Project, Program, Benefits, and Strategic Management

B.1 OVERVIEW

This appendix offers a brief background outlining of the differences between change management, project management, program management, strategic objectives, and benefits management.

Program management, project management, and benefits management are considered some of the key tools used to manage any given change initiative.

Whenever I conduct any training, I often find there is confusion between change management and both project management and program management. Even though the differences are clear (at least for me), as I attempt to clarify, the more it becomes apparent that my audience remains confused by the similarities between business and operational perspectives.

B.2 PROJECT AND PROJECT MANAGEMENT

B.2.1 Overview

Building a new university is just a project; however, building a new university could be part of a change initiative if it strives to achieve the objective of applying a new philosophy to the education system, or providing long-term benefits related to improving the education system. Realizing the short and long-term benefits is more relevant to change management than to project management.

A project ends upon delivery of the required outputs (solution or deliverables), i.e., establishing a new system or finishing the construction; while a change initiative ends when the benefits are fully realized.

A change initiative contains at least one project. The projects of the same change initiative must be designed to help achieve the change objectives and goals.

B.2.2 Definition

Project and program management definitions, disciplines, and processes have been established by professional bodies such as, the Project Management Institute (PMI) and the Association of Project Management (APM).

According to PMI, a "project" is a temporary endeavour undertaken to create a unique product, service, or result, and is defined by the APM Body of Knowledge (APM, 2013) as a unique, transient endeavour undertaken to achieve planned objectives.

"Project management" is defined by the APM Body of Knowledge (APM, 2013) as the application of processes, methods, knowledge, skills, and experience to achieve the project objectives.

Referring to the above definitions, we can point to the following important points:

1. The project has a definitive beginning and end.

2. The produced outputs of a project are a unique combination of one or more products, services, or results.

3. The main goal of project management is to achieve the objectives within the predetermined scope.

B.2.3 Project Life Cycle (PLC)

Each project has its own project life cycle (PLC). PLC's vary depending on the size of project. Figure B-1 presents a standard PLC with five phases and five milestones. Standard phases of a project are the initiating phase, planning phase, designing phase, implementation phase, and the closing phase.

PMI defined the phase as a collection of logically related activities that culminates in the completion of one or more deliverables.

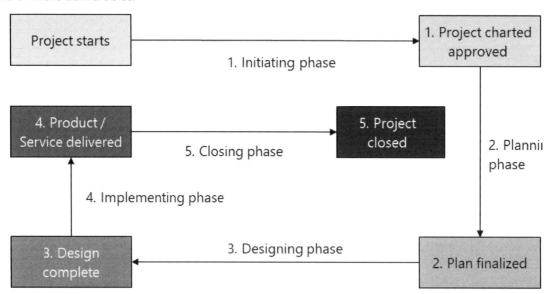

Figure B-1. Standard 5-Phase PLC

As presented in the above figure, approving the project charter is the milestone of the initiation phase and finalizing the plan is the milestone of the planning phase.

B.2.4 Work Breakdown Structure (WBS)

When it comes to project management, relevancy of the term "work breakdown structure" (WBS) is important to understand, as it is a primary concept. As the name implies, WBS is simply breaking down the main activities or deliverables into smaller activities or deliverables.

To understand WBS, suppose that the initiating phase, in Figure B-1, has three main deliverables:

business case, scope document, and project charter.

The WBS of the initiating phase is shown in Figure B-2.

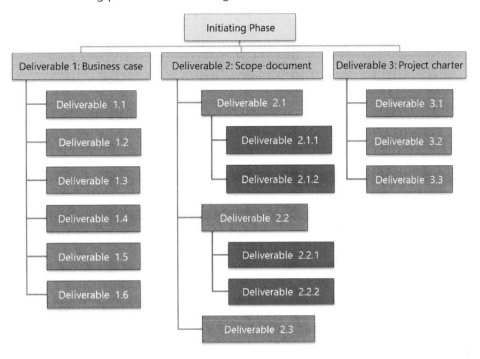

Figure B-2. WBS of Initiating Phase

B.2.5 Project Management Knowledge Areas

According to the Project Management Body of Knowledge (PMBOK® Guide), Fifth Edition, 2013, project management has 10 knowledge areas. Each knowledge area has logically related processes that can be implemented to achieve specific objectives. A summary of the 10 knowledge areas, together with sample processes, is presented in Table B-1.

Table B-1. *Project Management Knowledge Areas*

Name	Description	Sample Processes
Integration Management	Project integration management includes the activities and processes needed to coordinate all project management process and activities within the project lifecycle.	▪ Develop Project Charter ▪ Develop Plan ▪ Monitor and Control Work
Scope Management	Defining project scope is the process of developing a detailed description of the project, service, and product. This should also serve to define the project boundaries. Initially, the project scope is developed during the initiation phase through the Project Charter.	▪ Plan Scope Management ▪ Define Scope ▪ Create WBS
Quality Management	Quality management is the process of identifying quality requirements and standards for the project and its deliverables, as well as documenting how the	▪ Plan Quality Management ▪ Manage Quality

Name	Description	Sample Processes
	project will demonstrate compliance with these requirements.	
Time Management	Project schedule management includes the process of developing the Project Schedule and to manage timely completion of the project.	▪ Estimate Activity Durations ▪ Develop Schedule
Cost Management	Project cost management includes the processes to estimate and control the costs of a project so that it can be completed within the approved budget.	▪ Determine Budget ▪ Control Costs
Resource Management	Resource management includes the processes that organise, manage and lead the project team.	▪ Plan Resource Management
Communications Management	Project communications management encompasses the processes required to ensure the timely and appropriate generation, collection, distribution, storage, retrieval and disposal of project information.	▪ Plan Communications Management ▪ Monitor Communications
Procurement Management	Procurement management includes processes to purchase or acquire resources (staff, equipment, products or services) from outside the project team to perform the project scope of work.	▪ Plan Procurement Management
Risk Management	Risk Management is intended to identify challenges that may occur in the future and determine their probability of occurring and the impact on the project or business.	▪ Identify Risks ▪ Plan Risk Responses ▪ Monitor Risks
Stakeholder Management	Project stakeholder management encompasses the processes that identify, analyse, and manage stakeholders and their expectations.	▪ Identify Stakeholders ▪ Plan Stakeholder Engagement ▪ Monitor Stakeholder Engagement

B.2.6 Project Management Objectives

Project management is used to ensure the following objectives are met in the related projects:

- Providing consistent processes to managing projects.
- Unifying project terminologies and language.
- Providing tools for planning, tracking, and estimating.
- Providing related knowledge and skills.
- Assuring the quality of the deliverables.
- Documenting positive and negative lessons learned.

B.3 AGILE PROJECT MANAGEMENT

Agile is an iterative and incremental method of planning and delivering the outputs of a project; agile being a flexible approach that is needed when a project faces any of the following:

- Excessive ambiguity related to the project.

- Expectation of numerous changes.

- Unclear capacity forecasting and demand.

- Challenges in resource utilization.

It is clear from the above-mentioned issues that the Agile approach is practical within transformational programs.

Agile planning is considered as value-based planning vs. activity-based planning, which is practical for the change exaction. If Agile planning is adapted, the change initiative should have a high-level plan, while the detailed plan can be finalized incrementally at the beginning of every iteration and/or phase.

If a transformation change is not implemented following Agile, failure can be expected. The main benefit of Agile planning is its ability to respond to new changes arising throughout the project.

Agile's principles are quite suitable in conjunction with any change – its primary principles being:

- Increasing collaboration and involvement between the team members.

- Obtaining feedback as early as possible.

- Welcoming and adapting to change.

- Simplifying planning and estimation for increased efficiency.

- Ensuring continuously increasing understanding of project status.

- Maintaining continuous risk management.

- Assuring team motivation and commitment.

- Providing quick wins (value) as early and frequently as possible.

- Focusing on quality and technical excellence.

- Ensuring continuous utilization for all roles.

As change comes with uncertainly and resistance, it is better to be implemented in Agile way to make sure it is on the right track and help start early realization of the change benefits. Agile approach also helps create a value culture inside the organization. We will see how we measure the change value later in this chapter.

As an Agile practice, during any iteration, there should be a short daily meeting to make sure everyone is aligned. At the end of every iteration, there should be an iteration meeting to prepare the final plan for the next iteration.

As an Agile practice, activities are to be categorized as: Backlog, In-progress, to be verified, or Done. Each activity must also have acceptance criteria.

Summary of the high-level planning

Based on Agile, below is a summary of the high-level planning that was discussed:

1. The change is to be divided into a number of projects.

2. Each project is to be divided into a number of releases.

3. Each release is to have a major achievement/deliverable.

4. Specify the number of activities (called user story in software planning) for each release.

5. Estimate the effort required for each activity.

6. Conduct a release planning.

    o Specify the number of iterations in each release (based on best practices).

    o Decide on the value provided by each iteration.

    o Distribute the activities among the iterations.

For each activity, define the detailed tasks and the acceptance criteria, and categorize its status as: Backlog, In-progress, To be verified, and Done. Figure B-3 shown the Agile high-level planning for a project.

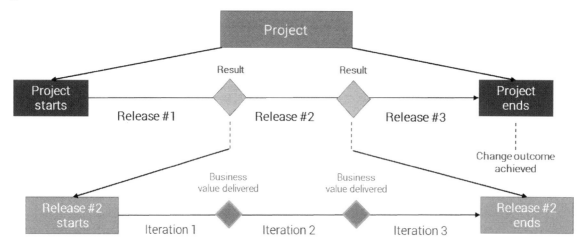

Figure B-3. Agile Planning

A comparison between Agile and traditional project management is presented in Table B-2 below:

Table B-2. A Comparison Between Agile Project Management with Traditional Project Management

Criteria	Agile Project Management	Traditional Project Management
Requirements	Project requirements are not totally identified. They are developed within the planning process.	Project requirements are perfectly identified before the project begins.

Outcomes	The final outcomes could be different from those expected at the beginning.	The final outcomes could not be different from the ones expected at the beginning.
Customer involvement	Part of the process is to involve the customer and consistently request feedback.	Customer is mainly involved towards the end of the project.
Flexibility	Teams can alter their direction to ensure they meet changing needs.	Teams cannot change direction easily as they are governed by an agreement with the customer.

Example B.1 - ACE Assessment Project

In order to explain the concept of Agile planning, let us suppose that we want to conduct the individual ACE assessment for 120 employees in a certain organization. This process will include the following four phases:

1. Phase 1: Communication with staff

2. Phase 2: Conduct ACE measurement

3. Phase 3: Identify gap analysis

4. Phase 4: Recommend action items

Figure B-4 presents the above-mentioned phases.

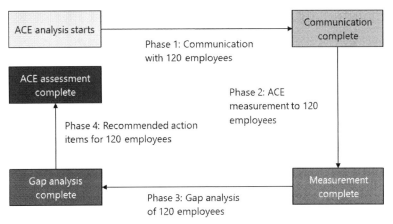

Figure B-4. Standard Project Cycle

To apply Agile planning to this example, the project could be divided, for example, into three releases. Each release will have the scope of 40 employees. Therefore, the roadmap plan will be as shown in Figure B-5.

Example B.1 - ACE Assessment Project

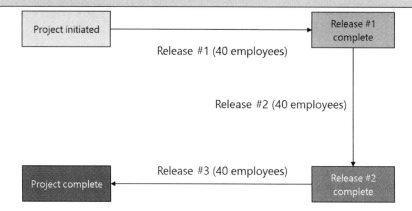

Figure B-5. ACE Assessment Roadmap Plan

The 40 employees involved in each release can be divided into two batches, as follows:

- Batch 1 (B1): 20 employees

- Batch 2 (B2): 20 employees

The release plan will be as shown in Figure B-6.

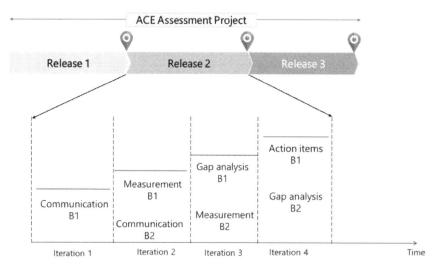

Figure B-6. ACE Assessment Release Plan

The benefits of using Agile planning for this ACE assessment example are:

- Value is provided early.

- Stakeholders are more engaged when they see an early sample of the end result.

- The process for the subsequent release is more refined and efficient.

- Better management of time.

- Good level of risk mitigation if there is not enough time to conclude the recommendations.

B.4 PROGRAM AND PROGRAM MANAGEMENT

B.4.1 Overview

As indicated in Managing Successful Program (MSP, 2012), program management is a key tool to enable organizations to deliver their strategy and manage their transformational change.

Change management and program management are more similar than change management and project management. Accordingly, a change and a program are more similar than a change and a project.

The change initiative may have a number of programs; each program may have a number of projects. Each project has its own scope and objectives; each project is to be managed according to the project management process of the organization.

B.4.2 Definition

The program is defined by the APM Body of Knowledge (APM, 2013) as a group of related projects and change management activities that together achieve beneficial change for an organization.

Program management is defined by the APM Body of Knowledge (APM, 2013) as the coordinated management of project and change management activities to achieve beneficial change.

Important Note

In program management, change management activities must be part of any program components.

Change management will aid in achieving the following goals when added to any program:

* Assessment of impact and readiness.

* Management of the "people side" of the change.

* Management of change within the culture.

* Management of the resistance.

* Implementation of change within operations.

* Quantification of the realization of change benefits.

B.4.3 Distinguishing Between a Project, Program, and a Portfolio

All the projects of the same program should be related through a common goal to deliver the required business value. The change will have a number of programs; each program has some projects; each project is to be managed according to the project management process of the organization. Programs may also include other non-project components or activities.

When a group of projects have separate goals with no relationship between business values, such projects are better managed as a portfolio rather than a program. Portfolio refers to a collection of projects, programs, and operations that do not share the same business value but aim to achieve the strategic objectives of the organization. Figure B-7 below illustrates the relationship between components of a portfolio.

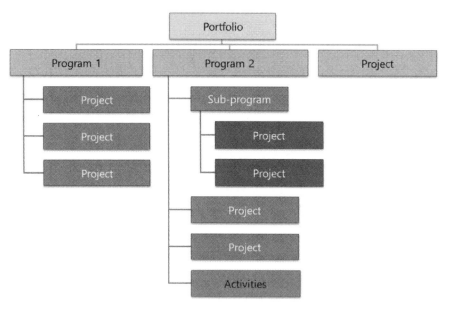

Figure B-7. Components of a Portfolio

B.4.4 Program Management Objectives and Principles

According to "Managing Successful Programs" (MSP, 2012), program management is used to ensure the following:

- The identification and delivery of benefits.

- Quality assurance.

- Delivery of the desired outcomes.

- Managing risks.

- Aligning with organizational strategies.

- Leading the "people side" of the change.

- Identifying and communicating vision.

- Focusing on the realization of change benefits.

- Adding value by combining different projects.

- Designing and delivering a capability that is released into operations.

B.4.5 Program Management Themes

According to MSP (2012), program management themes are as presented in Table B-3.

Table B-3. *Program Management Themes*

	Theme Name	Description
1	Resource Management	Managing resources to be consumed by the program such as people, systems, accommodation, and facilities.
2	Monitoring and Control	How the program will monitor progress in terms of expected and actual delivery of outputs, outcomes, and key milestones.
3	Information Management	How program information will be catalogued, filed, stored, and retrieved, and how the program will create and manage information.
4	Time Management	Program time management includes the process to develop the schedule and to manage the timely completion of the different projects that belong to the program.
5	Cost Management	Cost management includes the processes to estimate and control the costs of the projects so that they can be completed within the approved budget.
6	Quality & Assurance Management	How the delivery of quality activities will be incorporated into the management and delivery of the program.
7	Risk Management	How the program will establish the context in which risks will be identified and assessed.
8	Issue Management	How issues will be managed consistently across the program and how any resulting changes will be managed.
9	Stakeholder Engagement	Who the stakeholders are, what their interests and influences are likely to be, and how the program will engage with them.
10	Benefits Management	The delivery framework for identifying, prioritizing, and achieving benefits.

B.5 BENEFITS AND BENEFITS MANAGEMENT

B.5.1 Overview

Benefits should be the main rationale for investing in change initiatives. Benefits management is used mainly to ensure that the intended change benefits are realized, and to demonstrate the return on change initiative investment, while analysing non-benefit aspects of change – or negative effects anticipated as a result of change.

Important Note

Benefits management serves as an invaluable tool that should be used to assure successful implementation of the change.

B.5.2 Definition

A benefit is defined by the APM Body of Knowledge (APM, 2013) as any measurable improvement from change initiatives that are positively perceived by any stakeholder and contribute toward achieving the strategic objective.

A dis-benefit is defined by "Managing Successful Program" (MSP, 2012) as a measurable decline resulting from an outcome perceived as negative by one or more stakeholders.

Benefits management is defined by the APM Body of Knowledge (APM, 2013) as the identification, quantification, analysis, planning, tracking, realization, and optimization of benefits.

Referring to the above definitions, the following points are important to observe:

1. Benefits management is used within the change management framework to assure identifying, quantifying, tracking, and measuring the change benefits.

2. Change benefits should be aligned with the strategic objectives of the organization.

As mentioned earlier, change is about realizing specific benefits. Thus, change leaders should learn how to use benefits management, or other similar concepts, while implementing any change initiative.

Improperly defining the benefits of the change can result in a negative impact on the change initiative.

According to Jenner (2012), benefits management include five practices:

1. Identify and quantify
2. Value and appraise
3. Plan
4. Realize
5. Review

B.6 STRATEGIC MANAGEMENT

B.6.1 Overview

Generally, at the beginning of a change management training session, I dedicate extensive time in reviewing the strategic management process. Change management learners must have a grasp of strategic management principles in order to understand how they relate to change management. Typically, a change initiative is one of the strategic initiatives implemented to serve certain strategic objectives, thus, change and strategy must be cohesive.

Strategic management consists of five areas or processes:

3. Process 1: Developing strategy
4. Process 2: Planning strategy
5. Process 3: Aligning strategy

6. Process 4: Executing strategy

7. Process 5: Reviewing strategy

Figure B-8 below outlines the objectives of the five strategic management processes.

P1: Developing Strategy	P2: Planning Strategy	P3: Aligning Strategy	P4: Executing Strategy	P5: Reviewing Strategy
The objective of this process is to reaffirm the company's mission and vision, understand the business environment, and the company's position from the operations, financial, and value proposition perspectives in order to formulate a strategy.	The objective of this process is to translate the vision and strategic goals into specific strategic objectives that can be measured by specific targets and executed by strategic initiatives.	The objective of this process is to align and cascade the strategic objectives with the different business units. The strategic objectives are to be reflected in all units' objectives, indicators, activities, and initiatives.	The objective of this process is to execute the strategy by implementing the strategic initiatives. Continuous monitoring of the progress must be ensured.	The objective of this process is to measure and update the strategic targets, realize the benefits, and do corrective strategic actions.

Figure B-8. Strategic Management Processes

Change management practices are needed to assure the successful execution of the strategy.

B.6.2 Developing Strategy

In the developing a strategy process, the following questions must first be answered:

1. What business are we in, and why?

2. What are the key strategic drivers?

3. What is our strategic positioning?

4. How can we compete?

Figure B-9 shows the required four steps to develop the required outputs: (1) Strategic foundation (mission, vision & core values), (2) Strategic drivers, (3) Business model, and (4) Strategic directions.

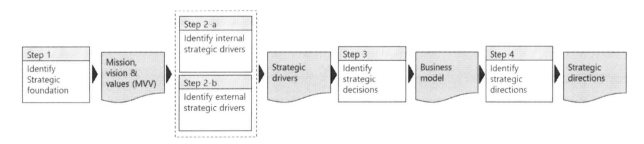

Figure B-9. Developing Strategy

B.6.2.1 Internal and external drivers

To identify the external drivers, we ask the following questions: "Are there new trends of sales channels?", "Is there a great change in competitiveness?", "Is there a new technology that will impact the ecosystem of our industry?", "Is there a change in standards of living?", "Will there be an economic change globally or locally?", "Is there a change in the characteristics of our target segment?", etc.

And to identify the internal drivers, we need to ask the questions: "Do we need to improve a business process?", "How good IS our relationship with our vendors?", "Do we have problems with the employees' engagement?", "Do we have a good employees' satisfaction?", "Do we have resistance in our new developmental programs?"

There are many tools that can be used for the internal and external analysis (Step 2) to get the strategic drivers

For internal analysis, the value chain model, gap analysis, or core competence analysis, can be used.

For the external analysis, we can use a tool line PEST analysis (Political and economic, social and culture, and Technological) is done to understand the strategic drivers for the macro environment that we have no control on.

We also can use a tool like Porter's 5-Forces (bargaining power of supplier, bargaining power of buyer, threat on new entrant, threat of substitution, and competition) for the micro environment that is related to a specific industry.

It is important to understand the strategic drivers that triggered the formulation of the strategic objectives.

Tables B-4 and B-5 show the external analysis outputs of both the PEST and Porter's 5-Forces analysis in order to define the strategic drivers.

Table B-4. *Using PEST Technique to Identify the Strategic Drivers*

Political and economic	Social and cultural
- We must adjust our accounting to be aligned with international standards - We must consider the current political conflict in the Gulf area if we go there. - If political instability happens in Egypt, it will be difficult to get external partners. - For next year, if the Egyptian currency keeps devaluating, we do expect major increase in export business. - High Inflation will reflect to the cost of our operations and activities.	- There is a great polarization in the Egyptian society. - Good professionals are few and are demanding high salaries which has a negative impact on our cost structure. - It is very difficult to get statistics data in Egypt to prepare market studies and analysis.
	Technological
	- Need to be always on the forefront of technology. - We are better prepared to cope with business than technical trends - We are not technological driven

Table B-5. *Using Porter's 5-Forces analysis to Identify the Strategic Drivers*

1. New entrants	4. Suppliers' power
• High amount of capital required • Easy to have retaliation by existing companies • There are legal barriers • Difficult to get a brand reputation • No differentiation in provided services • Access to suppliers and distributors are easy • Economies of scale is easy to achieve • Government regulations are not complex	• Number of suppliers is limited • Suppliers size is small • Suppliers can easily switch to alternative resources • There are resource scarcity in some services/resources • Cost of switching to alternative service is high • There is a threat from the suppliers to integrate forward. • Prices can be forced down on them. • You can control and demand better quality. • Are you strategic to them?
2. Customers' power	**5. Competitive rivalry**
• Low number of customers • Switching costs to other companies is low • Have the connections with end customers • They can easily access to your suppliers. • They can have a backward integration strategy • Can force down prices • Can demand better quality or more service • They are price sensitive • Customer is loyal to us	• Competitive tension is high • We have a value added over competitors • Number of competitors is high • Cost of leaving an industry is high • Industry growth rate and size is high • There is no differentiation in services • Most Competitors' size is bigger that we are • Customer loyalty is high only for few big customers • Threat of horizontal integration (adding new services) • Have high level of advertising expense
3. Substitute products	
• There are many substitutes • Performance of substitutes is relatively good • Cost of changing to a substitute is low	

B.6.3 Planning Strategy

In the planning strategy process, we answer the following questions:

1. What are strategic objectives?

2. How do we measure our strategic plan?

3. What action programs does our strategy need?

This process has three steps to develop the strategic objectives, measures, targets, and initiatives as shown in Figure B-10 below:

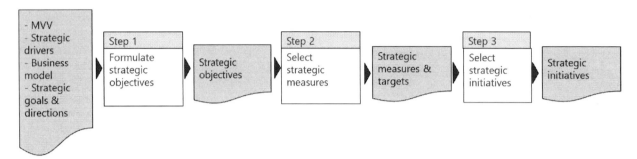

Figure B-10. Planning Strategy

The output of Step 3 in Figure B-6 (strategic initiatives) is typically the change initiative addressed in this publication.

Understanding the related strategic objectives and strategic drivers is essential in leading a change initiative.

Change benefits should be the link between the strategic objectives and strategic initiatives as discussed in benefits management.

I personally prefer to use the Balanced Scorecard framework to manage the planning strategy process, followed by introduction of the concepts of the Balanced Scorecard framework.

B.7 BALANCED SCORECARD FRAMEWORK

The Balanced Scorecard (BSC) framework was introduced by Norton and Kaplan in 1996. BSC emphasizes the usage of financial and non-financial measures for different business perspectives.

BSC consists of balancing strategy through four perspectives. Each perspective has its own objectives, measures, targets, and initiatives. Below are the four BSC perspectives:

1. The Financial Perspective defines the financial results of achieving the vision.

2. The Customer Perspective defines the value provided to customers.

3. The Internal Processes Perspective defines the means through which processes will achieve customer and financial objectives.

4. The People and Organization Perspective defines how to sustain the ability to improve and enhance tangible and intangible assets, i.e., people, technology, and culture.

Figure B-11 below shows the four BSC perspectives:

Figure B-11. BSC Perspectives. Source: Kaplan and Norton (1996). Balanced Scorecard

B.7.1 BSC Strategy Map

A strategy map shows the cause-and-effect relationships between strategic objectives based on the four BSC perspectives. Figure B-12 below outlines how the strategy map identifies the cause-and-effect relationships between different objectives.

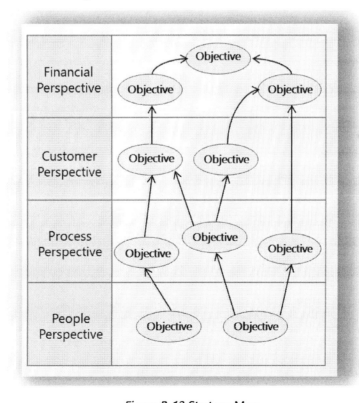

Figure B-12. Strategy Map

Example B.2 - Strategy Map

Figure B-13 shows a sample Strategy map. In this sample, demonstrating that improving the employee skills in the "people perspective" leads to improved process quality in the "process perspective." Further, the increase in customer loyalty in the "customer perspective" leads to an increase in revenue in the "financial perspective."

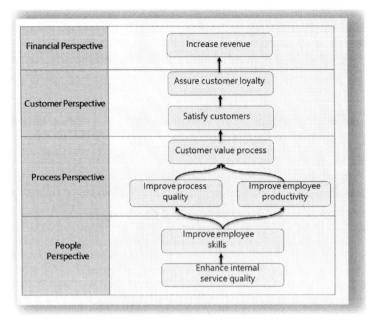

Figure B-13. Sample Strategy Map

Important Note

The strategy map is complete and mature when the chain of cause-and-effect relationships are established between the different objectives in conjunction with the four perspectives.

B.7.2 Measure and targets

Without strategic measures, objectives remain as passive statements or intentions that only point in random directions. The measures can be measured quantitatively, qualitatively, and by time (QQT). Table B-6 has samples of the measures that can be used for the selected change benefits or strategic objectives.

Table B-6. Sample Measures

Financial measures	Customer measures	Internal processes measures	People measures
▪ Return on investment (ROI) ▪ Gross profit ▪ Net profit ▪ Cost of sales	▪ Market share ▪ Market share in targeted segments ▪ Customer perception ▪ Customer acquisition	▪ Response time ▪ Production cost ▪ Percentage of re-work ▪ Number of complaints	▪ Percentage of employees trained in quality ▪ Innovation / learning culture

• Sales growth • Percentage of annual cost reduction • Amount of working capital • Return on asset (sales to asset ratio) • Percentage of administrative cost • Budget reduction	• Customer retention • Customer profitability • Customer satisfaction • Percentage of unprofitable customers • Sales from new customers • Percentage of unprofitable customers • Sales from new service	• Improvement of bottlenecks • Percentage of on-time delivery • Percentage of late orders • Cost of key resources • Percentage of waste eliminated • Percentage of resources utilization • Cost of storage • Number of new innovated Ideas • Percentage of uncollectible receivables • Percentage of customers who can track their orders • Lower unit cost • Value of time saved	• Employee retention • Employee productivity • Employee commitment • Employee satisfaction

Each objective should have at least one measure. The measures should validate the cause-and-effect relationships that were established between the objectives in the strategy map. For example, increasing the customer loyalty by 5% should lead to an increase in revenue by 15% and so on.

As Norton and Kaplan (1996) indicated, performance measures should also be balanced between outcome measures (lagging) and driver measures (leading).

Outcomes measures are used to measure whether the implementation of the strategy has been successful or not. Most of the financial goals are of this type, as they are derived from implementation of the remainder strategic objectives.

On the other hand, drivers measures are intermediate measures that allow managers to take actions in the event deviations are observed. They are the foundations of the higher level outcome measures.

B.7.3 Strategic Initiative

A strategic initiative is taken to help achieve one or more of the strategic objectives.

Table B-7 below shows a single balanced scorecard for the objective: Empower and develop talents; one of the objectives of the Global Trans case study. The objective has two measures and two targets, and three initiatives.

Table B-7. *A Single Balanced Scorecard*

Objectives		Strategic measures		
Ref	**Object name**	**Ref.**	**Measure**	**Target**
O1	Empower and develop talents	1	Number of certified talents	12
Description		2	Number of external certifications	10
It is mandatory to continuously develop our talents in their personal and professional aspects. Developing is done while empowering talent to be more delegated and responsible.				
Strategic initiatives						
Ref	**Name**	**Description**	**Start**	**Duration**	**Owner**	**Budget**
1	Develop internal certification program.	This initiative should lead to establish and maintain what is called: "The new Academy".				
2	Develop an orientation program for new comers.	This will be a training program that enables the new comers to experience all about the company.				
3	Empower talent while providing a coaching plan.	This initiative should set the internal guidelines and process of keeping coaching the talents while empowering them all the time.				

Example B.3 - Global Trans Balanced Scorecard

Reflecting on the Global Trans case study, Figure B-14 below shows a balanced scorecard as well as the strategy map of the company's strategy.

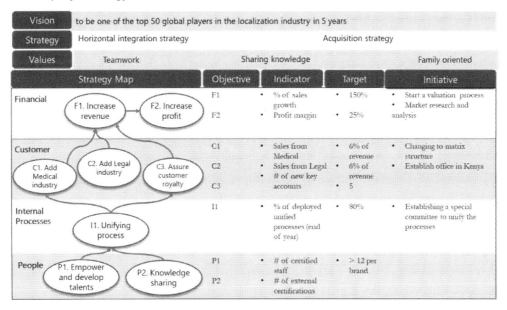

Figure B-14. Global Trans Balanced Scorecard

For the Increase Revenue objective, the following can be selected as its measure and target:

8. Measure: Percentage of sales growth

9. Target: 15%

For the Assure Customer Loyalty objective, the following can be selected as its measure and target:

10. Measure: Number of new key accounts

11. Target: 5

B.8 SUMMARY

- Program management, project management, and benefits management are considered some of the key tools that are used to manage a change initiative.

- Transformational change should follow the project management process by having a well-defined plan with a schedule, phases, milestones, activities, and deliverables.

- Project management largely avoids the "people side" during the implementation, i.e., organizational politics, hidden agendas, cultural barriers, motivation issues, lack of communication, conflict resolution, resistance to change, ambiguous roles and responsibilities, poor leadership, and insufficient sponsorship.

- It is better to have an Agile plan for the change; change plans never begin as a complete plan.

- A program is a group of related projects and change management activities that together achieve beneficial change for an organization.

- Benefits management is a very valuable tool that should be used to assure successful implementation of the change initiative.

- BSC is balancing the strategy through four perspectives. Each perspective has its own objectives, measures, targets, and initiatives.

- Change should not be implemented in isolation from the strategy. Therefore, the link between the change and its benefits with the strategy must be clearly identified.

Appendix C – Expected Behaviors in Organizations Based on Cultural Measurements

This appendix contains the tables that have the expected behaviors inside organizations based on the score of the six cultural dimensions of the Hofstede Multi-Focus Model.

Table C-1 shows the expected behaviors in organizations based on the score of the Means-oriented vs. Goal-oriented cultural dimension.

Table C-1. *Means-oriented vs. Goal-oriented*

Dysfunctional means-oriented	Means-oriented	In-between	Goal-oriented
Score from 0 to 34	Score from 35 to 44	Score from 45 to 54	Score from 55 to 100
Employees identify enormously with the "*how*"	Employees identify with the "*how*"	In-between	Employees identify mainly with the "*what*"
Employees exert no effort in their jobs	Employees exert minimum effort in their jobs	In-between	Employees put in maximal effort
Employees avoid risks and are uncomfortable with unfamiliar situations	Employees are probably uncomfortable with unfamiliar situations	In-between	Employees are comfortable with unfamiliar situations
Employees are told what to do	Work is usually not challenging	In-between	Challenging work; leaders show initiative
Too many rules; damaging internal competition	Rules and regulations exist in most departments	In-between	Entrepreneurial environment
No inspiring leadership	No inspiring leadership	In-between	Inspirational leadership
Continuous monitoring	Continuous monitoring	In-between	Employees seek to be pioneers

Note. Source: Waisfisz (2015); Hofstede Insight website.

Table C-2 shows the expected behaviors in organizations based on the score of the Internally Driven vs. Externally Driven cultural dimension.

Table C-2. *Internally Driven vs. Externally Driven*

Dysfunctional internally driven	Internally driven	Moderately to fairly externally driven	Very externally driven
Score from 0 to 29	Score from 30 to 49	Score from 50 to 74	Score from 75 to 100
Customers are completely out of focus	Company knows what is best for the customer	Employees do what the customer wants	Employees do what the customer wants, even if it is not in the best interests of the customer
Employees are continuously busy ensuring that their business ethics are watertight	Employees have high standards of business ethics	Employees have moderate to high standards of business ethics	Employees are not concerned with business ethics
Employees believe they are the best; there is no room for improvement	Employees believe they are the best, but there is room for improvement	There is room for improvement	There is always room for improvement
Employees are extremely normative	Employees believe they are consistent	Employees are flexible in what they say and do	Employees are extremely pragmatic
Employees hide behind the rules; procedures must be followed even if they negatively impact the results	Procedures are usually prioritized over customers' demands, unless they negatively impact results	Customers' demands are usually prioritized over procedures, unless they go against business ethics	Customers' demands are always prioritized over procedures
Employees believe that stakeholders are happy that the company exists			The customer is king

Note. Source: Waisfisz (2015); Hofstede Insight website

Table C-3 shows the expected behaviors in organizations based on the score of the Flexible vs. Strict cultural dimension.

Table C-3. *Flexible vs. Strict*

Dysfunctional flexible	Flexible	In-between	Strict
Score from 0 to 14	Score from 15 to 44	Score from 45 to 54	Score from 55 to 100
Extremely sloppy; few work standards	Easy going	In-between	Punctual and meticulous
Extremely informal	Informal	In-between	Formal - more unwritten codes about dress and respectable behavior
The company is the subject of a lot of jokes	The company is the subject of jokes	In-between	Employees are serious when having conversations about the company
Could be innovative	Innovative	In-between	Culture does not motivate innovation
Little control and discipline	Not burdened by control and discipline	In-between	A lot of control and discipline
No cost consciousness	Costs are of little concern	In-between	Cost conscious
Cheerful and relaxed	Cheerful and relaxed	In-between	Not a relaxed culture
Planning is not emphasized	Planning may not be emphasized	In-between	Planning is emphasized

Note. Source: Waisfisz (2015); Hofstede Insight website

Table C-4 shows the expected behaviors in organizations based on the score of the Flexible vs. Strict cultural dimension.

Table C-4. *Local vs. Professional*

Dysfunctional local	Local	In between	Professional	Very professional
Score from 0 to 19	Score from 20 to 45	Score from 46 to 55	Score from 56 to 75	Score from 76 to 100
Employees identify with their direct boss and/or work group	Employees identify with their direct boss and/or work group	In-between	Employees identify with their profession	Employees identify with their profession

Dysfunctional local	Local	In between	Professional	Very professional
Newcomers who are different are rejected	Newcomers who differ from us should adjust	In-between	Diversity is welcomed	Diversity is encouraged
A critical attitude is not acceptable	A critical attitude is not appreciated	In-between	A critical attitude is OK	A critical attitude is essential
Inward-looking	Inward-looking	In-between	Outward-looking	Outward-looking
Managers want subordinates to be loyal	Internal loyalty is important	In-between	Internal loyalty is not important	Internal loyalty is not important
Very short-term directed	Short-term directed	In-between	Fairly long-term directed	Long-term directed
Competition and mistrust between units is strong	Competition and mistrust between units is common	In-between	The norm is cooperation and trust between departments	The norm is cooperation and trust between departments
Employees do not care about competition	It is not important to know what competitors are doing	In-between	It is important to know what competitors are doing	It is very important to know what competitors are doing
There is a strong social expectation to be like everybody else	There is a social expectation to be like everybody else	In-between	There is no social expectation to be like everybody else	There is no social expectation to be like everybody else
Employees do not learn from their mistakes	Employees may learn from their mistakes	In-between	Employees learn from their mistakes	Employees learn from their mistakes

Note. Source: Waisfisz (2015); Hofstede Insight website

Table C-5 shows the expected behaviors in organizations based on the score of the Open vs. Closed system cultural dimension.

Table C-5. *Open System vs. Closed System*

Very Open System	Open System	Closed System	Dysfunctional Closed System
Score from 0 to 24	Score from 25 to 45	Score from 46 to 75	Score from 76 to 100
Outsiders feel immediately welcome	Outsiders feel welcome	Newcomers and outsiders alike do not feel all that welcome	Outsiders are not welcome
Those who fail are given the benefit of doubt	People are normally given the benefit of doubt	Those who fail are normally assumed guilty until proven innocent	Those who fail are assumed guilty
Not secretive	Employees are not good in keeping secrets	Employees are good in keeping secrets	Very Secretive
Everyone feels well-informed	Information can be easily acquired	It takes an effort from an employee to acquire information, unless he is part of the old network	It takes an effort from an employee to acquire information
Employees talk with their boss without any inhibitions	Employees tell their boss what they think	Employees will not tell the boss what they think if they find themselves in threatening situations	Employees never tell their boss what they really think

Note. Source: Waisfisz (2015); Hofstede Insight website

Table C-6 shows the expected behaviors in organizations based on the score of the Employee-oriented vs. Work-oriented cultural dimension.

Table C-6. *Employee-Oriented vs. Work-Oriented*

Employee-oriented	In-between	Work-oriented	Dysfunctional work-oriented
Score from 0 to 39	Score from 40 to 55	Score from 56 to 75	Score from 76 to 100
Personal problems are taken into consideration	In-between	Personal problems are not considered	Management is interested only in employees' output; personal problems are never considered
The organization takes co-responsibility for the employees' welfare	In-between	Everybody is responsible for their own welfare	Everybody is responsible for their own welfare

Employee-oriented	In-between	Work-oriented	Dysfunctional work-oriented
Important decisions are made by groups; management is consultative	In-between	Most important decisions are made by individuals	Important decisions are made by individuals
People are not put under extreme pressure for no good reason	In-between	Management believes that if they do not put people under pressure, nothing will get done	People are put under extreme pressure for no good reason at all, at least that is how it will be perceived
No danger of burn-out and/or silent resistance	In-between	Danger of burnout	Danger of burnout and/or silent resistance
It is difficult for employees to get fired	In-between	It is not difficult for employees to get fired	It is easy for employees to get fired
The company has an interest in the community	In-between	The company has no interest in the community in which its facilities are located	The company has no interest in the community in which its facilities are located

Note. Source: Waisfisz (2015); Hofstede Insight website

Appendix D – Research Methodology of ElKattan's Model

From 2012 to 2016, qualitative research was conducted on the 5-Theme Model under the supervision and mentorship of Swiss Management Center University, with support from ITIM International, trading as Hofstede Insights in Finland and the Netherlands.

After completing the interviews and quantitative and qualitative surveys with more than 150 participants in two different case studies, I collected, coded, and categorized the data into themes and sub-themes. I then designed the 5-Theme Model along with its themes, components, deliverables, lifecycle, and workstreams.

After the model's research and development was concluded, it was introduced in my doctoral dissertation in 2016. In 2017, the 5-Theme Model was published in a paper in the Arabian Journal of Business and Management Review under the title: The Five Themes of Change Management.

After nearly three years of writing, editing, and review, the most recent version of the model is published in this book.

The two case studies: Global Trans and News Media, introduced in Chapters 1 and 3, were included in the research and will be revisited throughout. Table D-1 summarizes basic details of the two companies.

Table D-1. *Basic Information About the Two Case Studies*

Components	Global Trans	News Media
Annual Revenue	US $6.0M	US $6.0M
Number of Employees	450	250
Industry	Content and Website Development	Language Services
Head Office	Arab Gulf	Egypt
Type of the Change	Transformational	Transformational
Magnitude of the Change	High	High

During the research, face-to-face interviews were conducted with four change management experts as shown in Table D-2

Table D-2. *Change Management Experts*

Name	Title	Experience	Organization Size	Types of Change Experienced
Mr. Mohamed El-Hamamsy	CEO, Vodafone Egypt	45-years	1,500 employees Revenue: US $150M	Restructuring, Mergers & Acquisitions, Culture Change
Mr. Nagy Hamamo	Transformation Change Manager – PWC	15-years	2,000 employees Revenue: US $700M	Restructuring, Process Improvement
Mr. Wael Amin	Chairman & CEO – IT Works	20-years	1,000 employees Revenue: US $30M	Restructuring, Downsizing, Spin-offs, Acquisitions
Mr. Ibrahim Sarhan	Chairman & Managing Director – eFinance	35-years	800 employees Revenue: US $28M	Restructuring, Mergers, Spin-offs, Acquisitions

During the research, between the two companies, roughly 210 employees participated in a survey conducted using the ITIM International's proprietary online questionnaire. This questionnaire was based on the survey that was used by Hofstede to develop the Hofstede Multi-Focus Model (refer to Chapter 6 for more details). This questionnaire consisted of three parts, with a total of 76 questions. The survey also included face-to-face interviews conducted with 10 employees from both companies.

Upon the completion of the interviews, quantitative and qualitative surveys of two case studies, I collected, coded, and categorized the data into themes and sub-themes, and came up with the five themes of the model as well as their components.

Appendix E – ACE Survey - Leadership

Awareness Survey

Table E-1 shows survey questions that could be used to measure the Awareness 'A'.

Table E-1. *Awareness Assessment Survey*

	Criteria	Strongly disagree (1)	Disagree (2)	Neutral (3)	Agree (4)	Strongly agree (5)
1	The vision of the change initiative was clearly communicated to me as part of the organization's strategy and vision.					
2	I am aware of the reasons for implementing the change initiative.					
3	The benefits of the change initiative have been well communicated.					
4	The risks of not having this change initiative implemented were explained clearly.					
5	I clearly understand my role and what is expected from me to implement the change initiative.					
6	Practices of providing change sponsorship and support were clearly communicated.					
7	It was communicated how conflict or disruption with other programs and day-to-day operations will be managed.					
8	I am aware that the lessons learned from the previous initiatives have been studied and taken into consideration.					
	Awareness score					

Competence Survey

Table E-2 shows survey questions that could be used to measure the Competence 'C'.

Table E-2. *Competence Assessment Survey*

	Strongly disagree (1)	Disagree (2)	Neutral (3)	Agree (4)	Strongly agree (5)
1. I need to enhance my KNOWLEDGE of the below competences.					
Results driven					
Knowledge sharing					
Building trust					
Motivation					
Change management					
Strategic management					
Change specific competences					
2. I need to enhance my SKILLS of the below competences:					
Results driven					
Knowledge sharing					
Building trust					
Motivation					
Change management					
Strategic management					
Change specific competences					
3. I am emotionally and rationally convinced to apply the following competences in the change initiative.					
Results driven					
Knowledge sharing					
Building trust					
Motivation					
Change management					
Strategic management					

	Strongly disagree (1)	Disagree (2)	Neutral (3)	Agree (4)	Strongly agree (5)
Change specific competences					

Engagement survey

Table E-3 shows survey questions that could be used to measure the Engagement 'E'.

Table E-3. *Engagement Assessment Survey*

	Criteria	1	2	3	4	5
1	I feel the **urgency** to implement the new change right away.					
2	I am very **dissatisfied** with the status quo the initiative aims at changing.					
3	I feel very **energized** to start working on the requirements of the new change.					
4	I have a great **hope** for the change to end up with great results.					
5	I have no **doubt** we have the required capabilities to implement the change initiative.					
6	I strongly **trust** that our leadership is committed to the success of the program.					
7	I strongly feel that everyone will carry the spirit of: "**we are all in it together**" while implementing the change.					
	Engagement Score					

Appendix F – The Model's Components, and Deliverables

Table F-1 shows the list of the components and deliverables of ElKattan's 5-Theme Model.

Table F-1. *The 5-Theme Model Components and Deliverables*

1. VISION & GOVERNANCE THEME				
Theme components	1. Developing the change statement	2. Developing the change vision	3. Managing the change outcomes and benefits	4. Developing sponsorship governance and CM methodology
Deliverables	• Change definition • Change statement	• Change Business case • Future desired state gap analysis • Change objectives and goals	• Change success criteria • Change outcome/benefit profile sheet	• Sponsorship governance framework • Change impact • Change management methodology • Change management Inception plan • Communication plan – Readiness phase

2. ASSESSMENT THEME				
Theme components	1. Assessing stakeholder readiness	2. Assessing culture	3. Assessing organizational alignment	4. Assessing communication
Deliverables	• Stakeholders influence analysis • Stakeholder register and map • Stakeholder readiness assessment (ACE assessment) • Change energy index • Sponsorship assessment	• Culture readiness assessment • Value assessment • Decision-making assessment • Leadership assessment	• Organizational elements assessment • Resource analysis • Risk analysis	• Channel assessment • Stakeholder narratives assessment • Communication climate assessment

3. STRATEGIZING THEME				
Theme components	1. Developing the stakeholder management strategy	2. Developing the culture management strategy	3. Developing the organizational alignment strategy	4. Developing the communication strategy
Deliverables	• Involvement strategy • Motivation strategy • Managing resistance strategy • Stakeholder management objectives (ACE objectives)	• Direct vs. indirect change strategy • Culture management objectives • Leadership objectives	• Organizational elements objectives • Resource objectives • Risk management strategy	• Two-Way communication strategy • Communication theme strategy • Relationship strategy • Narrative strategy

4. TACTICS THEME				
Theme components	1. Identifying the stakeholder management tactics	2. Identifying culture management tactics	3. Identifying organizational alignment tactics	4. Developing communication management tactics
Deliverables	▪ Coaching tactics ▪ Involvement tactics ▪ Stakeholder management tactics ▪ Sponsorship management tactics	▪ Culture management tactics ▪ Tactics auditing sheet	▪ Organizational alignment tactics ▪ Risk management tactics	▪ Relationship tactics ▪ Change narrative tactics ▪ Change meetings and workshops ▪ Communication management tactics

5. PLANNING AND APPRAISING THEME				
Theme components	1. Developing the change management high-level plan	2. Appraising change	3. Developing the change charter	4. Developing the change management plan
Deliverables	▪ Change management high-level plan ▪ Change management objectives analysis	▪ Change budget ▪ Cost-benefit analysis	▪ Change charter	▪ Change outcome/ benefit measurement plan ▪ Change management plan

REFERENCES

References

Alas, R., & Vadi, M. (2004). The influence of organizational culture on attitudes concerning change in post-soviet organizations. Journal for East European Management Studies, 9(1), 20-39.

Association of Change Management Professionals. (2019). ACMP's standard for change management.

Bashir, J. & Afzal, S. (2008). Ethics based model for change management. Digital Paper. Retrieved from http://www.highlykeen.com.

Bhola, H. (2010). The employee engagement: The influence of change management implementation in mergers. MBA dissertation, University of Pretoria, Pretoria, South Africa.

Burke, W. (2010). Organization change: Theory and practice. Thousand Oaks, CA: Sage.

Chiloane-Tsoka, E. (2013). The influence of corporate culture on organizational change of first national bank of Namibia. International Journal of Business & Economic Development, 1(3), 15-24.

Cohn, M. (2006). Agile Estimating and Planning. New York: Prentice Hall.

Creswell, J.W. (2009). Research Design: Qualitative, Quantitative and Mixed Methods Approaches. Thousand Oaks, CA: Sage.

Dastmalchian, A., Lee, S., & Ng, I. (2000). The interplay between organizational and national cultures: A comparison of organizational practices in Canada and South Korea using the Competing Values Framework. International Journal of Human Resource Management, 11(2), 388-412.

Devers, K. & Frankel, R. (2000). Study design in qualitative research: Sampling and data collection strategies. Swiss Management Center University, Switzerland. Retrieved from: http://swissmc.blackboard.com.

ElKattan, A. (2016). Cultural Influence on the Implementation of Corporate Change Management Initiatives: A Comparative Case Study. Swiss Management Center University, Switzerland.

ElKattan A. (2017). The Five Themes of Change Management. Arabian J Bus Management Review. 7:305.

Gordon, G. (1991). Industry determinants of organizational culture. Academy of Management Review, 16(2), 396-415.

Keller, S. & Aiken, C. (2011). The inconvenient truth about change management. Mckinsey & Company. Retrieved from: http://www.mckinsey.com.

Kotter, J. (1996). Leading change. Boston, MA: Harvard Business Review.

Kotter, J. (2008). A sense of urgency. Boston, MA: Harvard Business Review.

Kotter, J. (2014). Accelerate. Boston, MA: Harvard Business Review.

Petschnig, S. (2011). Identification of change in small and medium-sized enterprises in Austria: A qualitative research. International Journal of Management Cases, 13(3), 105-111.

Sun, T. (2009, January). Mixed methods research: Strengths of two methods combined. Swiss Management Center University, Switzerland. Retrieved from http://swissmc.blackboard.com.

Heerden, C. & Barter, C. (2008). The role of culture in the determination of a standardized or localized. University of Pretoria. Republic of South Africa.

Herkenhoff, L. (2004). Culturally tuned emotional intelligence: An effective change management tool? Strategic Change, 13(2), 73-81.

Hofstede, G. (1984). Culture's consequences. California: SAGE Publications, Inc.

Hofstede, G., Neuijen, B., Ohayv, D., Sanders, G. (1990). Measuring organizational cultures: A qualitative and quantitative study across twenty cases. Administrative Science Quarterly, 35(2), 286-316.

Hofstede, G., Hofstede, G., Minkov, M. (2010). Culture and organizations: Software of the mind. USA: McGraw-Hill.

Martinsons, G., Davison, R., Martinsons, V. (2009). How culture influences IT-enabled organizational change and information systems. Communications of the ACM, 52(4), 118-123.

Merrell, P. (2012). Effective change management: The simple truth. Management Services, 56(2), 20-23.

Murtezaj, V. (2011). Understanding the role of emotional intelligence in negotiating agreements and diplomatic conflict management behavior. Digital Dissertation. Swiss Management Center University, Switzerland. Retrieved from http://swissmc.blackboard.com.

Latta, F. (2009). A Process model of organizational change in cultural context (OC3 model): The influence of organizational culture on leading change. Journal of Leadership & organizational Studies. Sage Publications Inc., 16(1), 19-37.

Park, M. (2006). The lived experience of Asian international students in online learning environments in higher education. Digital Dissertation. Swiss Management Center University, Switzerland. Retrieved from http://swissmc.blackboard.com.

Pihlak, Ü. (2013). Change management in Indian organizations compared to Chinese and Estonian organizations (2009-2011). Baltic Journal of Economics, 13(1), 111-112.

Pihlak, Ü. & Alas, R. (2012). Leadership style and employee involvement during organizational change. Journal of Management & Change, 29(1), 46-66.

Pyszka, A., Pilat, M., (2011). Applying Trompenaars typology of organizational culture to implementation of CSR strategy. Journal of Intercultural Management, 3(2), 113-125.

Selvadurai, A. (2013). Change management in the public sector. Department of Communication. University of Ottawa.

Sun, T. (2009, October). Knowledge required to achieve an entrepreneurial success. Digital Dissertation. Swiss Management Center University, Switzerland. Retrieved from http://swissmc.blackboard.com.

Waisfisz, B. (2015). Constructing the best culture to perform. Helsinki, Itim International.

Wilkins, L. & Dyer, W. (1988). Toward culturally sensitive theories of culture change. Academy Of Management Review, 13(4), 522-533.

Printed in Great Britain
by Amazon

68245654R20233